The Education of
an Old Doc

The Education of an Old Doc

The Story Of My Practice In A Wilderness

RICHARD OHMART, M. D., F.A.A.F.P.

iUniverse, Inc.
Bloomington

The Education of an Old Doc
The Story Of My Practice In A Wilderness

iUniverse books may be ordered through booksellers or by contacting:

iUniverse
1663 Liberty Drive
Bloomington, IN 47403
www.iuniverse.com
1-800-Authors (1-800-288-4677)

ISBN: 978-1-4620-1474-3 (sc)
ISBN: 978-1-4620-1475-0 (ebk)

Printed in the United States of America

iUniverse rev. date: 05/09/11

Contents

PART II: ARTICLES WRITTEN BY DOCTOR OHMART

Also by Richard Ohmart, M. D.;
When I Died, An Amazing Adventure; 2002

To my wife

For many years my wife of fifty-two years, Carol, has encouraged my writing. Although she has not always been happy in Oakley, she has never criticized me in choosing Oakley for my practice. After I had a head injury followed by a stroke in 2001, she stood by me while I was hospitalized for almost a year in Denver. Without her love and support I might never have regained my abilities to walk, speak and write. I now have more time and am telling the story of our life in Oakley. I have loved her for fifty-five years. I look forward to many more years together.

Preface

This book tells of the education and development of a rural physician. It describes how I cared for my patients and what my patients taught me in the thirty-seven years I practiced in a rural community. After four years in medical school and a year of internship, I had an excellent basic medical education, one firmly grounded on caring for my patients. My instructors taught me the value of every individual, large or small. Kindness, gentleness and thoughtfulness were to be treasured. Along with teaching me those things they also taught me the value of the science of medicine.

I found in Oakley a mentor, an office staff and a hospital staff that had much to teach me. The older staff members were replaced by those of my generation, then a generation younger than I. They continued to educate me. The staff at my office and the staff at the Logan County Hospital became my friends and colleagues. We worked together. We laughed together. And, occasionally, we wept together. We forged a team that made my practice a joy.

I don't believe a young medical student now receives the same education I received. The students now have too much to learn, too many demands on his or her time. I hope the students have time to relax, reflect on medicine and its position in the world. They need time to discuss with their peers and faculty what medicine is all about. I had that time. I hope my little time as a preceptor for students has exemplified the qualities I have acquired in my practice. I hope each of those students has absorbed these traits to some small extent.

PART I

LIVING IN OAKLEY

Chapter 1

Why I Became a Rural Physician

This was written in 1997 and taped for college students who might be interested in medical school and a career in medicine. I was then the Director of Medical Education, Northwest Region, University of Kansas School of Medicine.

I Am, and Have Always Been, a Kansan

"I was born in Kansas, I was bred in Kansas,
And when I am married I'll be wed in Kansas"

I played my tuba in the University of Kansas band for three years, listening to students at football and basketball games sing those words, but I really paid little attention to them. Now I know how true they were, and how true they remain. I was born in Kansas, raised in a small town in Western Kansas, and educated at KU, where I attended both undergraduate and medical schools. My wife happens to claim the San Francisco Bay area as the place where she grew up, but we both attended junior high and high school in Scott City, Kansas. We were married in Danforth Chapel, on the KU campus, when I was a senior and she was a freshman at KU. Her California yearnings have been an occasional thorn in my side, but I

3

have, over forty years of marriage, managed to avoid that sting most of the time.

I entered medical school in the fall of 1958 with no money, a pregnant wife, and high hopes. That was fairly typical of my class, although many students already had children. I finished medical school in June of 1962 with two children, many debts and undiminished high hopes. The years between were filled with many highs, a few lows and lots of hard work, probably not much different from the years a student spends in medical school today. I spent my first year on the Lawrence campus, as the school was not yet combined on the Kansas City campus. Memories of that year are of the terrible stench in the basement of Haworth Hall where our cadavers resided. We spent nine months dissecting said cadavers. We enjoyed standing in front of Haworth Hall, observing and commenting on anatomy in motion as the coeds walked past. When there were no girls to ogle we wished Wilt Chamberlain had returned for his senior year to play basketball for KU.

Our first son was born in November, the weekend before our first set of "block exams" (exams in all of our courses; the exams required two days). At the party after the exams one of the instructors asked me what I was going to do with the experimental animal I now had at home. I was numb, exhausted and so relieved that Dale had avoided being born with any of the anomalies we had been studying in embryology that I could do nothing but mumble.

Carol continued taking classes at KU, so I did a bit of baby-sitting. On several occasions I took Dale, in his infant seat, to physiology lab with me, where he either slept or watched as we did terrible things to dogs and cats. Fortunately Carol didn't know exactly what I was exposing her precious son to.

My second year, in Kansas City, was a bit more exciting. Carol and I added another son to our family. I spent most of my time in the lecture rooms and laboratories in Wahl Hall. Pathology, pharmacology, microbiology; all were suffered through in a sleep-deprived daze, as I tried to study with two little children at home. As did many of my classmates, I suffered from all of the diseases whose symptoms we studied. I was enthralled with the manner in which the pathologists seemed to have all of the answers, and decided I would become a pathologist. With that in mind (and for the $15 I was paid for every assist) I became a *deiner*. This is an historic term for flunky at the autopsy table. I prepared the body for the prosector, helped as much as I was able, and cleaned up afterward.

My first experience as a *deiner* was almost my last. I was called in the middle of the night and hurried to the morgue, to find a body lying on the cold steel table, and the pathologist fuming because of a delay in securing the proper permission papers. The patient had been the father-in-law of the Dean of the Medical School and had been pronounced healthy by the Chairman of the Department of Medicine. About a week after the exam the man suddenly died, probably from a heart attack. (This was not particularly uncommon then as the examination of a heart consisted of auscultation, percussion and, probably, a resting ECG.) The irritated prosector went out for a cigarette, leaving me with the body, since he didn't think the corpse should be left alone. He came back. Still no papers. More fuming!

Finally he went to his office to do some paperwork, again leaving me in the morgue, alone with the body, to call him when the messenger delivered the papers. I was twenty-three years old. My knowledge of morgues and bodies had been derived from countless stories of mad scientists, Dr. Frankenstein, etc. These thoughts were not comforting. The cadaver I had dissected last year had carried various shades of gray, long immersed in formalin. This was a man still having the hues given him by nature, recently deceased. My imagination ran rampant! Every squeak was a moan from the corpse. Every rattle in the building was either a breath (How did I know he was *really* dead?) or a movement of those not yet cold limbs.

I did manage to refrain from bolting from the room, but not by much. Finally the papers arrived. I called the prosector and we set to work. By this time it seemed as if I was helping in the dissection of an old friend, but I did manage to complete the task at hand. Rarely have I spent such a night!

I remember a lecture about the sanitation of outhouses from Public Health probably better than anything from classes that year. I had grown up in one of the most rural areas of Kansas, and when we sought outhouses to tip over on Halloween, we found them hard to find. The few that I knew of were on farmsteads, but even those were rare. I wondered what I would do with the knowledge gleaned from that lecture.

My first day in Physical Diagnosis class was also memorable. I was one of six boys (young doctors?) in a group sent to the "clinic" to see and touch our first live patient. In those days "clinic patients" were what we might now call "economically deprived" and were treated essentially for free. The price they paid was that they had to suffer the indignities of having many inexperienced hands poke and pry on their vulnerable, sometimes hurting, bodies. Occasionally the spouse of an employee or student would be seen in the clinic. They, too, paid little or no fee. And they received no special privileges.

Our patient turned out to be the wife of a lab tech. I do not remember what brought her to the clinic, but I wager she never returned. She was a very pretty young woman, who turned red at the sight of a physician accompanied by six young men, all about her own age, entering the room. As part of teaching us the importance of a thorough exam, we proceeded through the ritual of a breast exam. After she had shed her top, extended her arms and been pawed by all of us, in the benefit of our education only, she was an even deeper shade of red. We were all a bit embarrassed, too, but we were, after all, learning! She fled, with prescription in hand, while we made jokes to cover our own discomfort. Later, in OB

6

Clinic, I would encounter my first pelvic exam, and be put in my place by an experienced clinic patient.

Years three and four were the clinical years. I spent those years seeing patients, many of whom knew more about their illnesses than I did. Most of the inpatients I saw had already had a staff physician, a resident and an intern take their history and do a physical exam on them. They did not appreciate my bumbling efforts. Pauses to look at my cue cards for the next question were met with either "I already answered that question three times" or "Doc, I've got cholecystitis. Why don't we skip this foolishness?" My unskilled hands-on tasks tended to draw an "Ouch," "That hurts," or an occasional "God Damn it!" Even the mildest expression of discomfort was enough to send me reeling back from living flesh. After all, why was I, a mere student, hurting one of those patients? I wanted to cure, not heap more indignities on my unfortunate patient? Understanding, but I hope not callousness, came with experience. I still do not like to do unpleasant things to people, but I know that sometimes it is necessary.

Gradually my skills and knowledge grew, although at continuing discomfort to both my patients and myself. I learned that the older, more experienced patients often played games with us, probably their way of maintaining some semblance of dignity and self-respect in what they must certainly have interpreted as a degrading situation. Some were helpful, knowing enough about their diseases to coach us in what to do and find. Others probably fed us stories about their history, symptoms and physical findings. A few could manage to embarrass us, or otherwise let us know that they were still in some semblance of control, even though they were more-or-less experimental animals.

Two examples come to mind, both from OB/GYN. After talking to a patient, pregnant for her seventh time, one of my classmates asked her "Why didn't you use birth control?"

My classmates probably averaged two children per medical student, so I don't know why anyone had the gall to raise that question. At any rate the woman replied, "Oh, yes sir, Doc. But them little wiggle tails swim right past my diaphragm," leaving my classmate speechless.

The second instance occurred after I had done my first pelvic exam. Five or six students, all male, had examined the same woman. These students were probably not feeling a thing that we were supposed to find. Of course all of us were nodding in agreement with what the resident had said we should find. After the last exam the patient sat up and said, "If there had been one more of you boys, you would sure have rung my bell."

We retreated hastily, leaving her triumphant in the exam room!

Graduation arrived on time. Our wives received their PHT (Putting Hubby Through) certificates. We all swore to observe the original Oath of Hippocrates at a ceremony in Battenfeld Auditorium, then adjourned to the Bigger Jigger for one last celebration. The following day we walked through the Campanile and down the hill on the Lawrence campus, delighted and proud of our green hoods and tassels. At last we were doctors, ready to enter the real world, heal the sick and comfort the afflicted! Little did we know what awaited us!

What awaited me was ten days as the only doctor in Oakley, the small rural community where I had precepteed, and where I now practice. Although today I tremble at the thought of my temerity, this was not unusual in those days. We finished school in May, and our internships started on July 1st, so there was a month to be spent doing something. Since I needed the money, I worked. I also learned a lot. And I was only frightened on one or two occasions, a tribute to how much I didn't know. One of those was an overdose of barbiturates. After calling the physician in the next town, about thirty miles away, I pumped her stomach and put her to bed.

Fortunately this had not been a serious suicide attempt and everything turned out well.

The other was the care and probable delivery of my first solo baby. The young woman was about my age and due while Dr. Marchbanks was gone. Pregnant with her second child, she knew more than I did and depended more on her mother than this obviously inexperienced doctor. Her mother was certain that each twinge of abdominal pain heralded the onset of labor and would bring her daughter in for me to check. Although we were well acquainted by the time I left, I didn't have the privilege of assisting in her delivery. We have since become good friends and have laughed on many occasions about my inexperience and terror at the thought of having to deliver her.

*   *   *

Carol, my wife of fifty-plus years, has been my lover, mentor, mother of my children and caretaker after I had a stroke. Oakley was my choice of practice location, not hers. We have made a life in Oakley, usually pleasant if not idyllic. We dated as teen-agers; now we are in our seventies. This tells how I managed to wed this wonderful girl.

Truly In Love

I had gone to KU along with several of my high school classmates, one in particular, Mona DeWeese. We were very good friends but rarely dated. I hoped to snare her while we were both at KU. She was in love with another of my classmates, our outstanding high school athlete, who also went to KU. However Mona was taking care of me. She knew a cute blond in Scott City whom Mona had kept her eye on for me.

I had known of this girl as a skinny little kid who came into the drug store where I worked. She either ordered a lemon phosphate or a chocolate soda. Those both required a bit more preparation than many drinks I served. I didn't care for the extra effort, or the brat who forced me to exert that effort.

Fall 1954

The Scott City High School held a school carnival in the fall to raise money for student activities. Kelsey Bodecker, the vocal music teacher, usually created a nightclub (actually the library decorated appropriately) where patrons could sit at a table sipping soft drinks, dancing and watching students perform. I was a freshman at KU but had returned to watch Bob, my brother, play football Friday night. Saturday evening I went to the school carnival where Ruby, a senior in high school and my heartthrob, was singing in the triple trio as one of the acts. Mr. Bodecker asked some of the high school or college boys to dance with the triple trio members. He hoped the dancehall girls in the triple trio could encourage others to dance.

I thought that was a great idea. I knew any high school girl would be delighted to dance with me, a college man. Even though I was not a good dancer I thought my college mystique would impress the girls. The only problem was that Ruby was not allowed to dance. I had known, and dated, most of the nine members while I had been in school. So I danced with the other members. There was a slim high school freshman singing soprano in the triple trio, Carol Socolofsky. The girls had been teasing Ruby about me throughout rehearsals. When Carol realized Ruby couldn't dance she asked me to dance with her. After all, Kelsey wanted dancers on the floor. Hence we danced. Carol was a wonderful dancer. I had two left feet. I took Ruby home after the carnival and promptly forgot about Carol.

Easter Break, 1955

One Saturday night two friends, Karl Lindemuth and Jerry McDonald, and I were roaming around town. Carol and a friend, Glenda, were in Carol's dad's car. As teenagers do, we ended up with all of us in the same car. Karl, the boy Carol had dated last year and wanted to date again, said he wanted to go home. So Karl left us. This left two couples in Jerry's dad's new business car. "Let's go rabbit hunting!"

Believe it or not, this was an actual "sport" in those days. We would, after dark of course, drive around in a pasture and shine our spotlight on a rabbit. Blinded by the light, the rabbit would sit still and let us shoot him, or at him. We rarely hit anything, but it was an excellent reason to drive a girl out into the country after dark. Carol and I were in the back seat when we heard a colossal "thump" and the car stopped! It was stuck! Jerry's dad's new car rested on its frame. It had fallen into two badger holes; both right-sided wheels were in holes. (And it only took four hours for Jerry and me to dig the holes just right that afternoon.)

Neither of the pair in the front seat was at all happy about this. Jerry had his dad's new car stuck, maybe damaged. Glenda was supposed to have a date with her steady about 9:00 that evening. Carol just giggled and I also thought it was funny. I was stuck with a girl in the back seat of a car. What could be better? We were having so much fun they made us leave them. Wandering off to look for help, we finally found some boards and carried them back to the car. With Jerry's assistance we were able to jack up the car, slide the boards under the tires, and drive the car out. By the time we extricated the car it was after midnight.

We headed for Scott City, one teenage couple giggling in the back seat, another couple in the front seat worried. Glenda was upset that she had been out with someone other than her steady boy. By the time we got the car out Jerry was frantic about his dad's car. Carol and I were both having a great time, although it was somewhat later than the time her parents had expected her home. On the drive home I told her that she had better think of a good excuse for her being late, because her parents would never believe the truth. For some reason Carol thought that was extremely bright and funny. I walked her to her door, wondering whether I dared attempt to kiss her goodnight. We stopped at the door. She opened the door to be certain the door was not locked, thinking it would be bad form if she allowed me to kiss her goodnight, only to find herself locked out. It was open. She leaned toward me. I was ready to kiss her. Then I looked into the room. Just inside the door her father, a large, formidable man, was sitting staring at me. No kiss! I didn't even shake her hand. I just said "Goodnight" and ran.

Years later Carol told me Charles had been sitting there working on his taxes. He hadn't been angry with me.

Summer 1955

After my first year at KU I returned to Scott City to work for a farmer during the summer. One Sunday evening at Methodist Youth

Foundation (MYF) one of my friends, Clifford, told me he had a problem. He had a date but no car; I had a car, but no date. Would I get a date, take them to the movie, and then go park somewhere, while they were doing whatever they wished in the back seat. He said they would leave my date and me in the front seat alone. I wondered what I was supposed to do in that seat but I could figure out something. My reply, "Sure."

I asked all the girls I knew at MYF. They either had dates or refused to go with me. Leaving MYF we drove to the pay phone and I called all of the girls I could think of. No one wanted to see the movie with me. Finally Judy, Clifford's steady, suggested Carol to me. Judy had asked Carol at MYF if she would go with me if I asked her. Carol had told Judy she would, as a favor to her friend. I remembered our rabbit hunting experience. Carol giggled a lot. I didn't want to face her father again. And I wasn't certain I even wanted to be in the same movie theater as this girl. But I acquiesced. Unfortunately, Carol was already at the movie.

Clifford and Judy went to the show. There Judy asked Carol if she would walk out to the lobby—Carol says that Judy looked so woebegone that she just couldn't say "No." So Carol went to the lobby where I asked her if she would go to the movie with me. Of course she accepted. I paid for my ticket and, as we entered, I slipped into her hand the fifty cents she had paid for her admission. Again she thought I was extremely humorous. She giggled. The movie was *The Caine Mutiny,* a show I had seen in Lawrence. I told her that Ensign Keith gets hanged at the end. This, of course, is not how the movie ends; he does not get hanged. She was quite irritated that I misled her.

After the show we went to park somewhere. While Clifford and Judy were making out in the back seat I didn't know what to do. As a first date (kind of) I hoped to get a kiss or two from Carol. We chatted for a short while. In our cold car we both remarked that our feet were cold in bed. Each of us thought it would be nice to have a spouse on whom to warm our feet. Then we each had a vision of two people in bed, each trying to place their feet on their partner's back. That started us laughing, so we laughed while our friends in the backseat snuggled. I had a good time, but really knew little about Carol; she thought I was funny, fraud that I was. But I did get a goodnight kiss that evening.

Fall 1955

That fall I again came home to watch Bob play football. I had a second reason for going home. I was planning to ask another girl to go steady with me. She, however, had a rule that she would not accept a date unless she was asked twenty-four hours in advance. It was Friday afternoon. The ball game was Friday evening. So I knew she would not go to the game with me. I asked Bob who might go with me on such short notice.

"Socy (Carol's teenage nickname shortened from Socolofsky) will go with anyone" said my brother.

I had already had some experience with her "I'll go anytime with anyone" approach. "Sure" she said when I called. "But I have to march to the ball game and sit with the band."

"That's OK" I replied.

So I watched my date march into the game, then I sat down with her in the bleachers. The director didn't throw me out so I remained with Carol in the band. It was cold so she had me sitting on her feet to keep them warm. He didn't like that, but that didn't slow Carol down. After the game Carol and I raced to my Mom's car, the only time I could outrun her, and took Mom home. Then we had Mom's old Chevvy. We headed for the football field again, but not for another ball game. Again we stayed out later than her parents had wished. I never got around to asking the other girl if she would go steady with me. Saturday evening Carol and I went to a movie, then again sat in Mom's car at the football field. I asked Carol to write me in Lawrence and let me know what was happening in Scott City High. And again we stayed out too late.

I don't have any idea why her parents would let their daughter go out with me again. Charles and Caroline were planning to go to Manhattan for a KSU-OU football game, K-State's homecoming. Neither K-State nor KU had football teams to brag about. Oklahoma and Nebraska were at the top of the heap, but both Carol's parents had attended K-State and Charles had coached there. Caroline and Charles invited Carol and Judy to go to the game at Manhattan. They also asked me if I would like to go to the game with them. I, however, played in the KU band and we were going to Lincoln to play in the KU-NU ball game. I worked it out so that I would ride with Mona to Manhattan Friday evening. (I owned no car.) She would then let me drive her car to Topeka. At 5:00 AM Saturday I was to flag down the bus with the KU band and drive up to Lincoln. At the halftime of the game some of the KU band members had to leave to get back to Lawrence to play for dances. They said they had room for me and they would take me along. They were to let me out at Topeka where I had left Mona's car; then I would return to Manhattan. I had it all cleared with Dr. Wiley, the director, so I was set.

So that's what I did. I stayed with Lowell in his fraternity Friday night. I spent Friday evening with Carol, but had to get up very early Saturday morning. In the fraternity house, boys wondered why a KU band member was getting dressed when they were just coming home from their dates. I drove to Topeka, waited for the band. I stood beside the road as the first bus passed me. The second bus zoomed by me also, leaving me standing by the road. The third, and last, bus slowed, and then came to a stop. The assistant director in the bus asked me if I had been expelled from the first bus as too rowdy. After I explained he let me on the bus.

We played during the first half of the game, marched in the halftime show; then I left in the car going to Lawrence. I'm certain I slept most of that drive. After I got to Manhattan Saturday evening I used Mona's car and Clifford and Judy used Carol's parents' car. They kept the radio on and ran the battery down, unable to return to Judy's motel. So Carol and I had to find them, and then push the car to start it. We took the girls and Carol's parents' car to the motel where her parents were. Another short night!

I spent the night with Clifford where he had a room in a private home. Someone knocking on our door early Sunday morning awakened us. The racket proved to be the girls, again giggling, but determined. They informed us that we four were going to church. We thought we'd just go back to sleep. As usual, the girls won. I didn't know what Carol, now a sophomore in high school, might have expected from a college man. Most of the time I spent in her presence I was asleep, both Saturday evening and Sunday morning. What a hot date I was!

When I drove Mona's car to pick her up to go back to Lawrence, she and the girl with whom she had spent the night asked me if I had invited Carol to come to the KU homecoming game next weekend. When I said "No" both girls jumped on me, "What kind of a college man are you?" they laughed.

I didn't know; I was just sleepy. By the time Mona and I had driven back to Lawrence I had been convinced that inviting Carol to Lawrence sounded like a wonderful idea. But I didn't imagine that her parents would let their daughter go to a KU game. Her parents might have taken her to a K-State game, but going to a KU game without a chaperone was an entirely different matter. I thought I had little chance of them permitting their daughter, alone, to take the train to join me in Lawrence for a weekend. Having both attended K-State they knew that all KU boys were wild party animals.

Actually I was about as far from being a party animal as I could have been, and still am for that matter. But they said "Yes." They were to drive Carol to Oakley, where she would take the train to Lawrence. I made arrangements for her to stay with a Scott City friend, Pat Ellis, a KU freshman. Sunday morning Carol would take the train back to Oakley where her parents would again meet her in Oakley and they would all drive back to Scott. I don't remember much about that weekend, either. Carol was staying in a girls' dorm so she could stay out until 1:00 Sunday morning, so I didn't get much more sleep in Lawrence than the K-State homecoming game.

It was the KU-K-State game. This time it was her chance to go to a game while I played in the band. As a tuba player I sat in the last row of the band so Carol joined me. The band was sitting in the stands playing after the game when three drunken pre-med students rolled (literally) into the band. All three were from Goodland, Gary Nitz, Dale Vermillion and Terry Poling. Gary and Dale were KU students whom I had met in classes. Terry was a K-State student. Dale went to Harvard for medical school; Gary and Terry became classmates of mine at KUMC. Following that experience I knew Carol would never be allowed to come to Lawrence again, unless she failed to inform her parents of the drunks falling into the band.

One of Carol's classmates, Ruth, had told her that she would not help her in Latin class unless she brought my high school class ring home with her. Carol spent enough time with me to carry that ring home as a trophy. After that I was hooked!

Later that year I joined a fraternity. As a pledge, then a member, I had a few social duties. Although I knew I was going steady, I had to escort a girl to certain affairs. I often took Mona as a date. Occasionally I took Coralyn, a girl I had dated as a freshman. Both knew I was in love with Carol but I enjoyed both girls' company so we dated frequently. Once Carol's parents had let her come to that first KU game and dance, they found it hard to refuse Carol's requests to come to KU. She made several trips to Lawrence for parties, etc. during my sophomore and junior years.

15

In Scott City Carol also dated boys there, but if we were in the same town we were steadies. Home for Christmas break one winter, I had to wait in her home with her parents until her date brought her home from the high school winter ball.

During the summers I enjoyed driving a tractor. I didn't have to think. As usual when Carol was around, I was sleepy. She didn't have to get up in the mornings; I usually had to start work at 6:00. When I got home in the evening I had to shower, eat and spend time with Carol. I was at best half asleep. She who had been alone all day was always bright and perky. I doubt she thought I was funny that summer. Most of my thoughts were of falling asleep, toppling from the tractor and slicing myself into small bits. Those fantasies helped keep me awake.

Fall 1957

That fall I returned to KU for my senior year, refreshed and eager to finish college, but no definite plans for post graduate work. Carol, whose entire family had attended K-State, went with me to KU. She had a room in GSP, a woman's dorm. Carol also didn't relish the idea of a roommate so she had a single room. Her father brought her to school with a car filled of her necessaries. Boys were standing around, volunteering to help girls carry their possessions to their rooms. This provided a chance for the fraternity men to meet attractive girls. Charles, following the rules, asked permission for him to carry Carol's things to her room. He was told that men were *never* permitted into the halls and the rooms of the girls. So Carol carried her own supplies to her room, watching as boys carried other girls' luggage to their rooms. Carol started off with a bad taste in her mouth for dorm life.

Charles headed for Scott City; Carol and I went to the movie that evening, *The Ten Commandments*. As we left the dorm Carol asked the girl who was manning (womanning?) the desk what time she needed to be in. She was told midnight was closing, because school had not yet started. We went to the movie, a three hour movie; then one of my friends had a car so we went to have a drink. We drifted in slightly before midnight. The entire dorm was in chaos. One of the freshman girls had not come in at 10:30 as required. The housemother had a fit when she saw Carol.

"Where have you been? What were you doing? I was ready to call your parents!"

Again, Carol had a problem with dorm life. She had been told that she didn't need to be in until midnight; the proctor thought she was an upperclassman, whose rules were more lenient than the freshmen. The fact that she followed the directions given her meant nothing to her housemother. We were careful to get Carol in by closing time for the rest of her dorm year. We were married in April that year. Finally Carol could stay out as long as she wanted; I was at home so she was content. We had no money to waste on entertainment. We stayed home and studied. This was my only straight A semester. Both of us were happy.

I Go To Oakley As A Student

After spending the summer in Kansas City in the KUMC ER I was ready to finish the fourth year of medical school, receive my degree and start my life as a doctor. I thought I wanted to be a general practitioner, although internal medicine was a strong contender. I was interested in people; quite curious about their thoughts and ideas——maybe I would be a psychiatrist. As in college I enjoyed each of my rotations, thinking I could make a career in that field, although surgery was never considered. Also, as in college, I thought I might spend my life as a student. Carol insisted that, now that I had a wife and two sons, I had to make a living.

My first senior block was the precepteeship. The precepteeship had been established to allow fourth year students to live with a practicing doctor. The students were assigned to a small community, originally with a population of 2500 or less, usually where a KUMC graduate practiced. Rural Kansas desperately needed physicians. The "Murphy Plan," sending students to those small towns, was to show the students that such a life might be enjoyable. Scott City was one of the sites to which students were sent.

However, students were not allowed to return to their hometowns. Carol and the boys were to spend September and October in Scott City with our parents, forty five miles from Oakley. Harold, my younger brother, was playing football for Scott City High School. With that in mind I traded with a friend and managed to spend my precepteeship in Oakley,

September of 1961. James Marchbanks, M.D., was my preceptor. Oakley had a fairly new hospital. I was familiar with the area. I was content.

I was to see all of a small town doctor's life. Jim had a room in the basement of his home where I slept. Paula, Jim's wife, fed me with their family. I could read in my room, or, if I chose, sit in their living room and read or play with their kids. Their older daughter, Kathy, was a few years older than Dale. Their boy, Pete, was about the same age as Dale so I played with him. Their second daughter, Leslie, was a lovable little girl, a year or two older than Dale and Pete. She enjoyed crawling into my lap and being held. I liked that so I didn't miss my boys as much as I might have. I don't think there was a TV; I certainly don't remember one. Jim had an extension to his phone in the room where I slept and told me to pick up if the phone rang and listen to what was said. If it was a medical call I was to listen to his response, then get dressed if we needed to leave. If it was a personal call, hang it up.

Jim was an avid golfer. On Sundays he arose early enough to make rounds at the hospital then play a round of golf before church. I had never golfed but he expected me to accompany him. I would rather have slept in than walked around hitting a little white ball. But he was the boss and insisted that all doctors had to play golf; saying I had better learn. Then he took me to church. Thursday afternoon was his day out of the office. Often we would play a round of golf, drink a beer at the country club, and then make rounds at the hospital.

Saturday evenings we went to the country club for dinner. Again we had a drink or two with dinner then spent some time on the dance floor. Seeing the doctor take a drink in public, then go to the hospital to see a patient, was a new experience for me. I knew that the doctors in Scott City might take a drink. They would drink in a friend's home, never the American Legion club where the dances were held. I thought this as hypocritical as Dad smoking in our home in Buhler or Scott City as a coach/teacher but not smoking in public. As I matured I realized this was not as hypocritical as I then thought.

Jim had office hours on Saturdays as well as Monday through Friday. He made house calls on Saturday afternoons, giving many patients an injection of mercuhydrin. "What is mercuhydrin?" you ask.

It's a mercury compound (a diuretic) that was used to remove water from a patient in congestive heart failure. In my second year I had been taught about Diamox®, an oral diuretic that was so new that it was not yet listed in my textbooks. Mercuhydrin damaged the kidney so that water leaked from the vascular system into the urine, ridding the patient of excess water. The patient would lose lots of water for three or four days after a mercuhydrin injection, then the kidneys would recover and again retain water. Next Saturday Jim would give the patient another injection. Even after the advent of Diamox® many patients needed the mercuhydrin injections, as oral Diamox® was not strong enough to rid the patient of enough water. Jim referred to those Saturday afternoon rounds as "pee rounds."

Terrell Pierson, Jim's good friend, was the hospital administrator. They played golf together, often spent Saturday evenings at the country club and enjoyed a drink together. While I was there Terrell was repainting the rooms in the hospital. He also repaired some of the mechanical problems. Although his title was that of administrator, he was a jack-of-all trades, a mechanic, carpenter, bookkeeper and he signed the hospital payroll checks. The maintenance man, Vernon Hurst, was superb at constructing anything Jim asked—physical therapy aids, shelves, etc. Vernon's wife, Leola, washed and repaired the linens and gowns in the hospital basement. The three of then kept the hospital going.

I don't remember having any medical adventures (misadventures?) that month. A boy made a pipe bomb and blew two or three fingers off his hand. A farmer caught his hand and arm in a grain auger. There was a car wreck or two. Jim took care of all of the trauma patients who wandered in to the Oakley hospital. There was no surgeon near Oakley, and he had been trained in the military to handle trauma. And his license said he was a "physician and surgeon." I still didn't like surgery. He delivered a few babies, did a few tonsillectomies, and a bit of other surgery. I still (2010) remember Larry, the boy with the bomb and Ernie, the man with the lacerated arm.

I did manage to diagnose a ruptured spleen in a high school boy who had been stretched over the seatback of a school bus rupturing his spleen. He was bleeding to death inside his abdomen. Jim called Dr. Reynolds, the surgeon in Hays, and he drove to Oakley while Jim prepared the boy and the hospital. The boy needed blood! The hospital used a walking blood bank. It consisted of a list of volunteers who would be on call, appear at the hospital and donate a unit of blood when needed. The donors' list included their name, address and their A, B and O blood group, and Rh positive and negative type. The patient's blood would be tested for ABO and Rh then mixed with a donor's blood cells with the same ABO and Rh. If the donor's blood did not agglutinate (clump) the match was considered compatible and the blood could be transfused. We knew nothing of hepatitis A, B and C nor of HIV. This came later.

Once in the OR I found I was first assistant. Jim gave the boy an anesthetic; I stood opposite the surgeon, following his instructions. The only approach to stopping the bleeding was to remove the boy's spleen. As soon as Dr. Reynolds opened the boy's abdomen he started scooping partially clotted blood out of his abdominal cavity, most of it splattering on my gown. He needed to see and simply threw the blood away from him as quickly as possible. He was in a hurry and had no time for such niceties as protecting me. Once he could see, Dr. Reynolds clamped the splenic artery and the bleeding slowed, then stopped. He removed the spleen, closed the boy's abdomen and we were done. Dr. Reynolds smiled at me and told me never to stand across the table when he was in a hurry! The boy did well, and I occasionally saw him in Oakley during my practice.

Even though I had fathered two boys I knew very little about delivering a baby. My OB rotation was yet ahead. When Jim delivered a baby my task was to sit at the head of the table and offer moral support for the woman delivering her infant. Frequently Jim asked me to hold an ether mask over the woman's face. I was not to anesthetize the patient. A little ether might relieve a bit of her pain. Occasionally Jim would give the patient a spinal, a procedure where an anesthetic was injected into the fluid around the spinal cord. This spinal anesthetic numbed the nerves below the injection. The paralyzed sensory fibers would not carry the pain stimuli to the woman's brain, which was what he wanted. But the motor fibers were also paralyzed. Until the nerves recovered her mother could not move her legs. Both of us learned to do a "saddle block," which theoretically anesthetized only the mother's perineum, the area a rider would sit on a horse. That worked wonderfully well, except that a mother in labor often pushed with her abdominal muscles. That muscular pressure often pushed the anesthetic higher in her spinal canal and paralyzed the nerves at a higher level than we wanted, essentially giving her a spinal.

*　　*　　*

Jim was not the first family doctor to mentor me. Dr. Preston Palmer was the long-time physician in Scott City, where I grew up. I wrote this in 1984.

Old Doc Palmer

There he sat, Doc Palmer, the man who had been my doctor for many years. Regarded by my high school contemporaries with a mixture of fear and reverence, he was the man after whom I had chosen to pattern my life. Never had I expected to see him thus, ensconced on the porcelain throne, with the bottoms of a scrub suit around his ankles.

I was in college, a pre-med, and had volunteered a unit of blood for the woman on whom he was about to perform a C-section. In turn, Dr. Palmer had asked her permission for me to watch the operation. I was about to have my introduction to surgery and there sat my god, in that most mortal of all positions. The small-town hospital boasted a doctors' "lounge" consisting of a single room with a partially screened toilet at one end. The nurse had told me to go in and change into a scrub suit. I entered, unaware of the view that awaited me.

Dr. Palmer grinned and said "Come in, Dick, and get into a suit. You always want to be sure to take a leak and a good crap before scrubbing or you'll be sure to regret it."

Thus did I receive the first of many sage words of advice given me by my preceptors in medicine. While I claim no special monopoly on any of this advice, and in fact many of them are of classical origin, I think they are nevertheless of value, worth repeating for the benefit of younger and less experienced physicians. Many of them were given to me in the oral, apprenticeship tradition of medical lore, others I have taken from various sources and applied to my practice. I hope you find them helpful, and perhaps entertaining.

"Why do you hate me? I only tried to help you." How many times have I pondered a similar thought as a patient whom I had gone out of my way to help asked to have his or her records transferred to another physician? Usually I was certain the new physician would not have made any unusual effort to offer help such as I had provided. I have found that one of the surest ways to lose a patient is to offer assistance above and beyond the usual, especially if there is no way for said patient to pay you for those services. Gratitude may be eternal, but it often makes it hard for the recipient of such services to maintain a sense of dignity or equality in future dealings. The same holds true if I learn too many of a patient's secrets. Often they then have difficulty in facing me. While this effect is no doubt exaggerated in our small community, I am certain that it holds true in all practices. Do I continue to go out of my way to help? Usually I do, after all I am a member of a "helping profession." I just try to avoid making the recipient of my largesse feel he owes me something, either in money or gratitude, more than my usual fee. And I hope not to be upset if that same recipient soon sends me a request for his records.

"Is it urgent, or merely important?" This question came from an excellent nurse practitioner that I have been fortunate to have working with me. During the time my own children were growing up I was often faced with decisions as to whether I left one of their activities to go see a patient at the hospital. After greater or lesser anguish I would make a decision, but I never was comfortable with the idea that a non-urgent drop-in at the ER was more important than my family. Now I realize that urgency sometimes must take precedence over importance, but that does not imply that the laceration at the hospital is more important to me than my grandchild or wife.

"If I don't take care of myself, no one else will." Nor will I be of much value as a physician if I fail to take proper care of myself. That doesn't mean that I don't skip meals, go without sleep and leave in the middle of a movie. But during the many years I have been the only physician in Oakley I have learned that if I do not get away on occasion, and leave the worries and pressures of twenty-four hour call behind, I begin to make mistakes. First I begin to feel pressured and hurried. Next I grump at Carol, my wife, and growl at my children for transgressions that I would usually ignore, or at least gently correct. (I was never, of course, wrong in any position I chose to take.) Finally, if I did not find relief, I would begin to make medical mistakes. I now know the early symptoms of such impending crises and I am able to find relief before they become too onerous. Somehow those moments always coincide with a play in Denver or a ball game at the University of Kansas, activities I always find enjoyable.

"Be not the first by whom the new are tried,
Nor yet the last to lay the old aside."

This was written three centuries ago by Alexander Pope, a poet not a physician. But nowhere is it more important to follow this precept than in medicine.

"Be not the first . . ." How many medicines have been greeted with hosannas as the newest panacea! How many blood tests have been trumpeted to the heavens as the test which will reveal cancer before any other signs or symptoms can be found! How many surgical procedures, once proclaimed the answer to our problems, have fallen by the wayside!

"Nor yet the last . . ." Holding to outdated modes of therapy is as devastating to one's life and practice as is continually jumping on the latest bandwagon. Somewhere between these two extremes lies the proper approach to acceptance of the new diagnostic and therapeutic discoveries. I am certain that I waver from one side to the other of this golden mean, but equally certain that it exists and I must continually seek it.

"This above all, to thine own self be true."

Not restricted to medicine, this advice from Polonius to Hamlet stands in good stead to all. I learn and relearn it regularly. Without fail, every time I fudge on a diagnosis, insurance report, etc. I regret it. Without fail, every time this lesson fades from my memory and I again try to "help" a patient I regret it. Without fail, if I forget this maxim I find myself in a position hard to defend. But, with age comes, if not wisdom, at least experience. My experience tells me that if I can not sign a paper or agree to do something without feeling uneasy about that action I had best not follow that course, for I will later regret it. I know no more certain way to make myself uncomfortable than to do something that I may feel guilty, or even dubious, about doing.

Although I am descended from a long line of preachers, I have not meant this to be a sermon. Rather I believe it to be a distillation of my experience and hope it may prove useful to young physicians, helping them avoid some of my mistakes. I am certain, however, that there are plenty of other mistakes lurking in the shadows, waiting to pounce on an unwary physician. No matter the number of HMOs, PPOs and other alphabetical organizations demanding "quality of care", medicine, by its very nature, must remain a trial and error profession. To those of you who follow me I can only say "Good Luck" and be sure that you keep your bowels and bladder empty.

Playing Doctor In Oakley

I had a two-week stint in Oakley to take over Jim's practice while he took a vacation. If a lone rural practitioner wanted a break he had to hire someone to cover his practice. At that time a new doctor, although not yet licensed, was often hired to cover a practice for a short while, allowing a single doctor to get a few days of vacation with his family. Herman

Hiesterman and Karl Gunter, physicians in Quinter, said they would back me up if I needed their assistance. Carol and the boys stayed in Scott City with her parents. I remember three events in Oakley during that stay.

The first was Carol Bosserman. She was pregnant with Troy and was due either during or just after Jim's vacation. I was terrified at the thought of her going into labor and I would have to deliver her. My OB experience consisted of nine deliveries, supervised by a resident or staff man. Many of the KUMC deliveries were women who had six, eight or more babies and no longer required the assistance of a physician. After a woman had a few babies her pelvic muscles had been so stretched that an infant popped out like a cork from a champagne bottle. Those were the mothers a medical student was allowed to deliver. This was Carol's second pregnancy. If she went into labor with Jim absent I was going to have to handle it by myself. I had been taught to make an episiotomy (a small incision enlarging the woman's vaginal introitus.) before many deliveries, but I had never repaired an episiotomy. The residents always repaired those.

Carol and her mother made twice weekly visits to Jim's office during those two weeks. Her mother kept encouraging Carol, and me, telling us that we would be fine if I had to deliver the baby. I wasn't so sure about that. I don't think Carol, either, was very enthused about this kid, not much older than she was and with minimal training, delivering her. Fortunately her pregnancy lasted until Jim's return. I delivered no babies during that stay.

One night the nurse at the hospital called me and said there was a young woman in the ER who had tried to commit suicide. On my arrival I found a semi-conscious young woman, obviously pregnant. She had taken an overdose of barbiturates. I knew how to handle that. During my summer in the KUMC ER I had handled a lot of overdoses.

Pump her stomach! Put a tube down through her nose into her stomach. Pour water through the tube into her stomach. After the water was in her stomach I then sucked the water out. Repeat the process. Repeat it again. And again. This was to wash the pills that remained in her stomach out, not allowing more of the drug to enter her blood stream. Once the remaining drug was removed from her stomach there was nothing further to do for her.

The next morning she was awake, although a bit groggy. At KUMC we had been taught that a suicide attempt had to be reported to the police, who then carted the patient off to jail. I was not certain that was what I should do in Oakley. My expert on this was Terrell, the hospital administrator. We decided that we would simply do nothing, just tell Jim when he returned. He then could handle the situation.

The final problem(s) arose over a court case concerning moving the Logan County courthouse from Russell Springs to Oakley, the last county seat battle in Kansas, perhaps the last in the United States. Earlier in the spring the voters in Logan County had voted to move the courthouse. In order to approve the move the "yes" supporters had to provide a two-thirds majority of the registered voters. It passed with a bare two-thirds majority and those against the move had sued the county, saying that fraud had carried the election. The trial was to start while Jim was on vacation.

The court was asking many women to testify—some about deceased relatives still on the voting roles, at least one who had been in a mental hospital for years, etc. Most didn't want to testify. Someone had said that if a woman didn't want to testify that if a doctor had a written statement that her testifying would damage her health she would not have to appear in court. I received several requests for such statements. Nowhere in medical school had I been taught about that situation. I looked at Jim's records, usually somewhat scanty, and signed the statements. I was in Wichita when the case ended, but the courthouse was to be moved. The actual moving of the records occurred after we were living in Oakley.

Chapter 2

I Become a Doctor In Oakley

Now I'm a Real Doctor!

I began my practice in Oakley after my internship and a short trip to California. My license said, and still says, I am a physician and surgeon. After completing my internship and receiving my license I, and many others of that era, felt we were prepared to conquer the world with our newfound education. I was aware I was not prepared to operate on hearts but had many skills and a substantial amount of knowledge. I had labored to acquire that wisdom. Now I could actually use this book-learning and those techniques I had been taught to help people.

As a skilled young physician establishing a practice I was certain I knew all there was to know. Hadn't I graduated from the University of Kansas with honors, two majors, one in chemistry and one in English, receiving honors in English and chosen membership in Phi Beta Kappa? Hadn't I graduated from the University Of Kansas School Of Medicine in the top ten percent of the class, higher if I had ignored my wife and two children and spent more time studying? And many of my classmates and physician/teachers at Wesley said I should have received the award as the best intern that year. I was ready! I had a lot to learn.

Every doctor needed a doctor's bag. Jim bought a bag and gave it to me. It was a hard case, about 24 inches long, 12 inches high and 8 inches wide. The bottom was simply a box in which I placed a stethoscope, oto/ophthalmoscope, tongue blades, a few syringes (initially of glass) and a few bottles of injectable and oral medications. The tops of the box opened to the sides and had four small compartments to hold a few other medications, needles and small bandages. It contained everything a doctor might need on a house call. Most doctors carried such a bag, a target for thieves wanting narcotics. This was not much of a problem in Oakley. Radiologists, pathologists and other hospital-based doctors carried no bag, but the doctor I wanted to be was to make house calls and treat sick people. That bag was my portable office.

*   *   *

Jim left on his long awaited family vacation to Alaska. I was on my own, the one and only doctor. Jim had left a few patients in the hospital so I made morning and evening rounds, a practice I continued until my retirement. All of the doctors I emulated made morning rounds at the hospital; in Wichita some physicians had patients in two or three hospitals. They then spent the day in their offices and made evening rounds at the hospital(s) before they went home for dinner. Jim's schedule was to start rounds at the hospital about 8:00 in the morning. After making rounds we had coffee with the hospital administrator and any other staff members who dropped in. Jim's first appointment at his office was 9:30, but he and I usually didn't get there until about 10:00. Theoretically he had a noon break from 12:00 to 2:30, scheduling appointments from 2:30 until 5:00. He then made evening rounds and went home, unless he had house calls to make. Practically his schedule never worked.

Already late to the office at 10:00, he never caught up. And if a patient needed more time than allotted, he spent the necessary time. He never chased a questioning patient out or refused to see a walk-in. So his lunch break often began at 12:30 or 1:00 PM. Scheduling patient appointments at 2:30 gave him a bit of time for lunch and a nap. Afternoon walk-ins were seen until they were all cared for. He usually wrote a short note on each patient's chart immediately after seeing the patient. It might be 6:00 or 6:30 when he left the office. He was still holding office hours all day Saturday, but did not schedule Saturday appointments. Shortly after I arrived we stopped the Saturday afternoon hours so we could watch the football games on TV. Theoretically, one of us was off duty on Saturday and Sunday, alternating the weekends. Whichever of us was on call made rounds twice daily on Saturday and Sunday. Practically, everyone called Jim if he had a problem. Only if Jim were out of town was he not summoned first. I was the second team doc.

That was the approach to the medical practice I joined. In medicine a sixty-hour workweek was the norm. A hard-working rural doctor might spend much more time than that. As any physician, Jim needed time to study and learn outside of the office hours. I usually had study time at the office until Jim died. Then I was overwhelmed!

I changed the schedule a bit after Jim's death. I made morning rounds at 7:30, still had coffee with the hospital staff but tried to get to my office at 9:00. I hoped to finish seeing patients by 12:00, but had entries to make on charts, and phone calls to return. If I was finished at 1:00 I had lunch and a twenty to thirty minute nap and was back at the office at 2:00. Again I didn't do my charting until I had seen all the patients so I then had my office charting to do, return phone calls and make evening rounds at the hospital. I then went home for dinner. Often that was 7:00 or so. That was the way my mentors lived. That was what I had expected when I entered medicine.

This, of course, led to some problems within our family.

"Carol, that call is from the hospital. I have to go. Keep supper warm!"

"Carol, I'll be late. I can't go to Dale's program"

"Carol, will you take care of the dog?"

I thought my practice was more important than anything else was. "After all, I was saving lives."

Truth be told I was rarely saving lives, or even easing pain. But I was earning a living and caring for my patients; this was what I had wanted and been trained for. Quickly family life devolved into Dick practicing medicine, occasionally having time for his family. Medicine was my job. Carol's job was to care for the children and me and maintain our home. That era didn't last long!

I began to realize there was more to life than medicine. I enjoyed our children so I spent more time with them. With small children in the house Carol and I didn't have much time to share but she remained the girl whom I had married, the woman I loved. I enjoyed the minor tasks in our home, as long as they were a man's task. Cleaning, washing and cooking, of course, were women's tasks. Carol attempted to teach me that a marriage was a communal project. Intellectually I agreed with that idea. I simply thought my man's job, especially as a doctor, was certainly more important than whatever Carol was doing or wanted. With time I was better trained.

*   *   *

Oakley is not now the community into which we moved. Jim and Bill Funk, the dentist, had built a new office at 418 Hudson, where Terri Albers, DDS, and Rich Loftus, DDS, now have their practices. The hospital was half a block south of their office. Kenny's Drug Store was where The Bank now resides. There was a second drug store, Pennington's that became Paul's Pharmacy for years; it is now part of Farm and Home. Both drug stores had a soda fountain. The Farmers State Bank has replaced the Kaufman Hotel, the place where everyone ate Sunday dinner (lunch). There were two pool halls, two barbershops, and two theaters on Center Street. There were three liquor stores in town. The two drive-in theaters in Oakley closed just before we moved to town. Girls in Scott City liked to drive to Oakley to shop for clothes in the elegant clothing stores in Oakley. There were two grocery stores, two or three hardware stores and two lumberyards. The Curiosity Shop His drew in boys and young men from fifty to one hundred miles to buy their up-to-date clothes. An office call was either three or four dollars. Medical insurance was only for hospitalizations or major accidents.

*   *   *

Shortly after I arrived in Oakley a preceptee and I were standing in the hospital hall with Jim discussing one of the patients. A sweet little lady walked by this small group and said "Good morning Dr. Marchbanks."

Then she added "Good morning, boys" without the deferential tone when spoken to the real doctor. I was crushed!

George was installing a freezer in our new home. Attempting to be nice to the new doctor's wife, George said he had made an appointment and seen me the day before. He had made an earlier appointment to see Dr. Marchbanks but his wife became sick so he gave his wife his appointment and said he would see Dr. Ohmart. He didn't want his wife seeing the young whippersnapper but it was OK if he saw the young doc. Carol laughed at that interchange for days. Her somewhat stuffy husband didn't care that much for Carol's chuckles.

During my early months a nurse told Jim I didn't know how to deliver babies. Another patient told me she would see me because anyone could deliver a baby. Many of Jim's older patients called his preceptees the "sample doctor." I, too, was considered the "sample doctor" until I had spent enough time and shown enough skill in Oakley that Jim's patients would remove the "sample" from the title and I then would become the real doctor. For many that appellation remained until Jim's death.

*   *   *

There were many lessons to be absorbed in Oakley. I gained a lot there, from Jim, from physicians in the surrounding communities, and from my patients. Later I began to write short articles about Oakley and my experiences. This occurred early in my practice in Oakley.

Youth and Love

Once, when I was young and bright and handsome (or at least so I thought) I felt certain that love was only for those of us who were young. I don't know where I got that idea, perhaps I simply grew up with it, certain that all such youthful pursuits belonged only to those who were young enough to appreciate them. I moved to Oakley and began my practice of medicine, still bright and young, ready to take on the world. Little did I realize that the world might have more to say to me than I to it.

Along with the young and pretty women who flocked to my care came some older people, individuals who needed my attention much more than did the attractive obstetrical patient, or her sick child. While they certainly were not as appealing at first glance, they often had much to teach me.

Bill and Gertie formed one such pair. I met Bill first. He was overweight, often smelled as if he needed a bath, certainly needed to eat less garlic, and had tobacco stains in his handlebar mustache. He talked incessantly, but many of his stories were interesting, at least the first time I heard them. Dressed in overalls and a long-handle shirt (This was before the young people adopted this dress and made it stylish.) he would lean on the doorframe and spin his tales, oblivious to my need to get on to the next patient. He fished, not for sport, but as a necessity, so many of his stories involved fishing.

One tale that I particularly remember involved Bill sitting on the creek bank, throwing his line in and relaxing. Then, with actions to accompany his words, he would relate how he felt something moving beneath him. He leaned over to show how he looked between his legs to see what was there, almost toppling over in my hallway. What did he see but the head of a rattlesnake! This may sound unbelievable to those of you raised in the city, but I have always thought it possible, if not too likely. At any rate there he sat, afraid to move for fear of startling the snake, afraid not to, because the snake might grow tired of the weight upon him. Ever so cautiously Bill reached into his tackle box, grasped his knife, and drove it between his legs into the snake's head. I have always wondered at his accuracy, being afraid I might perform a simple, but painful, operation on myself had I tried such a remedy, but drastic situations do sometimes call for chancy solutions. The story improved each time I heard it—the snake grew larger, the head shorter and Bill's aim more accurate.

I met Bill's wife when I hospitalized Bill with pneumonia. Gertie was even more distressing than Bill. She had a speech impediment and had not been allowed to go to school because no one could understand her and they had assumed that she was too slow to learn. I realized early on that this was not true; she was uneducated but not ignorant. When I learned to understand her, she too had tales to tell. She needed dental work in the worst way, smelled worse than Bill, with even more garlic on her breath. She had decided that she was more easily understood if she spoke directly in your face, so I had no trouble detecting the garlic odor. But she was truly concerned about Bill, who was seriously, but not critically ill. Bill recovered and our relationship continued. They had little money, a shanty for a home and a generally hard life. Amazingly, they always had a smile for me, a gift I did not appreciate in its entirety.

Bill asked if he could pick the dandelions that grew profusely in my yard, because he had heard me say that Carol would not let me spray them. He wanted to make dandelion wine, and everyone else poisoned their crop. I was quite happy to have him pick all the dandelions he wished, but never had the courage to taste his wine; I kept seeing the quarter inch of dirt he wore beneath each fingernail.

Gertie developed breast cancer, and had a slow, lingering death. Not particularly painful, but, as was common in those days, she spent a long time in the hospital dying. Bill spent a lot of time there, also. They had no children and little other family, so Bill was almost the only visitor Gertie had. He would spend hours holding her hand, saying very little; there was very little that any of us could say. Nor was there much to do other than watch nature taking her course.

One evening Bill caught me at the nurses' desk. Try as hard as I could I was unable to gracefully extricate myself, so I braced myself to hear about the rattlesnake again; or perhaps it would be some other story. By this time I had heard them all. Or so I thought. But Bill was in a different mood this time. He told me about how he had met Gertie, about how she had not been allowed to go to school. She had been kept at home as a manual laborer, a not unusual script for someone too "different" to go to school in those days. He said that he had fallen in love with her, which I in my callowness found hard to believe, but at least I had the kindness to hide my lack of understanding. He had taught her to live in a world outside of the farm where she was born. He had lived with her for a good many years, and had taken care of her when she was sick. Together they had faced a world harder than any I had known. Slowly I came to realize that this was real love, that everyone has his own idiosyncrasies and that it is not only the young and beautiful who find meaning and love in life.

"Doc," he said, "I know she ain't much, but she's all I've got and I've loved her for a long time." He had tears in his eyes as he spoke.

So did I.

*   *   *

Sometimes I learned from my inability to communicate. Shortly after my arrival in Oakley a widow came to see me. Whatever her problem was I thought I should refer her to Hays to a physician and hospital. She was not eager to see a doctor there, and certainly was not going to St. Anthony's in Hays. She said her husband had died from the "staff" at St. Anthony's hospital. I tried for years to convince her that the "staph" (staphylococcus aureus) was responsible for the infection that resulted in his death, not the "staff" at the hospital. It might, however, be true that a "staff" member carried the "staph" to him and infected him with the bacterium. I think she carried that belief to her grave.

*   *   *

Occasionally the young doctor was correct. There were new things in medical school I had been taught that Jim hadn't been taught. Medical knowledge had been exploding, and this material continued to grow exponentially throughout my career. There was not enough time in the day to practice medicine, spend a bit of time with a wife and children and attempt to assimilate the new techniques and information disseminated throughout medicine.

Jim delivered an infant one evening. The next morning he asked me to look at the infant. Its genitalia was quite ambiguous, neither male nor female. It had a small penis, perhaps a scrotum but containing no testicles. In school I had learned of the adrenogenital syndrome. This genetic defect is in the adrenal gland where one of the steroids (17-hydroxyprogesterone) is not converted to cortisone. With a deficiency of cortisone the adrenal gland makes a larger and larger supply of the 17-hydroxyprogesterone. An increase of this leads to an increase of testosterone, virilizing a female infant. The syndrome may also decrease the manufacture of aldosterone.

A lack of aldosterone results in a high rate of sodium loss in the urine. A low serum sodium may lead to death.

I examined the infant and thought it was a virilized female and she might well have the salt losing problem as well. I felt we should immediately send her to KUMC where I had been taught about this. If she began to vomit or have diarrhea her low sodium would be lowered even further in her stools or vomitus, killing her. Jim was unaware of the salt-wasting, virilizing syndrome. He thought it was a male infant who needed to be taken to a pediatrician in the future, determine the gender of the infant and let him mature and then have reparative surgery as a child.

Since it was Jim's patient nothing was done. He sent the infant home with his/her mother, warning mother that the infant should be watched closely and returned to the hospital if ill. Two weeks later mother brought the infant to our ER *in extremis*. I was on call and rushed to the hospital. There was nothing I could do. The infant died. Her mother was disconsolate at the hospital. I was unable to respond there to her sorrow. I was unable to speak for fear I would break into tears.

Jim and I autopsied the child that evening. It had a uterus, ovaries, an enlarged clitoris and a markedly hyperplastic adrenal cortex. She had been a girl! She died of the salt wasting adrenogenital syndrome. Jim was devastated! I, although having a bit of pride in my acumen, was also aware that a woman's infant had died. As Jim performed the autopsy he told me that, with experience, I would learn to address a patient's sorrow, both verbally and physically——a hug can do wonders. I never could speak of a death without my voice quavering, or even breaking. As time went on I simply gave up, weeping if need be, but attempting to respond to questions and offer solace as best I could.

*   *   *

With Jim's death and my lack of an associate I retreated into "I'm too busy to take care of the lawn."

"Feed the kids and I'll eat later."

"Take the kids to the movie and I'll get there later, if I can."

I matured as our children did. I learned what was essential and what was merely important and to separate them. I spent more time with Carol and the kids. I learned to manage my time better. There were times when I had to stop what I or we were doing and go to the hospital——auto accidents, heart attacks, deliveries—things that took precedence over all else. But most of the time I, at least, was able to do what I wanted, both as a father/husband and doctor. Looking back now (2010) Carol and I agree that we each had a job—mine as the doctor, Carol's was to care for the kids and me. But we worked together. We did that, not without some serious discussions, but we fit into the mold of most physicians and physicians' wives. Nevertheless we constructed a strong, lasting marriage.

The preceptees were certainly of assistance in my practice, especially after Jim's death. If I were extremely busy, e.g. cold or flu season, a good preceptee might examine and treat a patient without my seeing the patient. Usually the student would visit with and examine the patient while I saw another patient, made a phone call or completed a chart. Then the student would tell me what he had found and what he thought we should do. Together we would see the patient. I would examine the salient findings the student had pointed out to me and I would write a prescription. A student managed many night calls at the hospital with only a phone call to me. A good student, and almost all were good students, saved me time. I taught them small town office medicine. I learned something from most students. I certainly enjoyed them and, and at least most of them, enjoyed their stays in Oakley.

*   *   *

As I aged, both in years and experience, women were more at ease in questioning me. A seventy-five year old woman, obviously quite uncomfortable, had a question for me. She had recently remarried a man of her own age. I had taken care of them for years. I congratulated her on her nuptials, trying to relieve her anxiety about her question. That made her more troubled. I had no idea what she was screwing up her nerve to ask.

Finally she asked her question. "Doc, we want to have sex. Is it all right for us to do that?"

That was not a medical question; they were basically healthy. She was asking permission, was it OK for people her age to have, and enjoy, intercourse? I hid my smile and answered "Of course it is. There's no reason to avoid sex if you both desire it."

I could see her relax. The doc didn't ridicule her question. I responded with the answer she had hoped to hear. I cared for them for several years before they died. I think they were a happy couple, enjoying their time together

Many of the older women were hesitant about questioning a male physician, particularly as a young man, about certain problems. An older woman whom I was treating for her blood pressure asked me to look at her buttocks. "I have something on my bum."

She was embarrassed even to ask me about it. She noticed it when bathing and had tried to ignore it but it continued to grow. I asked the aide to help her on the table and help uncover her *derriere*. Once situated I was ready to examine her. She had something on her left cheek, a lesion I thought might be a basal cell skin cancer. I anesthetized the area and removed the lesion.

She asked, "What causes those things?"

I hesitated only for a second, glad she couldn't see my smile, and replied "Too much sun causes these skin cancers."

I could hear the laughter in her answer "Doc, if the sun ever saw my bum it was when I was a baby!"

Sometimes I was the elder in an exam room. A young woman wanted a prescription for oral contraceptives. I told her she would need a physical examination, including a pelvic and Pap smear. She had been in the military service; I assumed she had been through this rigmarole in the army. All went well during the early exam. Then my nurse placed our patients' legs in the stirrups and I sat down between her spread legs.

"Dr. Ohmart, you don't leave the lights on during that, do you?"

Now old enough to laugh with a patient, I said, "Yes. If I turned the lights out now most women would scream and flee from the room, even if unclothed."

Patient, nurse and I all enjoyed the laugh. Our patient was more relaxed during the exam. And we completed the process. I later delivered two infants for that young woman and we always chuckled overt her initial pelvic exam.

Chapter 3

A Physician and Surgeon

My license said, and still (October 2010) says, I am licensed to practice medicine and surgery. When I completed my internship and received my license I felt I was prepared to handle most of the problems in Oakley. Only my good sense limited me. I was aware I was not prepared to operate on hearts, remove cataracts or perform urological procedures. But I had assisted in a couple of gall bladder removals, been first assistant in a C-section, and watched as a cardiologist in the ER opened a chest to attempt cardiac massage. This was the era of "Watch one, do one, teach one. Then you are an expert!"

During my internship I had to spend many nights in the ER, both at Wesley and the Sedgwick County Hospital. An intern was usually the only physician in the Wesley ER. Most of the patients who came to the Wesley ER had their personal physician. We were instructed to call that physician and ask him what he wanted us to do. We were often told to do whatever we thought appropriate. A few instructed us in what to do and a very few came to the ER to care for a patient. If that were so, rarely did we get to do anything; we had to stand by as the physician appeared at the ER and treated the patient. Often we believed we knew better what to do than the attending but we dared not criticize those men.

At the County Hospital an intern was the sole decision-maker. Often the experienced nurses were more knowledgeable than we were, so we learned a lot from them. One of the lessons was how to handle obstreperous patients. If it were an adult patient a policeman was called and calmed down the patient. If it were a child and we needed to repair a laceration the nurses taught us to give the child a sedative—usually we used Demerol®, 50 milligrams, and 5 milligrams of Compazine®. That combination slowed most kids down, often to sleep, while we sutured the laceration or removed the foreign body. At Wesley I had learned to watch one of the attendings use hypnosis to calm down his patients in the ER. I tried it at the County Hospital but never made it work. In Oakley I was often able to talk a kid down and take care of a terrified child, but I don't think I really hypnotized the child.

*   *   *

Fortunately I had no interest in considering myself a surgeon. I had joined Jim, a fairly young man and an excellent GP surgeon, in Oakley. I had two months' training in anesthesiology. I would pass gas while Jim operated. And both of us had something many surgeons did not have—good judgment. But I stretched those bounds.

Lane's parents brought him to the ER one Sunday afternoon. He had been riding his bike and the spokes of his wheel had caught the back of his ankle. He couldn't plantarflex (bend down) his foot. He had a small laceration but it had severed his Achilles' tendon, the tendon that pulls his foot down. It had to be repaired. There were orthopedic surgeons in Hays. But I had repaired a couple of small tendons in the KUMC ER. I thought I could also repair that tendon; I had been taught how to do it. Lane was a trooper. I anesthetized the skin around the cut and a small area above his laceration. I made an incision a short way above his ankle so I could reach the contracted tendon. I then pulled it down and sutured the fibrous tissues surrounding the tendon together. After putting a splint on his ankle to maintain the plantarflexion in his ankle so as not to stretch the repaired tendon, he was ready to go home. He was probably on crutches for four to six weeks then was able to walk and run.

Lane was a couple of years younger than Dean so I had many chances to watch him play ball in high school. I could see no signs of any disability. I often wondered if he had any problems with my repair. I asked Lane's father in December 2008 if Lane had any problems following my suture job and he replied that as far as he knew he had never had a problem.

Dean, playing basketball as a young man, ruptured his Achilles' tendon. Admittedly a sharp laceration is quite different from a torn, shredded tendon, and a young boy is different from a thirty year old adult, but Dean had a general anesthetic, a ninety minute operation, and was in a cast for two or three months, followed by an extended period of rehabilitation. Both recovered.

Still a brave (foolish?) young doctor I cared for a trucker involved in an accident near Oakley. He had several lacerations but the most consequential was a small cut on his right elbow. It looked quite unimportant until I explored the laceration. There I discovered he had severed his ulnar nerve. The ulnar nerve carries the impulses to the muscles that flex (close) the muscles of his fingers. I had been taught how to repair that laceration. I approximated the severed ends and sutured them together. Then I splinted his elbow to maintain the apposed ends. After I had repaired his other lacerations he spent a day or so in our hospital. His employer picked up the injured driver and his truck. I never heard what became of that repair, but I have frequently wondered about that bit of surgery. The nerve below the laceration would die. If my reconstruction had been successful the nerve would regenerate and he would be able to use his fingers. I had been told a nerve would regenerate an inch a month. If that is correct it would have taken my patient eighteen months to regain the use of his hand.

As a young man I did such things as those above that I would not have dreamed of doing ten or fifteen years later. Occasionally weather forced me to do procedures that I was hesitant about performing. But during my years in Oakley I became competent in other procedures and new techniques through my experience and continuing medical education classes

*   *   *

Anesthesiology Fits the Bill

When I moved to Oakley Jim, as most physicians then, was doing a lot of T&As (tonsillectomy and adenoidectomy). Jim was still using open drop ether, a comparatively safe anesthetic. However ether had other problems. As well as our patient, we all had to breathe the ether; it was an explosive and extremely slow to put a child to sleep. To avoid the kid fighting the ether, Jim taught me to use a liquid barbiturate, Pentothal®, as an enema. The child then could go to sleep in his mother's arms then be taken to the OR. There the ether would keep him asleep during the T&A.

The enema induction procedure was not very scientific; we just guessed at how much solution to use in the enema based on his weight. We also had little idea whether the kid expelled a little or a lot of the solution before he went to sleep or how sensitive the child was to Pentothal®. This technique also meant that the child might be quite slow to awaken from the Pentothal®.

Using an ether mask to cover the child's mouth and nose made the removal of tonsils difficult. My patient would breathe ether for a few minutes; then I would remove the mask, allowing the child to breathe air for a few minutes, while Jim tried to quickly remove the child's tonsils and adenoids. If the child started to awaken, I poured more ether on the mask and again covered his mouth and nose. When he was again appropriately anesthetized I would remove the mask allowing Jim to return to the T&A. The procedure was thus completed in fits and starts.

I had been trained to use open drop ether in Wichita where one or two older doctors wanted the ether used on their T&As. More physicians there used Cyclopropane®, also an anesthetic gas. Cyclopropane® was administered by use of a gas machine where oxygen and nitrogen, the two gases found in air, were used as a carrier for the Cyclopropane®. The anesthetist was able to control the patient's respirations by increasing or decreasing the amount of Cyclopropane® flow into the patient's lungs.

As part of the use of Cyclopropane® I was also trained to intubate patients. Once the child was asleep I would insert an endotracheal tube into his trachea and connect the gas machine to a tube with the gas going directly into his lungs. The tube prevented blood from the T&A running into his trachea and lungs. This also kept blood from entering his esophagus during the T&A. With less blood in his stomach our patient was less likely to vomit swallowed blood. Using the Cyclopropane® was safer, faster and easier to control than ether. But it also was explosive. We had to take precautions to avoid a spark. Jim was delighted to switch to the Cyclopropane® as soon as we had the supplies. We still used the Pentothal® for induction; then used Cyclopropane® to maintain the anesthetic.

*   *   *

One morning I was talking with another patient after Jim completed a T&A, still using Pentothal® and ether. I was in the south hall, away from the nurses' desk, when an anguished wail came from a room where a girl

41

and her mother rested after her T&A. I ran to the room and her mother cried "She's not breathing!"

She was not! She was already turning blue! I don't think anyone at that time had any training in CPR. Artificial respiration was for drowning. But she needed air. It was easy. I simply bent over her bed, placed my mouth over hers and forced my breath into hers. After a few breaths she gasped and breathed on her own. I had been taught, or told, that if a patient were not breathing he would have a last, gasping breath before dying and that breath would again start him breathing. I'm glad I didn't wait to see if that actually worked.

Operations seem to have their own fads. As mentioned, Jim did a lot of T&As when I first moved to Oakley. As time went by we did fewer and fewer T&As. Partly that was due to the use of the new and better antibiotics for tonsillitis. In medical school we knew only of penicillin and streptomycin. During the next few years a host of better antibiotics for tonsillitis were developed. Physicians also realized that not all sore throats were tonsillitis and that removing tonsils did not prevent sore throats. For a while physicians thought they should remove adenoids to prevent ear infections. That also went by the wayside. There remain excellent indications for removing tonsils and/or adenoids but not as many as we used to believe.

Carpal tunnel operations were rare in Jim's practice. I remember only one such operation he performed while during our years together. This procedure was done fairly commonly during the last few years of my practice. This may have to do with the computer age where many people spend hours every day typing with their wrists slightly cocked.

During my year in Wichita we interns joked at some of the surgeons of whom we said, "His reason for doing a hysterectomy is that the woman has a uterus." Since most doctors were male they could always find a reason for that procedure. Jim and I joshed a bit between us that a surgeon in Colby did hysterectomies for sterilizations in St. Thomas Hospital, the Colby Catholic hospital, where simple tubal ligations were forbidden.

In the 1960s and 70s it seemed that we were doing an appendectomy a month. And most of the path reports were read as "acute appendicitis." In school the surgeons told us that if we removed one normal appendix out of four clinically diagnosed as acute appendixes we were doing a good job in the diagnosis. Jim and I rarely removed a normal appendix. We waited until we were confident that it was truly appendicitis. Often we retained a patient in the hospital if his symptoms were questionable. If we sent someone home we assumed that, if symptoms persisted, our patients would return a few hours later. In the 1980s and 90s I rarely saw a suspected acute appendicitis. Whatever happened to those inflamed appendices? I never knew. Maybe they went to another physician who performed operations and would remove the offending organ. Or perhaps they healed without medical assistance.

*   *   *

Was I To Become a Surgeon?

I never cared for surgery, not in medical school, not in my internship nor in practice with Jim. I don't think my dislike for surgery came from my being responsible for a patient in the OR. I anesthetized many patients for Jim or the other doctors who practiced in Oakley. Occasionally one of the Colby physicians who practiced in the St. Thomas Hospital would bring one of his patients to the Logan County Hospital where the doctor would perform a tubal ligation. Either Jim or I would anesthetize the woman. After Jim died in November of 1971 I endeavored to become a surgeon, or at least some facsimile thereof.

At the time of Jim's death he had been caring for a pregnant woman who had planned on Jim's performing a tubal ligation on her following her delivery. She asked me if I would assume her care. Taking care of her prenatal care and delivery was no problem. Doing a tubal ligation was a bit different. But I had watched several done. It looked simple. Why not? I agreed.

The prenatal care and delivery went according to my plans. The tubal ligation was not as fear inducing as I had anticipated. All went well. I removed a segment of each Fallopian tube, sutured each end, and buried the ends of the tubes leading from the uterus in the muscles of the uterus. I thought, "Hey, this isn't so tough. And I can charge a surgeon's fees, not an assistant's or anesthetist's fee."

We sent the two specimens to the lab in Hays so I would be able to prove that I had, indeed, removed two segments of Fallopian tubes. The report was returned. As I expected one specimen reported that it was a right Fallopian tube. The second reported the specimen as "normal

43

thyroid tissue." Real surgeon or not, I knew that I had not been anywhere near her thyroid gland. Jim had operated on a thyroid rarely, but certainly not in months. No other surgeon had operated in Oakley. I called the pathologist and told him about the reports. The pathologist was certain they had made no mistake in the lab. I was, and still am, certain the lab made an error. I am still laughing about the surgeon who expected a report of thyroid tissue and whose report said left fallopian tube. I told my patient about the path report and was certain that I had severed two tubes and that she need not worry about a pregnancy. I took care of her and her family until my retirement. No, she did not conceive again.

About that same time a tourist family spending the night at the Camp Inn north of Oakley brought their teenage boy to the ER in the early morning. He had right lower quadrant abdominal pain, a white count of 15,000 and a low-grade fever. He had appendicitis! I also knew how to handle this problem. Again it was simple. A small incision, find the inflamed appendix, clamp it off from the cecum, sever it and drop the cecum back into the peritoneum. Sew up the skin and I was done. I once watched the fastest surgeon at KUMC do it in fifteen minutes. It took me forty-five. A couple days later the family was on their way, only delaying their vacation minimally.

The man worked for Purdue University and his insurance card appeared valid. I don't remember what the problem was but the insurance did not pay my fee. Nor did the family pay either the hospital or me.

Two for two in my surgical misadventures. My procedures yielded no medical problems, but the anxiety I spent over those two episodes convinced me that I would relinquish any dreams I might have in becoming a surgeon.

Jim had also asked me to assist in performing vasectomies in our office. He had done them alone before I joined him but said it was much easier for two to perform the operation. Jim always sent the two vas specimens to the pathologist to insure that he had severed the vas. He also asked his patients to bring a sperm specimen to the office after six-eight ejaculations to assure Jim that there was truly no sperm in the ejaculate. One morning my first visitor was a young woman whose complaint was amenorrhea.

In taking her history she said Jim and I had performed a vasectomy on her husband. Then I examined her. She was either pregnant or had a large uterine fibroid. This was much earlier than the ability of sonograms or pregnancy tests available in our office or from your local pharmacy to corroborate a pregnancy. Her blood was drawn and I sent it to Topeka to the lab there. A rabbit test confirmed her pregnancy! Her husband was quite upset. My patient swore that no man other than her husband had had sex with her. I looked at his records. His chart showed that we had submitted two specimens of vas, but had never returned for his post vas sperm check. Fortunately for all of us his ejaculate showed swarming sperm in the ejaculate. No one was angry. Jim and I found an accessory vas on each side of his scrotum and ligated those. This ejaculate showed no sperm.

Another man Jim and I performed the procedure on also failed to follow our instructions. The vasectomies were done in the morning and he was given instructions to go home, stay off his feet and put an ice bag on his scrotum. This was a football coach with a football game Friday evening. The coach went home, applied the ice bag and stayed off his feet until game time. He then went to the game where, as usual, he stood along with the high school players during the game. The next morning his wife called and asked me if I could come take a look at him.

I did. On his bed lay a football coach in pain. Uncovering his unclothed privates I found a football lying between his legs. A small vessel had bled during the game and after he went to bed. His scrotum was purple and literally the size of a football. The bleeding had ceased but there was nothing to do other than let his colorful scrotum regain its normal size and coloration.

After Jim's death I did a few, very few, vasectomies by myself. Standing at the operating table and performing that procedure made my own groin hurt so much that I decided it was not worth it.

I did however continue to do D&Cs as needed, along with almost anything I could remove under a local anesthetic. A D&C usually required a general anesthetic. Sometimes I asked a nurse to follow the patient after I gave her a barbiturate. Sometimes I asked a preceptee to monitor our patient. At KUMC they often did a D&C after a miscarriage by simply giving the woman an injection of Demerol®, a narcotic analgesic. They then proceeded with the D&C. I tried that once or twice but my patients didn't care for that—the analgesic left the patient with too much memory of the procedure. I later tried ketamine, a dissociative anesthetic, which I had used in children successfully. It was an extremely safe anesthetic. The books indicated that it was not usually used in adults because of hallucinations during and after its use. I tried it once. The young woman saw Santa Claus sitting on her bed for several hours and they had a fine conversation following her D&C. Neither I nor the young woman cared for that effect. I continued to use the barbiturate anesthetic or called in a nurse anesthetist from Colby.

* * *

I continued to learn surgical techniques using a local anesthetic and removed many skin lesions and repaired fairly large lacerations. With practice I became a competent plastic surgeon, although I always referred the patient if I thought I was not capable of handling the problem. As the Oakley population aged, many patients developed skin cancers, usually squamous or basal cell cancers. I wasn't at all concerned about basal cell cancers. Removing them usually cured the disease. Squamous cell cancers were a bit more worrisome. They might metastasize, spreading to a distant site through the blood or lymph system. I removed them but closely followed those patients for recurrences or metastases. I removed several malignant melanomas, although I usually preferred to biopsy the suspicious lesion then refer it to a surgeon for definitive therapy of a melanoma.

Melanomas were always extremely worrisome. My instructors at KUMC told me that if I were to see one melanoma in my career I would be surprised. I was told that sailors, spending their lives at sea usually going shirtless, were about the only people who developed those cancers. Farmers, also spending their lives in the sun, were the next most likely group to develop a melanoma. Most farmers, however, wore shirts, usually with long sleeves. I think the first patient I saw with that disease was a woman who presented to me with a lump under her left arm. I didn't know what it was but I thought it needed to be removed. So did the surgeon. He removed it in our hospital, and then told me he thought it was a "white" melanoma, a malignant melanoma that didn't have the melanin in the typical melanoma. "Do you know if she had a melanoma on her arm?"

"No, I don't. She had been Jim's patient, but I can look at her chart in our office."

The path report came back as an amelanotic malignant melanoma. Her chart told us that Jim had removed a small lesion from her left forearm some twenty years prior. Now it had shown up again! A chest

X-ray revealed that she had metastases in her lungs. She died of the melanoma. One of Dean's high school classmates died of melanoma a few years after they graduated from high school. I removed two melanomas from women's faces, one just in front of her ear and one in her eyebrow. The eyebrow lesion recurred and I again removed it. Neither of them had any further trouble. I diagnosed one on a woman's thumb, under her nail. This I referred to a surgeon who amputated the distal phalanx of her thumb. They all died years later of other causes. Probably during my years in practice I averaged about one per year, certainly more numerous than I had been taught. And I can, without searching my mind, recall four who died from a malignant melanoma.

*   *   *

At the nursing home two elderly men, roommates, had a fight at dinner, when one of them threw pepper in the other's face. They were separated, and then returned to their room for the evening. In their room the peppered man grasped his cane and swung down on his attacker's head, ripping his ear almost off. I was summoned to the ER and, after removing the bloody bandage from his head, realized he had almost had his ear severed. With time and local anesthetic I reattached his ear, wrapped his head in a tight bandage and sent him back to the nursing home. Surprisingly the ear survived, leaving very little scar.

Whether I thought I was capable or not, sometimes the weather forced me to make decisions and perform procedures I might have liked to hand off to a surgeon in Hays. During a snowstorm a local girl had her nose partially separated from her upper lip in an auto accident. The weather was terrible! I believed I could repair that, especially considering the weather. I talked to her parents and they agreed that I would repair it in Oakley. If the scar was disfiguring she could have it repaired later. I used all the skills I possessed; she healed well, and needed no further repair. After we had an ambulance, and later, airplanes and helicopters, it was easier to move patients from Oakley to a secondary or tertiary care center, even in bad weather. But I still had to repair some laceration I would have preferred to transfer.

My most amazing repair was an elderly man whose car had skidded across the median on I-70, hitting an oncoming car. The other driver was killed. My patient had a laceration starting with the corner of his mouth, running beside his nose and up to the corner of his eye. The lower end of the laceration was a through and through laceration of his cheek. He also had a back injury, although he had no neurological problems. An icy road was the cause of his accident. I would have been quite happy to send him somewhere else, but the same icy road prohibited that. It well might have been two or three days before he could safely be transported. It took me most of the morning but I repaired his laceration. It healed amazingly well, leaving him with very little scar. For years I joked with him that I should enter him as my sewing project in the Logan County Fair. He was always pleased when I showed a new student the face I had reconstructed. I knew that, although it was strange, the elderly healed with less scarring than children. I took advantage of that fact in caring for many of my patients.

*   *   *

Real Surgeons Visit Oakley

Zeferino Arroyo, M.D., a general surgeon in Scott City, was a welcome addition to the Logan County Hospital staff. He scheduled elective surgery in Oakley and would often come to Oakley for emergency surgery. I served as first assistant and learned quite a bit about techniques but I never again wanted to be "the surgeon." We had a nurse anesthetist, often from Colby, provide the anesthetic. Dr. Arroyo taught me to do EGDs—esophogo-gastro-duodenoscopies. He moved to Garden City, too far to drive to Oakley to see either emergency or routine patients.

Mike Lasley, M.D., then Ross Stadelman, M.D., both general surgeons, started to come to Oakley once a week. They did major surgery in Oakley: Cesarean sections, hysterectomies, cholecystectomies, and cancer surgery—mastectomies, gastrectomies and colon resections. Again I was first assistant, with a nurse anesthetist. During the time in my practice the number of major operations declined. Thus we provided medical services in Oakley for almost forty years.

Chapter 4

Now I'm an Obstetrician, Too

Oakley was our home! I was a doctor! I was not just any doctor; I had found an excellent mentor and soon-to-be partner. My salary was more than I had imagined. In the mornings I drove to the hospital whistling, ready to go to work!

Jim left on a long overdue vacation. He had told me he had left me two or three pregnant women. He said they had all had delivered babies before and he expected no problems if I were to deliver them. He had no concerns about my abilities. Of course, the women might have been less confident of my abilities. They chose Jim as their doctor. Now he was going to leave them in the care of some kid, a wet-behind-the-ears doctor, if he actually was a doctor. It would be a new experience for Jim's patients to have a doctor younger than she deliver her baby. However, I too, was now confident of my ability. I had delivered more than two hundred babies in medical school or during my internship. And birth was a natural process. What could go wrong? All I needed to do was act confident, catch the infant, and hand him to the mother.

*　　*　　*

Ass-Backwards Babies

If only it had been that easy! My first delivery was Norma Lee. Early in labor all went well. As I examined her I realized something didn't feel right. No head presented! What I was feeling was a butt! That's not the way baby's are to be born. Of course I had been taught how to deliver a breech. But I had never even seen a breech delivery! Off to the books to bone up on the technique. I told Norma Lee that I could feel the baby's breech, that it was a boy and what was going on, but she didn't seem upset. After all, I was the doctor.

After a somewhat longer than usual labor she was ready to deliver. There was the breech, with his legs up beside his head. Just as my book had instructed me to do I put my fingers beside one leg, flexed the knee, and then removed that leg. The other was easier, more space. But the danger is that the aftercoming head might compress the umbilical cord between the head and her pelvis. I knew what to do—you should flex the infant's neck and use my first two fingers to hold the infant's neck flexed and use this to gently, but quickly, extract his head.

I had very little to do! With having had prior deliveries she knew what to do. She pushed! And the boy was born! Everyone was happy, no one more than I. Shawn was born on August 3, 1963, the first of the slightly more than one thousand babies I delivered in Oakley.

In the summer of 2008 I bumped into Norm Lee while both of us were in the New Frontiers waiting room. I knew who she was; I even remembered her name (no mean feat for me at age 72). We reminisced on our first meeting. I told her how terrified I had been in being faced with my first breech delivery alone. She told me she and her husband said I had appeared to have all the confidence in the world. Many times those acting skills carried me through a nerve-wracking few minutes.

* * *

Three of my first five deliveries were breech deliveries. An older nurse told Jim that the young doctor didn't know how to deliver babies. I no longer feared a breech presentation. But the approach to delivering a breech baby changed during my years in Oakley. After my first three breech deliveries in Oakley I felt confident in that procedure. Those three women had all had a prior cephalic delivery. A primip (primipira—initial delivery; multipara—multiple deliveries) with a breech presentation posed a somewhat different problem than a multip. A breech delivery needed a bit more room in a mother's pelvis. The doctor needed to ascertain that her bony pelvis would accommodate the butt first delivery. In a primip her tissues had not been stretched by a prior delivery. And, whether or not true, if the baby had any damage the courts would ascribe the problems to the physician's care in delivery. After twenty years in Oakley I had delivered primip breeches with no problems, but obstetricians strongly recommended physicians discovering a primip breech presentation do a C-section delivery. They also recommended considering a C-sections on a multip breech presentation.

I had cared for Paula (not Paula Marchbanks) throughout her pregnancy. As the time for delivery approached I thought she might be carrying a breech baby. At that time there were two ways to determine the position of the fetus—by feeling the fetus through the mother's abdominal wall or by X-raying her abdomen to determine the baby's position. No one wanted to submit a fetus to X-rays if possible; if necessary it should be done as close to the delivery date as possible. It felt to me that the baby was breech. I discussed our options with my patient. If we were going to do an elective C-section it should be planned on Wednesday, the day the surgeons were in Oakley. The week before that I had X-rayed her abdomen. Yes, the baby was breech and a C-section was scheduled for next Wednesday morning.

Paula went into labor Tuesday! When I examined her I thought I felt a crown (head) presenting in her vagina. Could that kid have turned around? Another X-ray of her abdomen showed the baby had, indeed, turned itself upside down. No C-section, just another vaginal delivery.

I had delivered Elaine's first infant. Now she was pregnant again. Her first delivery was uneventful. This time I thought she might be carrying a breech baby. Now there were sonograms to show the baby's position. Yes, it was breech. Elaine and her husband discussed the situation with me. They knew of the advice of doing a C-section for a first infant. But this was a second delivery. Should she have a C-section? They wanted to avoid a C-section if possible. Should they request an obstetrician to deliver her breech baby? We called an obstetrician in Hays. Would he deliver Elaine vaginally, although a breech delivery? His reply was that he had never experienced a vaginal breech delivery. He would be glad to do a C-section but not a vaginal breech delivery. I delivered Elaine's infant in Oakley, breech and all. No problems.

* * *

Obstetrics became my favorite part of medicine. That was partially because the young woman to appear before me was usually healthy and happy. Most had a fortuitous outcome. I count two who were delivered elsewhere, one at home and one in the ambulance on the way to Hays, among the thousand I have delivered.

Having a baby in Oakley was held to be a natural event. The mother-to-be came into the hospital when her labor began and labored until she was ready to deliver. The woman, her husband and probably her mother and other family members were all at the hospital, waiting patiently. Actually most families waited impatiently. When her delivery was imminent, a nurse and I (unless I was in a hurry to change into scrubs), assisted by her husband and other sundry family members, helped her move from her bed to a stretcher. We then trundled her to the delivery room where, after chasing everyone but the nurse from the delivery room, we reversed the process with the cart. We had her clamber from the stretcher to a cold metal delivery table, put her "up" and we waited.

"Up" is the correct position. This was for the comfort of the delivering physician, certainly not the comfort of the laboring woman. She was laid on her back and her legs were strapped into stirrups. In this position the stirrups flexed her hips, flexed her knees and spread her legs. Then the officiating doctor sat down on a stool between her legs, staring at her perineum. And thus we waited, sometimes for hours. As I became more experienced I managed to shorten the wait, occasionally only to seconds, but we usually had some time to commune with each other. I got to know the woman quite well. Or at least her perineum. I have been screamed all the epithets a shipload of sailors might have heaped on me, but once the baby was in mom's arms I was told how great I was. It's no wonder doctors acquire a God complex.

*   *   *

Mothers-To-Be Dislike Pain

There were various anesthetics that could be given to relieve the mother's discomfort. Early in labor, but not too early as it might stop labor, Demerol® could be given to the woman. I was taught that the mother should not be given her Demerol® within an hour before the delivery as it might suppress the infant's respirations. During my internship in the height of "twilight sleep" craze I saw two infants die because of the baby's respiratory suppression. I wanted no even mildly suppressed babies in my delivery room. Thus if I gave the woman her Demerol® too soon it would prolong labor; if I thought it was too late for me to give her a shot she went cold turkey.

Once in the delivery room a woman had some choice of an anesthetic. There was the "grin and bear it" approach as in the Salvation Army Hospital for Unwed Mothers. At KUMC I had been trained to give spinal and/or saddle anesthetics and a spinal certainly relieved her pain. She was also paralyzed below the level of her anesthetic, paralyzing her legs until the anesthetic wore off, usually a few hours. Most mothers given spinals could not discern when she had a contraction. Mother's assistance was important in pushing that baby out. So I would tell her when to push since I could feel the contraction on her abdomen. Theoretically I was trained to use a "saddle block" which was supposed to only block the feelings from the saddle area of her perineum. If I was lucky that worked. If the anesthetic got too high she was temporarily paralyzed. If too low she got only partial pain relief.

The obstetricians at KUMC also liked to use a pudendal block. This was an anesthetic injection given on each side of the cervix through her vagina. Much as a dentist blocks a tooth, it was supposed to block the pudendal nerves. Sometimes this worked well, sometimes it didn't. But it would not suppress the baby's respirations.

We also used gas. There was a Trilene® (trichloroethylene) inhaler. It was not flammable as was ether and not as dangerous as chloroform which frequently damaged livers. This was used in a handheld mask that the mother could inhale as she desired. She could huff and puff all she wanted with this. It didn't suppress the baby but it wasn't a very effective pain reliever, either.

A few years later we used another inhaler, Penthrane®. I used this as an anesthetic agent in surgery, a great step up from open drop ether. In the OR I placed the liquid Penthrane® in an anesthetic machine where it vaporized and, along with nitrogen and oxygen, would provide a surgical level of anesthetic. In OB I put a small quantity of liquid Penthrane® in a handheld inhaler strapped to the woman's wrist. She could breathe it to her heart's content. If it made her too sleepy she would drop her hand away from her mouth and wake up, then resume puffing. It seemed to work very well but this was the day of recreational drug use. The government declared Penthrane® was too easy for users to obtain and took this inhaler off the market.

I also used nitrous oxide, the laughing gas of many movies. I would prepare the anesthetic machine and the nurse would administer the anesthetic. This also did not put a woman to sleep, nor was it a particularly effective analgesic. This also became a drug of abuse but because it had to be stored in a tank and administered via a machine it was not so easily misused.

* * *

Somewhat later in my practice "natural childbirth" came into vogue. By this time fathers were allowed, actually encouraged, to go into the delivery room with his wife. Oakley was the first local hospital to encourage the LaMaze method of natural childbirth. This approach was to conduct prenatal classes, teaching what was to happen in labor and delivery and instruction in relaxation. Little medical analgesia would be used. The hope was that if the woman were relaxed she would have less pain and an easier and faster delivery. This was similar to the "grin and bear it" approach to childbirth at the Salvation Army Hospital. One of our nurses, Jeanita Losey, was trained as a LaMaze instructor. She held classes for expectant mothers and their husbands.

I thought this was the best approach to childbirth analgesia. Both of the parents were involved, not only in the conception, but also in the entire pregnancy and delivery. Although the mother had some (or much) pain, the couple had accomplished a joint project and their bonds were strengthened. We delivered many girls with the help of LaMaze training and a little local anesthetic for her episiotomy.

I am certain at least a few women felt this was her chance to get even with her husband's transgressions. She wanted him aware of what he was putting her through in a pregnancy and delivery. In these cases her husband was not the only recipient of epithets. Nurses, students and even I were lambasted, although we could easily forget about the words used. Her husband was not so fortunate. Shortly the title "husband" was replaced by "significant other," sometimes male, sometimes female.

One of my early experiences with the father in the delivery room was almost the last time I would allow a father into the delivery room. Labor and delivery went swimmingly. But the mother kept bleeding, losing lots of blood. I realized that her uterus had prolapsed. This means her uterus has turned itself inside out with it projecting through her vagina. I knew what the books said to do—push the uterus back through her vagina and into the proper position, with your fist! Of course we were first to put her to sleep, or better yet, she would already be asleep.

I had only a nurse for assistance, no anesthetist. I had not given here a saddle, just a little gas. I had no other choice. I said it might hurt a bit. Then I placed my fist against her uterus and pushed. Fortunately I have small hands. With a "thunk" from the uterus and an "Oh" from the patient, her uterus was replaced and the bleeding ceased. I looked at the father at the top of the table. He was bug-eyed! After repairing her episiotomy and taking her back to her room, he said "Was that what I think I saw?"

I replied "Yes."

That was about all that was said. Both mother and father did well. I knew that cows comparatively frequently prolapsed their uteruses and the rancher simply replaced them, but it was not common in women. And that father had not been a rancher; I think he was a minister, if I remember correctly. After that experience I knew I could handle whatever came up with the father in the delivery room.

*　　*　　*

My Own OB Patients

The first mothers I delivered had been Jim's patients, patients I had taken care of when he was absent, on his vacation or on a weekend. One of the first women who chose to see me was a woman who had already had several children. Jim had delivered those. But Jim was busy so she came to see me. She chose me! Proud as punch, I skimmed Eileen's old office chart, talked to her about this pregnancy and examined her. Yes, she was pregnant. I had been taught that I should now tell her about her care for herself and the baby. I began my little speech but she cut me short "I know all of that. I've been through this before."

Now what was I to do? She was four or five months pregnant, so diagnosing the pregnancy was not a wonderful feat. I really had little to offer on that first visit. I did give her a prescription for prenatal vitamins. Then I asked her why she had chosen to see me. She said, "Dr. Marchbanks is so busy I hated to bother him. Anyone can deliver a baby."

I was crushed!

When we dated her estimated date of confinement (EDC, the date when our calculators said the baby should be born) it said January 1. I often joked with my patients, telling them they had to plan the day so that deliveries, accidents, etc. had to be prearranged in advance so they didn't interfere with my plans. I told her she couldn't deliver on the first because I wanted to watch football games all day on the television with my boys. That was the way we always spent the day. We joked about it on her prenatal visits and she said that day wouldn't work for her, either, as she had to prepare a noon family dinner on the first. All went well, until Eileen phoned me on New Year's morning and said she was in labor. She stayed home, prepared dinner, and then drove to the hospital. The nurse called, "Yes, she is in labor."

My reply was "Call me when you need me."

The nurse phoned me later that afternoon and said she thought I should come to the hospital. I did so, examined Eileen and thought, "Yes, she is well into labor but not yet needs to be in the delivery room."

I walked to the lobby, where the only TV in the hospital rested, sat down and turned on the ballgame. The first half of the game ended, the nurse summoned me and I delivered the baby. I was home in time for the start of the second half. Eileen always said she had done a magnificent job of scheduling her day—she had dinner prepared and the family had eaten, so it didn't interfere with her family. Then she delivered the infant at halftime so it didn't interfere with my plans. Most of the patients in Oakley attempted to be as little bother as possible but no one has been more successful in that than Eileen's New Year's Day delivery.

*   *   *

The fall of 1963 a young woman entered our office. She thought she was pregnant. She had missed a period, and had a bit of morning nausea. Yes, she probably was pregnant, but she wasn't far enough along for me to feel an enlarged uterus. The only pregnancy test then available was to draw a tube of blood, send it to the lab in Topeka where a rabbit test was done, and then mail me the results. This took a week or so, depending on mail service, weekends, etc. Many couples awaiting those results, with a greater or lesser degree of anticipation or anxiety, had a haggard appearance when I finally relayed the results. Now there is an over-the-counter urine test, able to provide positive (or negative) results in a few moments, even before the woman has yet to miss a period.

That evening after examining Helen, Carol and I went to Dance Club. That was the social event of the month, a dinner-dance at the country club. Carol and I were new in Oakley and we were invited. The high school assistant football coach and his wife, Sonny and Helen, were also invited. After dinner the members started the dance with a number of mixers to acquaint the new members to the older——a circle dance, a broom dance and others all having to leave a partner when the music stopped, then finding another dance partner when it began again.

I found myself dancing with Helen. Both of us were a bit embarrassed. To break the ice this young woman said "I have never danced with a man in the evening after he has taken my clothes off in the afternoon."

After complaining that I had not been the one who removed her clothes, I said, "I have never danced with the woman I examined earlier in the afternoon, either. So it's a draw."

The ice was broken, we became friends and I had a new patient.

A few weeks later Helen called and said she had some fairly heavy vaginal bleeding. I told her to go to the hospital quickly and I would see her there. She was miscarrying. That was Friday afternoon. Her husband's first game as football coach was scheduled in Oakley for that evening. Jim gave her an anesthetic, I did a dilatation and curettage (D&C) later that afternoon and Sonny made it to the ball game. I don't remember whether Oakley won or lost, but I'll wager the new coach never forgot his first ballgame.

*   *   *

In November 1970, Rose came to see me. She was a tiny young woman. Her husband was quite a bit larger than I was and I was six feet tall and weighed two hundred and twenty pounds. We had delivered her first infant, five pounds and six ounces. I thought we could deliver a somewhat larger baby if this infant were a little larger. No. Rose came to the hospital in labor, six weeks early. I felt it would be a tiny baby. And she was ready to have her baby. Now! I had no time to transfer her. Delivering the baby was simple. The baby weighed two pounds and twelve ounces. Now what should I do?

The baby was little but seemed quite strong. I contacted the nearest pediatrician, in Denver. "What am I supposed to do in Oakley? Send mother and baby to Denver? How do I keep her warm in their trip to Denver? How do I feed her?"

Had this occurred thirty years later we would have flown baby and mom to Wichita or Denver. Even the pediatricians in Hays didn't want an infant that small in Hays. In 1970 we had no ambulance service, no Flight For Life.

The pediatrician said if all went well we should just keep her here, feed her and keep her warm. And there wasn't much more anyone could do even if the baby were in Denver. She was too small to suck. We had to put a tube through her nose into her stomach every two hours to feed her. I had learned to do that in Wichita but I had to teach the Oakley nurses how to feed her. None of them liked to do it, but all learned to insert that tube and feed her. The baby grew. And grew. When I last saw her she was a cute little girl.

*   *   *

Most deliveries were joyous occasions. I enjoyed caring for these expectant women throughout their prenatal care and delivery. Usually they were happy and healthy throughout their office visits and deliveries. But occasionally something went wrong. The coach's wife above was such an instance. This next incident was even more heart-wrenching to a young doctor.

About a year after I joined Jim in Oakley I was summoned to the hospital and was told that one of Jim's patients was in labor. Jim was out of town. She was not due for two months. But she was certainly in labor. At that time there was nothing to do for premature labor other than bed rest. Bed rest was not going to do anything for her. She was in active labor and was going to have the baby—quickly! I had delivered fifteen or twenty babies during that year so I was fairly confident about handling the delivery. Care for the mother would be a snap. Handling and delivering a small infant would be no problem. Taking care of a premature baby two months early was a different matter. There was no pediatrician to care for the infant. No one to assist me! I was it! In the delivery room labor quickly resulted in a pale, unmoving infant. There was nothing to do but tell the parents that their infant was dead.

There I learned why the older nurses kept a small bottle of holy water in the delivery room. She baptized the infant then handed it to his mother. I had been told in medical school that I should baptize a dying newborn, or any other dying patient, but had never seen it done. Later during my career I baptized a rare infant but was always hoping to have time to call a priest for that task.

I don't suppose that poor mother had laid her eyes on the young doctor who was now saying that her infant was dead. In tears because of the death, I was unable to speak. Her husband was obviously upset, too, attempting to comfort his wife. I had never been faced with such a situation as this. I could not explain the premature delivery and death. I knew I was supposed to request an autopsy. I certainly didn't want to ask the bewildered parents for permission to have an autopsy done on their child. But that was the only way we might obtain an answer to the cause of the infant's death. I managed to explain why we needed the autopsy and they acquiesced. My autopsy revealed that the infant had a congenital heart problem; that had been the cause of the child's death. I took care of both of them for many years.

I learned that I could survive a crisis, even a crisis that I could do nothing about. There was never any enjoyment in that kind of a task; it was my responsibility and I learned to do it. With experience I found I could do what was necessary and cry alone, at home. I also learned that faith was important to my patients, as on that morning. Many times during my medical career a priest or pastor would be my supporter in cases of injury or death.

*   *   *

Babies Rarely Appear As Scheduled

As a young doctor I was certain I was always correct. One evening I was making a presentation to a women's club. Most of them were mothers and had wanted to see a movie of an actual birth. Such movies were not easy to come by and certainly did not have such shows on TV as we now might see. I managed to obtain a Navy training film of childbirth which they used to show to expectant mothers. Halfway through the film the hospital nurse called and said a young woman was in labor. It was her first pregnancy. She was a small woman and I knew that her labor would last for some time. So I finished the film and asked for questions. The phone rang again and again I said there was no hurry.

The audience agreed that if they had seen the film prior to becoming pregnant they would not have had any kids. After dessert I headed for the hospital. As I walked in the door I heard the nurse scream "You better get to the delivery room!"

Fortunately the nurse had moved her to the delivery room without waiting for me. I hurriedly shed my clothes, ran to the delivery room and then she delivered a cute infant girl. More than once I wore street clothes into the delivery room, stripping shoes and shirt off as I entered. I might deliver the infant thusly clad. Often an aide would hand me a gown, tying it behind me as I reached for the infant's head. Neither the mothers nor infants ever complained to me.

*   *   *

Some women knew more than I about the timing of labor. At this time Carol and I took our kids to the Little Cafe for Sunday dinner (lunch). The restaurant was just across the block from the hospital. After church I went to the hospital to examine a woman in labor. I told her that I was certain I would have time to eat before she had the baby, and lots of time to take her to the delivery room. The woman told me that with her first delivery her doctor had left her on the first floor of that hospital while he went to the second floor to see another patient. She delivered that baby before the nurses could summon her doctor back to her room. "Don't do that to me again. Please stay here in the hospital. I know I'll do it again."

I was certain she wouldn't repeat the rapid delivery. I had everything under control. I drove around the block to the restaurant, following Carol and the kids into the restaurant. By the time I got into the restaurant the nurse at the hospital had phoned and was telling me to hurry back. I ran through the alley to the hospital. There, with a triumphant smile on her face, was my patient holding her infant. She was proud and happy with her infant. And she had also proved the doctor wrong!

*   *   *

Several years later I took care of Paula, Jim's wife, for her prenatal care and delivery. Her three previous deliveries had been later than anticipated, about two weeks beyond the standard forty weeks of gestation. Dale and Dean wanted to go to the wrestling tournament at Hoxie. Paula was due; it was forty weeks. But Jim told me she had always been late. She told us she had no signs of impending labor. So I took the boys to Hoxie. Halfway through the evening someone came to me and said I was wanted on the telephone. Jim said Paula was in labor. He said he would handle the delivery if needed, but would prefer me to drive home and take care of her.

Leaving my boys with someone to take them home I clambered into my Barracuda (a small car with a huge engine) and raced home. I assumed any policeman or highway patrolman would recognize my purple Barracuda speeding down the road and would not stop me. No one did. When I ran into the hospital, Jim was just cutting the cord on his dead baby son. The baby had had a knot in his umbilical cord and that tightened knot had prevented the needed oxygen from the placenta to the infant. Again I learned—just because something a bit unusual has occurred in the past does not mean that it will necessarily recur.

*   *   *

I should have learned not to trust a pregnant woman's lack of signs of labor. Again I left town, this time to have dinner with Dean on his birthday in Hays. This was her first pregnancy. She was due any day. A first delivery averaged eight to ten hours of labor. I was certain that if she were to go into labor her labor would take several hours. If she wasn't in labor when I left, she had lots of time for me to eat dinner and return. I talked to my patient and she told me she hadn't had any sign of labor during the day and I told her I was going to Hays to have dinner with Dean. She said that was fine and wished me a good evening.

At that time Alan Adams, MD, was my partner. We might both leave Oakley to go to Colby, but thought one or the other of us should stay nearby. Alan remained in Oakley. In Hays I had a wonderful dinner with Dean then drove home. When I got home Carol told me Alan had just delivered my patient. "Nothing to do about it now, but I have to face her in the morning."

Abashed, I entered her room. She didn't throw things at me, but *she* apologized to *me*. She had been having strange abdominal cramps during the day but it never entered her mind that she was in labor. Only when those pains became regular, at five-minute intervals, did she consider labor and go to the hospital. Sure enough, she was in labor. And she didn't wait for my return! She was so delighted with her infant girl that she was not angry with me. I again was shown I should not accept a patient's diagnosis of labor if I was thinking of leaving Oakley. Later I delivered her second baby.

One last obstetrical story concerning timing of a delivery. I was caring for a young woman whom I had cared for since she had been a child. She was in early labor that evening. Carol, a medical student and I wanted to see the movie. I told my patient we were going to the movie and I would return after the show. Her red hair glowed and her eyes flashed! She told me in no uncertain terms that I was her doctor and that I was not going to any movie that evening. I calmed her down a bit, and said I had lots of time before she was to deliver. This time I was correct. We watched the movie. I examined my patient and went home to bed. They did get me up from bed in the early morning hours to deliver her infant. But mother was still angry with me and remained so for a long time. I should not have told her my plans for the evening.

*   *   *

Jim used to tell me of the twenty-five mile drives to the Colby hospital with the father driving and the patient and Jim sitting in the back seat, hoping they would get to the hospital before the stork. A heavy snow made it even more exciting. After the Oakley hospital was completed Jim didn't have such exciting drives. I never had the chance to experience such a trip. With both the hospital and me in Oakley, only the weather posed transportation problems. I had several expectant mothers call and ask me if I would deliver her although I wasn't her physician. She had been seeing a doctor in Colby, Quinter or Hays and a blizzard was forecast. I always replied "I will be happy to deliver you."

I never was called upon in that fashion although I delivered two or three women who had been driving by and simply stopped at Oakley to have their deliveries.

I have had many mothers-to-be who lived on farms. Some have parked a car on a good road, saying that they could drive a tractor to the road if a blizzard or extremely wet weather prohibited her husband driving their car to the road. One or two have told me that they did have to use that tractor to get to the blacktop. Now the four-wheel drive pickups do a good job delivering laboring women to the hospital.

Early one morning my phone rang and a frantic husband said his wife was going to have her baby . . . soon! Many have told me that but few have been correct. I told him to take her to the hospital and I would be there. Before I could get dressed he phoned again. "She went to the bathroom and she had the baby on the floor!"

Putting my last shoe on, I rushed to the hospital, grabbed an OB pack and ran across the street to their home. Mom and baby were fine, so we wrapped them up and carried them to the hospital. The father, awake and aware she was in labor, had seen me leave the hospital earlier in the night. He considered calling me then but thought there was more time.

"You can never depend on a baby! Or a mother!"

I don't remember whether I put down the hospital or their home across the street as the site of delivery. This is the only patient who carried her newborn to the hospital, but many mothers have barely made it to the hospital to deliver.

*   *   *

I visited one of my patients in labor in the hospital. After examining her, I didn't think she was in labor but we were in the middle of a blizzard so we just let her stay in the hospital as she lived several miles from Oakley. I went home. Early in the morning the nurse at the hospital called and said my patient was in active labor. I scrambled into my car and headed for the hospital. I got three blocks. I was stuck! I finally managed to get to the hospital but the nurse had already delivered the infant. After Carol and I built a new house and Oakley had a new hospital, I learned that I could not put my car (now a 4-wheel drive Ram Charger) in the garage if it were to snow and blow. I had to leave my car on the street. Our driveway was always snowed in. I learned to park my car on the street, where the wind always blew the snow away from either the front or back of my car.

*   *   *

Along with me most of the community enjoyed the basketball team when Dean was a senior in high school. I loved to watch the team play. Again I had a woman in labor and his game was in Goodland, fifty miles away. I was prepared to miss Dean's game. The local TV channel always sent an announcer to provide audio access to Channel Four, the local news channel. I was at the hospital where I could hear both the girls' and boys' games, waiting for the baby. I was in a room next to the labor/delivery room listening to the end of the girls' game. Suddenly my patient screamed "It's coming!"

I rushed next door. The baby lay on mother's bed, crying her lungs out. After a few words spoken to the mother and the nurse I hurried to my car and sped to Goodland. Goodland is in the Mountain Time Zone so they are an hour behind us. I had an hour in which to get to Dean's game. I made it just as they tipped off. And of course they won. The baby did well also.

That TV got me into trouble at least once. Early in my career I used to joke with pregnant women that she had to fit her delivery in with the ball games on TV. In the old hospital I would sit in the lobby where the only TV was, the nurse calling me when needed.

In the new hospital each room had a TV. I always wanted to relieve as much tension in a delivery room as possible. The more relaxed the woman would be the easier and faster the delivery would proceed. Often the patient and her husband would have the TV on and we would joke about the program we were watching. (They could watch but my back was usually to the TV.) After being sued for my inability to deliver a healthy baby, their attorney claimed that I was in too big a hurry to deliver her baby. I had said, "Now the program is over. Let's deliver this baby."

I may well have said this but I had no idea anyone would believe that I was serious and act on that statement. A jury might well believe my joking comment. However I continued to attempt to relieve tension in the delivery room, using the TV as appropriate.

*   *   *

Similar to Jim's drives to Colby my most exciting drive was to take a patient to Hays. We now had an ambulance service. A young woman in active labor came in, but she was six weeks or so earlier than we expected. I thought the baby would be too small for us to take care of in Oakley so I told Kathy "This baby is too small for us to safely care for. I'll go with you in the ambulance and be there if the baby is born before we get to Hays."

The ambulance crew was quite happy to take me along, as they didn't want to take care of a newborn on the road. Sure enough, the intensity and frequency of her contractions increased and we obviously weren't going to get to Hays. I decided that we should go on, deliver the baby in the ambulance and take both mom and baby to Hays. I told Kathy "I have everything we need to deliver the baby, IV fluids, oxygen, you and me."

That we did. Both did well. The boy weighed slightly over five pounds and a few days later they came home. Then I received a birth certificate from the Hays hospital. Would I complete the certificate and sign it? Part of it was simple. But what should I list as where the baby was born? Finally I decided that, as coroner, I was used to completing death certificates and filling out the site of death as milepost XX on I-70. Thus this young man's birth certificate says the site of his birth is milepost 136 on I-70.

Another trip to Hays had a less sanguineous outcome. This mother-to-be was due, but she came into the hospital with heavy vaginal bleeding but not in labor. And she had severe abdominal pain. I decided she had a placenta praevia, a placenta that had separated, at least partially, from her uterus. This is supposed to happen after the infant is born, not prior to delivery. When this occurred (fortunately rare) the baby's blood could not carry oxygen to the baby through mom's placenta. Treatment was an immediate C-section.

We could still hear a heartbeat so we headed for Hays where an obstetrician would do a C-section and a pediatrician could care for the infant. We were used to calling the OBs when needed so they would be ready for our arrival. It took slightly over an hours' drive. In the hospital the staff there required an hour or so to be prepared for a C-section. By the time we arrived, the OR crew was ready and waiting. The obstetrician met

65

us at the ER, still heard a heartbeat and immediately did the section. The pediatrician was also waiting for us. But the baby was seriously depressed. She did survive but with severe brain injury.

*   *   *

In medical school we had no formal training in ethics. We just assumed we all were ethical and used good sense. We used to have bull sessions about those problems. Often we started off with "What would you do if . . . ?" One I remember was "What if you were taking care of a family of Jehovah's Witnesses. You have a child who needs a blood transfusion. What would you do?"

There were three responses. Convince the parents to allow me to give the child a transfusion. Do the best I could without any blood. And if the parents refused and I was certain I needed the blood, ask the courts to make the baby a ward of the court and let me transfuse the blood. None of us really expected to face this quandary.

Early in my career I had a couple come in to see me. She was pregnant for the first time. They said they were Jehovah's Witnesses, informing me they would not accept blood or blood components. "If you thought she needed blood what would you do?"

That was easy. I fudged. Rarely would a woman need a transfusion. And if such a woman had lost enough blood to need a transfusion she would probably have been transferred elsewhere, needing a surgeon. If we needed a transfusion in Oakley it took a bit of time. First we had to type the patient, then call a donor or two, draw his/her blood and cross-match the blood before we would even draw the blood from the donor. If I needed to give her blood I would have some time in which to urge her to accept that blood. I didn't tell them all of this. I merely said I would not demand that she be given blood.

The delivery went easily. Dad and Mom were delighted. The next morning the nurse told me there was blood in the baby's diaper. The baby looked pale. Her hemoglobin and hematocrit were quite low. She was anemic and losing blood, but why? I could find no reason. Other than her anemia she appeared normal. The parents said they would not allow me to give the infant blood. They wanted no transfusion given to her. I said that if the bleeding continued she might die. They remained adamant. Should I call the judge? I thought not. It really was their decision.

I phoned a pediatrician in Denver, explaining the situation. He told me "Sometimes a newborn develops a stress ulcer from the stress of her delivery. Feed the baby. That will usually cure the ulcer."

Mom nursed and we fed her frequently. The bleeding in her diaper slowed, then ceased. She was well. I think most of the Jehovah's Witnesses in the area became my patients. I never had to face that problem again, thank God.

*   *   *

We furnished a room as a labor and delivery room. There was a comfortable recliner in which the expectant father could sit. There was a TV in the room. There were pictures on the walls, drapes on the windows and other chairs in the room. If they had children they could come into the labor room and see how mom was doing. In early labor the woman could walk around, sit in a chair or, as labor progressed, lie in a comfortable bed. When delivery was imminent the foot of the bed could be removed. The cold steel delivery table and stirrups were replaced by padded supports for her legs attached to the bed. The woman was still forced to stare at the doctor for some time as he sat between her legs observing her perineum, but her physical discomfort was somewhat alleviated.

Many young women wanted their mother in the delivery room. I never objected to that. Another request, in at least one instance, was that the baby be delivered under water. I didn't even have to consider this very long. "No. This would mean putting the mother and me in a tub, delivering the baby, and handing it to a nurse. I'd have to shower before and after the delivery. Someone would have to clean up the mother. Then someone would have to clean the tub. No matter how hard we try, a delivery involves a certain amount of mess—blood, feces and amniotic fluid. I don't want to stand in that mess."

I was requested on more than one occasion to allow her children in the room during the delivery. Here I also put my foot down and didn't permit that. Although having a baby had become a family affair, most women did express some degree of pain and I didn't think young children should see their mother suffer. I remembered the women at their club meeting who had said they would never have become pregnant if they had seen a delivery prior to conceiving. What would these children think? I'm not certain my decision was correct, but it was what I believed

I usually acquiesced with most other requests from a pregnant woman, unless I thought it was dangerous. Rosa stumped me "I want to deliver on my hands and knees."

She had delivered her prior infant in that position and believed she was comfortable and had no problems. She had other requests, all of which I agreed to. "No, if you're on your knees one of us will be upside down. I'm too old to do things upside down. You'll have to do this my way!"

Labor progressed smoothly and rapidly. The baby's scalp presented. Then things stopped. The baby didn't progress down the vaginal canal. "Let me turn over and kneel. I know that will help."

"No, time will do the job."

A bit later "I'm sure this baby will come if I can just kneel."

Nothing had changed except my response. "OK. Let's give it a try. Turn over and kneel. I'll just try to hang on to the baby."

Five minutes later I was holding a screaming baby. Rosa was beaming and didn't even gloat.

*   *   *

Jim had told me that he was always surprised when twins appeared. Occasionally he would suspect twins but at that time the only way of being certain was to get an X-ray. We hated to expose a fetus to the radiation in an X-ray. I was alone at this time and didn't suspect twins. I had two women in labor. We moved the first woman to the delivery room and I delivered the baby. "Whoa. There's another baby in there!"

Then the nurse hurried in and said the second woman was about to deliver. We moved the second woman into the operating room. I cleaned up and delivered her infant. Then I hurried to scrub again and deliver the second twin. Three screaming babies. Two delighted mothers. Two, or at least one, overwhelmed father. Sometimes things do break very well.

Rarely was it a problem to be the only doctor in town. Again I had two women in labor. It looked like they were racing to deliver. If they tied I would deliver one and Dennis Elliott, a physician assistant (PA) who worked for me, would deliver the other if necessary. He was certainly capable of doing that. I hoped to do both of the deliveries because I always enjoyed that part of medicine.

I delivered the first and prepared to repair her episiotomy. The nurse scurried in and asked me to come over to the OR where Dennis had taken the other patient. He had a bit of trouble. So I had to leave her on the delivery table, scrub again and deliver the second mother. Then I had to return to my original task, repairing her episiotomy. Not an ideal situation, but there was no other choice. No one seemed to object. The mothers were happy at the wondrous bundles deposited on their laps. The babies were healthy. And the fathers were just happy that all the folderol was over.

*   *   *

I certainly enjoyed obstetrics. The parents were always happy, the outcome was usually good. We became friends. As the years went by I didn't care for as many expectant mothers as I might have chosen. Years ago Jim had told me that many young women whom he had cared for were choosing me to deliver their babies. He was now the old man. They wanted a younger man to care for them. Now it was my turn to be the old man. There were also many women physicians, PAs or nurse practitioners. A young woman might be more comfortable with a woman provider caring for her. Medicine was changing.

Two nurse practitioners, Tracey and Ramona, worked with me in New Frontiers and both delivered babies, although the practitioners always summoned me to the hospital for the actual delivery. A young woman physician joined us. Another young man joined us part time. And I was working for KUMC part time and often out of town. I was now the experienced older doctor, but there were new techniques in which I had not been trained. Many young women wanted a caudal anesthetic for pain relief. I hadn't learned that technique. Other women didn't choose the old man but a younger practitioner who would be in Oakley when she delivered. I missed the prenatal care, deliveries and care of the infants. But I didn't miss hurrying to the hospital for a deliver at 3:00 in the morning. I still, nine years after my stroke, miss that part of practice, even though I was scared out of my wits once in a while. Shortly after my stroke the providers stopped delivering babies in Oakley.

Chapter 5

Affairs of the Heart

In my early years in Oakley most patients with heart attacks came through my office, a few to the hospital ER, always surprising me. A patient might walk into my office door and say his chest hurt. Perhaps his family carried someone into the hospital and said he had just collapsed. Or maybe a neighbor didn't see her today and tried to call her or knocked on her door. If the neighbor could raise no one, the police were notified. Then the police would break in and deliver her to the hospital. Or they might find her dead in bed, in her chair or on the floor. Then the police called me and I had to make a coroner's call, pronouncing her dead and deciding what caused her death. The police chief and I decoded the signs surrounding the body and determined whether or not there were any suspicious circumstances concerning the death. If there were, the Kansas Bureau of Investigation agent in Colby would be contacted.

If none, and if I had taken care of the decedent and knew she had heart problems, I might just sign her out as a coronary. Another possibility was for me to go to the mortuary and do a partial autopsy. My year and a half of working in the pathology department at KUMC stood me in good stead in that task. I was used to inspecting a body and examining the body at KUMC. But I was not used to examining a recently deceased patient. I never learned to handle that with equanimity. But I learned to distance myself from examining the body of a friend and the autopsy I was performing. The procedure in Koster's basement was as follows. I would examine the heart, lungs and abdominal organs. If I found anything I questioned, I would take a segment of the tissue, place it in a bottle of formalin and send it to the Hays Path Lab. Eventually they would send me a report.

*   *   *

After there was an ambulance in Oakley and the Emergency Medical Service was formed, more heart attacks (or presumed attacks) were brought to the hospital by ambulance. We thought we were up to date when I could carry a pager. Not a pager we think of now, but one the nurse on duty at the hospital could send a short message to me. She usually simply asked me to call the hospital. I had no way to answer back to her on my pager. I had to hurry to the closest phone and call the hospital. If the nurse thought it was urgent she would simply tell me that I was needed at the hospital. The nurses had the responsibility to determine the urgency of the message. They did a wonderful job of sorting urgent from unimportant calls. If the nurse thought it was urgent, however, I had no idea whether it was a heart attack, a car wreck with half a dozen injuries or an imminent delivery.

The ambulances carried radios. I learned to fear the messages saying that the EMTs were bringing in a patient with chest pain. Regardless of what I was doing the EMTs believed that I should be at the hospital when they arrived. Their task was to initiate care, then transport people to the hospital; it was not to diagnose. Occasionally I was glad to be at the hospital, the chest pain did proclaim a heart attack. More often the patient had muscular pain, an unimportant fall or an upset stomach. But we always prepared for the true emergency. The nurse, respiratory therapist, an aide or two and I awaited the patient.

With the advent of cellular phones I could easily communicate with the nurse on duty and the EMTs. The nurse would tell me how long it would take for the ambulance to arrive and how urgent the incident. If it were a "heart attack" I tried to beat the ambulance to the hospital, even though I knew most of these would not prove to be a myocardial infarction. But none of us wanted to ignore a true emergency. Anticipation, not knowing what we might find, was much worse than actuality. Standing in the ER awaiting an ambulance was no fun for any of us.

*   *   *

When I was an intern we were just learning about heart attacks, arrhythmias and cardiac resuscitation. Hughes Day, M.D., at Bethany Hospital in Kansas City, was one of the earliest cardiologists to use electronics to monitor post-infarction patients. A huge bank of oscilloscopes, monitors and recorders covered an entire wall of their ICU. When I started practice in Oakley there was, of course, no such monitoring. If a patient had a heart attack we simply put him to bed, maybe back in the far corner so it would be quieter, and kept him in bed. I can't remember anyone being found dead in his bed in that corner. After two or three days of bed rest we would let him walk to the bathroom. After another few days he was allowed to walk in the hall. Finally he was dismissed, with strict instructions about what activities allowed and what proscribed. If the patient going home queried his doctor about sexual intercourse he was told he could have sex with only his wife, no one else. I assumed the extramarital sex might have been too exciting or too physically strenuous. Or perhaps it was meant to be a joke.

*   *   *

Practicing medicine in Oakley meant that I, alone, was responsible for caring for a patient. In facing most problems I had time to look for information in a book. As a student a KUMC physician told me to install a bookshelf in the bathroom and stock it with a few books. Thus I could excuse myself to go to the bathroom and bone up on the immediate problem. After a few years I simply told a patient I needed to look up a question if I needed.

Shortly after I arrived in Oakley I realized that a cardiac emergency usually left no time for me to read a book or call another physician to seek a solution. Cardiac problems often required immediate action. I had always been more interested in thinking than acting. Now I needed both. I began reading cardiology texts and attending cardiology conferences and became a fair to middling cardiologist. I learned to read EKGs, keep up to date on the new medications, and, as time went on, I learned when and how to use a defibrillator.

Of course, not all infarcts were an emergency. In the early 1970s Frank walked into my office Monday morning. I didn't know Frank at that time but we later became good friends. He told me he had developed chest pain Friday night. He hated to bother me that night, or during the weekend.

So he came in to see me Monday morning, after I was in the office. My office was only half a block from the old hospital so my aide and I put him in our wheelchair and wheeled him through the alley to the hospital. Yes, he had a two-day old coronary.

I put him to bed in the hospital, bed rest being the only treatment following a heart attack. After a week or ten days he went home. He spent many years in Oakley. He had more problems. A cardiologist thought Frank should be catheterized to examine his coronary arteries. During that procedure he had a stroke. He only partially recovered. He had other infarcts. Years later Herman Hiesterman, a Quinter physician who attended church in Oakley, followed the ambulance to our hospital. Frank was dead. Dr. Hiesterman said Frank had just collapsed, dying, in the church. At home I penned a rare poem.

> Nothing was left
> After the vomit, the blood and the shocks.
> Nothing but a body,
> Growing cold upon the cart.
>
> He had been a friend,
> This man with the thinning sandy hair.
> A friend who didn't call
> Until three days after his first heart attack
> Because he didn't want to bother me.
>
> Today the ER nurse called.
> "They're bringing Frank in from church", she said.
> "CPR in the ambulance."
>
> I beat him to the hospital
> For all the good it did.
> And we did all the proper things,
> Intubation. Intravenous. Cardioversion.
>
> But his heart had nothing left.
> Too many infarcts.
> Too little oxygen.

And I, my skill to no avail,
Had to say "Stop. It's no use."
And fight back my tears as I stepped out to see his wife.

Never have I felt more helpless.

Dec 11, 1988

*   *   *

In Oakley we purchased an oscilloscope that alarmed the nurse if her patient's heart stopped or an arrhythmia developed. We put that in the room closest to the nurse's desk, fifteen or twenty feet away. That was our coronary care unit! And Medicare also considered this a coronary care unit and paid the hospital more money than in a regular bed. During the night the entire hospital staff would often consist of an RN and an aide. They might be busy elsewhere; if the alarm sounded they might not hear it for some time.

Our new hospital, opened in 1976, had a two bed ICU across the hall from the nurses' desk. It was not only for coronary patients but used for anyone with a major problem—heart attack, arrhythmia, pulmonary problems, severe injuries or post-op patients. We even hospitalized a couple of drug overdoses in that room. If we had a patient in the ICU a nurse was required to remain in the room to monitor the patient. After two or three days in the ICU we would assume the patient was out of danger. The patient would continue to be monitored as we could attach a radio transmitter to a patient in any hospital room and transmit the heartbeats to a monitor at the nurses' desk. Thus he could walk around his room, visit another room, and be allowed to walk about as he desired.

*   *   *

One morning one of the aides in the old hospital called me and said they needed me stat (immediately) in the hospital. I raced down the alley and into the back door where the ER and CCU were. Everyone was excited but in no hurry. Betty Howard, the head nurse, had been in our CCU with a patient when her patient fibrillated. None of us had had any occasion to use our new defibrillator, but we had all been trained. By the time I had run to the hospital Betty had shocked him; he was awake and his rhythm was normal. He recovered and went home. I was glad someone other than I had the first experience with that process. During the ensuing years in Oakley many nurses and I used the defibrillator but I have always remembered the initial episode.

*   *   *

Sunday afternoon. Quiet. I was probably watching the football game. The phone rang. "Dr. Ohmart, my wife's awful sick. I called Dr. Marchbanks but Mrs. Marchbanks said you were on call. Could you come see my wife?"

"Yes. I will. Where do you live?"

"Five miles north of town, just east of the highway."

I drove to the house where an elderly man slowly shuffled to the door and showed me to his wife, sitting in their parlor. "Where do you hurt?"

"Right here!" she placed her hand, just over her left breast.

She was sweating with pain. It was an effort to speak. I knew she had had a heart attack. I gave her a shot of morphine for her pain. "I've got to take you to the hospital! I'll drive my car as close to the door as I can. Cal and I will help you to the door and drive you to the hospital."

We did that and I drove to the hospital where the nurses and aides helped her into bed and removed her clothes. I ran an EKG on her, a skill I learned in the veteran's hospital as a medical student. The EKG showed no heart problem! The morphine had eased her pain. The few lab tests available in Oakley showed only an elevated white count. Her pain again increased, and I had the nurse give her another shot of morphine. When she could lie still I again examined her chest and abdomen. Her chest was clear. Her upper abdomen was quite tender and that was where her pain was most severe.

The next morning her pain had localized to her right upper abdomen and then subsided. X-rays revealed she had gallstones. The next day Jim removed a badly infected gall bladder. She had an uneventful recovery. My diagnosis was incorrect, but I had done the correct things that afternoon. She was well and both she and her husband were grateful for my care.

*   *   *

November 13, 1971

My partner, Jim Marchbanks, and I were Boy Scout leaders. One or the other of us would usually go camping with the scouts when an adult was needed. Jim was camping at Ottken's Grove, five miles east of Oakley. One Saturday afternoon I was again summoned to the hospital. They told me Jim was the patient. When I got to the hospital Jim was lying in the back of a station wagon and one of the adult leaders was trying to resuscitate him. A fire had gotten away at the grove and they were fighting the fire. Someone noticed that Jim was lying at the foot of a tree, where he had evidently sat down. They loaded him into a station wagon and raced to Oakley. There was little anyone could do in the vehicle. By Jim's arrival he was dead. I was in tears. Again Betty helped me through the tough spots. Call Paula, his wife. Call our medical friends in nearby communities. Arrange for an autopsy. The autopsy revealed he had severe coronary artery disease and, probably, died instantaneously from an MI and ventricular fibrillation. I now was the lone doctor in Oakley!

*   *   *

One morning Dennis Elliott and I were called to the old hospital. A man had been brought in from the Camp Inn, five miles north of Oakley. He and his wife had spent the night there and were preparing to leave that morning when he collapsed. His wife rushed to the manager and they brought him to the hospital. We still had no ambulance in Oakley. But we did have the monitor and defibrillator. Using the rudimentary equipment we possessed we attempted to resuscitate him. After several shocks and medications his heart began to beat on its own. I didn't, and still don't, know how he survived the ride and our resuscitation, but he did!

His heart continued to beat. He was breathing on his own. An IV had been started. He had been intubated. But he didn't regain consciousness. I hoped he would respond during the afternoon, but did not. I phoned Dr. Crow, a cardiologist I had worked with in Wichita, and asked his advice. All he could offer was to maintain his fluid and electrolyte balance. After two or three days I again phoned Dr. Crow. My patient was from Oklahoma. Could I transfer the man to Dr. Crow at Wesley?

He said yes, but thought there was nothing anyone could do for him. "Hospitals have wards full of individuals whose hearts have been resuscitated but whose brains were not."

He was later transferred to a veteran's hospital in Oklahoma where he eventually succumbed. There was, and still is, no way to determine who would recover fully and who would not. We have to do everything we can, then pray.

*　　*　　*

Lee was brought to the hospital by ambulance. An elderly man, his heart rate was two hundred and forty beats a minute. While a young person might maintain that rate for a short time, Lee's aged vascular system would not supply blood and oxygen to his brain. He had collapsed and was unconscious when I arrived in the ER. We started an IV and moved him to the CCU. There I knew I had little time to waste. I applied the paddles to his chest, shouted "Clear" so no one was touching Lee or his bed, and pushed the buttons. With a whap! from the paddles Lee awakened and exclaimed, "Oohh shit!"

Never did I have a happier audience for that expletive. Over a year or two Lee had several similar episodes. We continually decreased the power, finally to ten joules. This minimal power setting converted him to a sinus rhythm but he never liked the process. And he often responded with the epithet.

*　　*　　*

I occasionally found heart attack victims other than in the hospital: my office, a ball game or at their home. Al wandered into my office one morning. He had some chest pain, but it was not severe. An EKG in the office however showed he was having a heart attack. Rather than call the ambulance and wait for its arrival I just asked him to get in my car and I would take him to the new hospital. That would be faster. However I had to cross the railroad tracks between my office and the hospital. I could see that there was a train, not moving, but blocking Second Street, which I needed to cross. I headed north on Center——Third Street was blocked, Fifth Street was blocked, Eighth Street was also blocked. I remembered that the Oakley Police Department could contact the trains in Oakley since the west side of the tracks housed our hospital but most of Oakley was east of the tracks. The ambulance also was housed on the east side of the tracks. I called the police department and asked the dispatcher to clear Eighth Street as I was about there. They then moved the train. I got Al safely to the hospital.

*   *   *

This is an essay I wrote involving a heart attack where we were not successful in resuscitating a man, a young man, too young to die. It was written in May 1991. It was published in *American Medical News*, Dec 9, 1991 (Copyright ©1991 American Medical Association. All rights reserved.) as

In a Rural Practice: Death, Rebirth and the Will To Go On

Discouraged and defeated I terminated the code. All of us felt the same sense of loss. Although we had known nothing about the young man when he arrived at our ER, he was obviously too young to die and we had fought hard for him. Our patient said that he had been working on an oil-drilling rig when he developed a severe chest pain. He told his boss who then brought him to our hospital. He fit the classic clinical picture of an acute MI, except that he was only 33 years old, the same age as my oldest son. "My chest hurts like hell!"

His skin was cold and moist, his BP was 104/52 and his pulse was 116. An EKG revealed ST segment elevation over the entire precordium. Age notwithstanding, off he went to the CCU. He coded on arrival there but prompt defibrillation restored a sinus rhythm. IVs were started, lidocaine was begun and his VPCs deceased in frequency. Then he developed V-tach. This responded to IV procainamide.

I obtained some history from him between bouts of frantic activity. He lived about 150 miles from us. He drove to Oakley to work on an oil rig, would put in 48-72 hours, and then return home for a day or two. His wife was at home, a diabetic and pregnant, expecting to deliver any day. He didn't want to die. His family needed him.

We called the cardiologist in Wichita, 270 miles away. We administered TPA. He developed further arrhythmias, PVCs, atrial fibrillation, ventricular tachycardia, another episode of ventricular fibrillation. Somehow they all responded to treatment. The AIRWATCH plane was on the way. I had a senior medical student with me and explained to him that this was a man worth fighting for—young, otherwise healthy, exactly the type of man these techniques had been developed for. And I thought he might do OK. Then he developed a bradycardia, followed by a flat-line EKG. Nothing we could do changed this. Beaten, we filed despondently from the CCU.

I could not face returning to the routine of my office.

Earlier I had seen a 34-year old teacher who had tried for several years to conceive. A month or so ago she had appeared at my office, hoping, yet afraid to hope. She hadn't had a period for three or four months. Could she be pregnant? A urine HCG was positive. Exam showed her uterus to be enlarged, at least four months' size. Her natural exuberance boiled into near mania, but she was delighted and delightful. Question followed question. Could her husband come with her next visit? He did, and there were more questions. Both were delighted with the unexpected pregnancy. This time my exam revealed a uterus definitely larger than her dates indicated. She was scheduled for a sonogram the next time our traveling unit came to town.

Despondent after the failure of our resuscitation attempt, I sat at my charting desk, trying to put words on paper. Somehow I had to compose myself, dictate the report of the code and get on with the day. My actions had not been that unusual, my responses were. In twenty-nine years as a rural physician I had seen death, sudden and unexpected, before. I knew that all I could do was my best, and that was not always enough. But somehow this young man's death had touched me in an unusual manner. Maybe because he was the same age as my son. Maybe because I had been on call for three months, with only one short weekend away from Oakley to relieve the strain. Maybe I just didn't want to admit defeat. At any rate it was harder for me to accept than most deaths.

Then I heard a familiar giggle from the room where sonograms were done.

It was my OB. After a few moments to collect myself I walked into the room where she and the tech were abuzz with laughter and vitality. They were looking at twins on the screen! Their enthusiasm was contagious. One by one the nurses, aides and ancillary people who had faced death with me a short while before filed into the room, viewed the screen and left, as I had, renewed and ready to continue our routine tasks. The mother-to-be does not yet know what she gave us that day, May Day, a day for rebirth. When I am sure that I can get through the story I will tell her how much her joy and the new life inside her meant to many of us.

*   *   *

Not all resuscitation efforts failed. One wintry December morning the ambulance deposited a cold, lifeless form at the ER. One of the EMTs had seen a man fall to the street. As he had been trained he rushed to the victim and began CPR. Someone else called 911 and the ambulance was summoned. The man was loaded into the ambulance and they sped to the hospital. I was at the hospital and was prepared to assist in his resuscitation.

We had excellent personnel. The EMTs continued chest compressions as the inhalation therapist bagged the man. I moved to the head of the cart and intubated him while a nurse started an IV. Then it again was my turn. I shocked him. Nothing happened. I gave him an injection of adrenaline. Shocked him again. Again nothing happened. I gave him injections of sodium carbonate, calcium chloride and more adrenaline. More shocks. More cardiac standstill!

We followed the monitor as we watched. Our five attempts to make his heart resume beating were followed by a minute or two of futile electrical activity, then activity ceased. I alone had the authority to say "Stop. It's not going to work. We'll give it up"

We had spent thirty or forty-five minutes of futile efforts. Thinking "I am ready to end the resuscitation efforts, but I will make one more attempt."

I gave the man another ampoule of calcium chloride, another of adrenaline and cranked the defibrillator to its maximum. Then I said "Clear."

The still form shook with the electrical impulse. As we watched the monitor it first had a fibrillation pattern, then a sinus rhythm. We could feel his heart beating! But I remembered the man we had resuscitated in the old hospital, the man whose heart had been resuscitated but whose brain had been dead. I dreaded that outcome. Perhaps I should have stopped the code before the final attempt. "Better to be a dead man than a living vegetable."

Our patient's wife was waiting at the hospital. They had been driving from an eastern state to Denver to spend Christmas with their daughter and family. One of the nurses had taken a brief history of our patient and had kept her informed of our lack of success. My task, both wonderful and dreaded, was to tell her of our partial success. I told her of the good news "His heart is beating. But he is not responding to us verbally. As yet, I have no answers to your questions about what to expect."

I went to the nurses' desk to contact a cardiologist in Denver and arrange a transfer to a Denver hospital. By the time I completed that and the EMTs were ready to drive him to Denver he was groggily responding verbally to his wife.

I wondered what had transpired after his arrival in Denver. The day after Christmas I phoned the CCU where he had been transported. The nurse on duty knew that I was the doctor who had sent my patient to Denver. She was willing to tell me "He walked out of the hospital with his wife and daughter yesterday."

It came a day late but I had a marvelous Christmas gift.

*   *   *

One night in the early 1980s I awakened, aware that my heart beat was out of synch. It was going beat-beat-KABEAT-beat-beat-KABEAT and the KABEAT was earlier than the regular beat-beat-beat-beat I usually felt. I felt fine; no pain, no shortness of breath. Only a bit of anxiety about this irregularity. I turned over and went back to sleep, assuming my usual rhythm would be normal when I awakened.

It had not! My heart still went beat-beat-KABEAT. I shaved, showered and went to the hospital where I asked the tech to do an EKG on me. At this time I had no partner, no assistant, and no student in Oakley. I was alone. A cursory glance at my EKG revealed a trigeminal rhythm, one that the books said might, at any time, turn into ventricular fibrillation, a deadly rhythm. Again inspecting my EKG, I confirmed the strange feeling. Yes, I was in trigeminy! Following a heart attack this rhythm often presaged ventricular tachycardia, followed by ventricular fibrillation. But I had no chest pain. The EKG was normal other than the rhythm. I had not had a heart attack. I had spontaneously developed a trigeminal rhythm. As usual, Betty was the nurse on duty. She wanted to put me to bed in the CCU and attach a monitor to me. I refused. I felt fine other than this strange rhythm. And there was no other doctor or PA in Oakley. Was I to care for myself? I didn't go to bed in the hospital.

I followed my usual schedule, seeing my patients in the hospital, then drove to my office. There I cared for the patients in my office, drove home, ate lunch, returned to the office, completed the day, visited my patients in the hospital, went home, ate dinner and again assumed the strange rhythm would revert to normal overnight. It did not. After several days of that I decided I was now a bit short of breath. I had used oral procainamide in several instances to control ventricular arrhythmias and treated myself with the small tablet. At a low dose my arrhythmia was abolished. I was cured!

Not exactly! At this time I was a pilot, owning an airplane and flying it. I also gave flight physicals for pilots. I knew that a pilot taking procainamide should not fly, as the pilot's heart was at far greater risk to precipitously stop than the average pilot's heart. I should have grounded myself when the trigeminy appeared, which I had ignored. But I doubted I could ignore taking the medicine forever. After a few days on the procainamide and having no further trigeminy I stopped the medication. I was certain the trigeminy would not recur.

No. It recurred immediately. Now I was in a quandary. I consulted a cardiologist in Wichita to whom I often referred patients and asked him to see me. Of course he said yes. I flew to Wichita, with my heart continuing to go beat-beat-KABEAT. A friend picked me up and asked me to accompany her on her usual evening walk, a rather rapid, long walk. I agreed. As we finished the walk she asked me why I was in Wichita. I said I had an appointment with a cardiologist because I had an irregular heart beat. She chastised me severely for our walk but there were no problems from our outing.

The next morning the cardiologist examined me, did a stress test on me and told me he could find no evidence of heart disease. But I still had the trigeminy. He told me not to worry, get more rest and he thought the arrhythmia would disappear. I flew back to Oakley and thought my flying days might be over. The next day the arrhythmia ceased and has never recurred. I now certainly get more rest than I did during my practice but I doubt I got more rest after my visit to him than before the visit. I think, and thought then, that his reassurance was what solved my problem.

*　　*　　*

I wrote the following in May 1997 that was never published.

Another Story Of A Heart Attack

I saved a life this morning. Nothing dramatic happened; certainly nothing that would be worthy of *ER*. I simply picked up a pair of paddles, applied them firmly to a young man's chest, and pressed two buttons. The squiggly line on his monitor settled into a regular pattern, Very shortly he was breathing and talking, as if nothing had happened. Do I deserve any special credit? No. Any nurse in our small hospital and many of the other employees could have done the same thing, and would have. I simply happened to be standing next to the bed and the defibrillator when our patient fibrillated.

While the above is quite true, it is not the entire story. Mike, our patient, is 46 years old, far too young to die of an MI. Yet that is exactly what would have happened to him when I began practice, almost 34 years ago. That was the era when open heart massage was novel, and external defibrillators were unknown. Hughes Day, at Bethany Hospital in Kansas City, had huge banks of monitoring equipment on the wall of his ICU. In Oakley we simply tossed a man with a coronary into bed, gave him some oxygen and morphine for pain relief. Most of our therapy consisted of watching and waiting. If he were lucky he would be dismissed after two weeks in bed and told to "take it easy." It is hard to believe that my short life has spanned the immense changes in coronary care that have occurred.

I have taken care of Mike as a junior high and high school athlete, a bull rider, and a motorcycle rider. As you might guess, this involved a number of fractures and other injuries, great and small. We usually saw only those of some import; like many of our young men he did not concern himself greatly with anything he thought might heal with only nature's care, perhaps a very rational approach to health. I had taken care of his wife and delivered at least one of his children. Truly a family doctor's story.

My practice, however, has slowly changed. As I have aged so has the age of the patients I see. I now practice only half-time; it is often hard to get to see me with an acute problem since most of my appointments are filled well in advance with follow-up visits, physicals, etc. Often these people are my age (61) or older. While I know them, like them and appreciate their strengths and weaknesses, there is seldom an immediate challenge in their care. Too often there is little to do but ease them and comfort their families as they progress through a terminal illness, usually a malignancy or a stroke. Through necessity I have become fairly proficient in this. Although I comfort them as best I can and ultimately grieve with them, it does not seem to me that this is all I should do.

It is not that I crave excitement. Quite to the contrary. When I was flying I heard a pilot's life described as hours of boredom punctuated by seconds of sheer terror. I much prefer the boredom, both as a pilot and a physician. I know that I could not now, and probably never could have, tolerate the life of an emergency room physician, or even someone who continually cares for critically ill patients. I like my family practice. I would not trade it. Yet sometimes I wonder if I make a "real" difference. This morning I did.

A little over two years ago, as a patient myself, I ran from our ICU, trailing my monitor wires, to assist in a code. We were unsuccessful, as is the case most of the time for us. The patient was Mike's father. As usual after such an event, I wondered what else I might have done. Probably not much. But the question is always there. Today I knew. There was something more. We do all we can. The rest is up to God or the fates. We had been successful this morning. Mike remained stable and was flown from our hospital to a tertiary care center where he will receive all of the benefits of contemporary care. All because someone, in this case myself, was looking at lines jumping around on a screen, recognized a major problem and pushed a couple of buttons. Not dramatic, but, for me, a chance to utilize my training in a more active, and in some visceral way, more rewarding manner than my usual practice.

Although my intellect tells me that discovery of a malignancy in a curable stage, smoking prevention, or treatment of hypertension may be just as life saving, there is something in my heart that exults, "Yes. This is what it is all about!"

Chapter 6

What I Learned From Women

I have never understood members of the female gender. My mother began my education about women. She was a quite bright, very determined woman. She earned a college degree in chemistry, a man's degree, in 1934. She worked for a year or so, married in 1935 and I was born in 1936. I, and later as Bob and Harold were born, was trained to use my mind. Mother always had the radio on while working in the house, habitually to the news or a baseball game. The St. Louis Cardinals broadcasts were the only one she could get, but somehow I became a Yankee fan. We argued incessantly with mom over the games or the news. She usually won! I learned a woman could be bright, knowledgeable and strong, as well as feminine. As I grew I encountered other girls and women, females who made me forget about my brain. These women taught me that a woman's more feminine attributes often lured me away from the "shoulds" I had learned at my mother's knee. I was, and have always been, a sucker for a woman.

In kindergarten I was enticed into walking home with a girl where we needed to cross a footbridge. My parents had forbidden me to cross that bridge. I don't remember the girl or the visit, but I remember the spanking I got when I arrived home. It was after dark when I returned. After assuring herself I was unhurt, Mother used her paddle on her firstborn. I don't remember the phrase this time but I remember Mother later in Wichita saying to me (or Bob) "This hurts me more than it hurts you."

I never understood that. It hurt my fanny, not hers. As an adult I realized what she was saying, but I certainly didn't believe it hurt her then.

In the second grade, in Wichita, I was still having to ask a girl to tie my shoelaces. In the third grade I learned to tie my own laces after the girls taunted, then taught me. I still followed girls home. Eventually I learned to phone home and tell mom where I was and when to be home. But I was choosy about whom I walked with. A neighbor girl followed me to school. Believing she was not the girl I wanted, I ran away from her. She was determined and ran faster than I! When she caught me I realized it had been the right girl. Hand in hand we entered the schoolyard, exhausted but happy!

During the war no one had gas (or a car) to drive kids to school. We walked, rain, snow or sunshine. We all had galoshes to put over our shoes in wet weather, tightly buckled over our trousers. One of the girls lured me into testing my galoshes in the puddles. I thought it was great fun to splash my friends. The girl stayed dry on the sidelines. I was wet from the waist down. My leather shoes, my galoshes notwithstanding, were still wet the next morning. The little girl laughed at me when she saw my still wet shoes at school.

Buhler, a town of six hundred people, was small enough I didn't get into trouble for following girls home. Everyone had a bike and went wherever we wished to ride. They had a noon whistle that was heard throughout the town. That was everyone's signal to go home for lunch, even the girls. Parents sent everyone home at dusk. I could run faster than the boys my age could. I could ride my bike faster than the boys my age could. But there were two girls who were taller, faster and stronger than I. They beat me in games such as kick the can, tag and ditch'em on bikes. They teased me mercilessly. Of course, they were the girls with whom I wanted to spend time.

They would run away or hide from me. If I found them we might play together a while, then again the girls would vanish. I would have to find them again. I concluded that girls were flirts, enticing then rejecting, almost at the same time. I'm sure they thought this was a fine game. I wasn't so certain of that. But I was learning about women.

In junior high we moved to Scott City. I was the new boy in town. The girls were interested in this strange boy, partly because many of the boys my age lived in the country and depended on older brothers or sisters to take them to school and home. During the summer the boys were working on their parents' farms. I was in town. I was a new target; the girls began experimenting with their newfound powers over men (boys).

"Dick, let's do this."

"Dick, let's do that."

"Dick, jump over the cuckoo's nest."

I was willing, probably eager, to do any girl's bidding. I was a Boy Scout. In the summer the Scouts sold cokes and candy at the car races and ball games at the fair grounds. I spent all my money (a minimal sum at best) on the girls who asked me to give them a coke or candy bar. When I ran out of money I would put her purchase on the cuff, if she were the right girl. Not being an athlete I spent lots of time with those girls, which I certainly enjoyed. But the girls' entice/reject approach continued to intrigue me. In spite of this, or perhaps because of it, I have always enjoyed a woman's company more than a man's. I never cared for hunting or fishing. I enjoyed music and art. And women continued to fascinate me throughout my career.

*   *   *

In high school I was no more athletically successful than in junior high. Nor was I more successful with the girls. I was always a friend, not a boyfriend. Throughout high school I worked in a drugstore during vacations and weekends. I bought cigarettes for girls who couldn't buy them. I bought cokes or ice cream for girls. Had we known about drugs and had I been able to obtain them I might well have been the local pusher.

I tried throughout my high school career to attract girls, endeavoring to play football, then basketball. After my junior year in high school I gave up football and became "trainer" for the football team. That initially consisted of picking up the locker room after games and practices and washing and drying socks, jockstraps and towels. As a senior I advanced to taping knees and ankles. I also kept the statistics for our football team—who carried the ball, how far did he go, who fumbled, etc. In basketball I always tried out for the team but was cut from the squad. My sporting successes were limited to playing in the marching band at football games and playing in the pep band at the basketball games. I realized that was no little consolation because I had a chance to spend time with the cheerleaders and the girls in the band. I learned a lot from those girls, more than I would have learned from sitting on the bench on a team

All the mothers knew me as that polite, helpful, responsible boy who worked in the drugstore. That's who I was. When I reached sixteen I acquired a driver's license. Mothers, and at least one girl's older brother, let me drive their cars, taking their daughters/cheerleaders to the out-of-town basketball games. I had a lot of fun, but I was always a friend, much as I wanted to be a boyfriend. On those drives I absorbed a wealth of information about feminine wiles.

I don't think I ever dated a cheerleader. Perhaps I knew them too well. Perhaps they were all dating athletes. I know they terrified me. They were pretty. They were popular. They dated the "big boys." I don't think I ever became a "big boy." After a year of college I was brave enough to ask Betty Ann to go to Garden City to the movies with me. She had been a classmate and a cheerleader. She said, "Yes."

I was amazed! We had a good time at the movie, *The Seven-Year Itch*. The only problem was that we had to sit in the second row of the theater. Seeing Marilyn Monroe on their large screen and that close to us was a bit overwhelming. I had a flat tire on the drive home. I was embarrassed but we managed to laugh through replacing the tire.

All the way home I debated. "Do I dare kiss her when I walk her to her door?"

I dared, and didn't get slapped.

$$*\quad*\quad*$$

At KU I rented a room in a private home. There were another boy or two there but they had their own friends and activities. I was lonely. I started hanging out at the Wesley Foundation, the Methodist student center. I met Coralyn. She was different from the girls I had known in Scott City. She was a year older than I, a good student and was more serious than the girls I had known in high school. She was my first serious romance. She had no entice/reject aspect to her. She was open and honest. We could discuss important subjects. She helped me mature. I helped her in gaining self-confidence.

She told me we should take advantage of the KU campus. We attended concerts, both pop and classical. We went to the art museum. We went to an opera in Hoch Auditorium, where the basketball team played. We made a good pair and dated for a year and a half or so. We still stay in contact.

After I joined a fraternity I played touch football and intramural basketball. I played, but not well. There were always a few girls at those games, girls who dated the boys on our team or our opponent's team. I was usually too shy to speak to them. I was never a star, and was uncomfortable during and after the games. If one of them spoke to me I was tongue-tied and unable to find anything to say. But I learned from them as well. Much later in life I realized most of those girls were as speechless and confused as I.

Then I met and started dating Carol. I had never known such a girl! Four years younger than I but ten years wiser than I. She also did not use the entice/reject approach. She was honest. She taught me to believe whatever she said and that I could depend on her. I learned to act on what information was available. She taught me that everyone did the best he or she could at the time. We were married in 1958; she was eighteen; I was twenty-one. The polite, honest, responsible boy matured into a polite, honest, responsible doctor. She has played a major role in my development.

Carol said that she had to act on a person's words, not attempting to read in meanings, facial expressions or actions contrary to one's words. She said she simply responded and reacted to words. I learned to do that also. I did, however, while basing my actions on a person's words, occasionally retained a slight question in my mind about the sincerity of those words. I would not go too far out on a limb based on the available verbal information. Thus I learned more about women, or at least one woman.

*   *   *

Honesty. As a boy I was probably no more nor less honest than any boy trying to avoid trouble. Lying to Carol, however, was always a mistake. As I practiced medicine I learned that lying to anyone had its own pitfalls. I had to remember what lie I had told, and to whom. I soon learned to avoid lies. I believed my patients should receive the truth from me. If someone questioned me I either told the truth or replied that "I can't answer that without breaking a confidence. I can't talk about a patient."

I did, however, have a few stock lies.

"Did your daughter ask me for a prescription for birth control pill?"

"No, of course not" was my stock response to that question. If I hedged that I couldn't talk about a patient, a mother accepted that as a "Yes."

"Has he (she) been drinking or using drugs?" A simple "Yes" or "No" might or might not afford the truth. That question frequently required a more nuanced response.

"Don't tell Dad he has cancer."

That was easy. I couldn't take care of a patient if I lied to him. If the cancer were treatable he should be told and treated. If incurable, Dad usually had a strong suspicion about the truth. And he needed to know the facts to make reasonable decisions.

*   *   *

In the 1960s if a young woman wanted to go to beauty school she had to have an examination form signed by a physician. It wasn't much of an exam; it consisted of a blood test for syphilis and a vaginal exam to prove she didn't have gonorrhea, both tests done by the state lab and signed out as negative. The blood test was easy, at least for most girls. The other was a different matter. Having some strange man standing between her legs while they were held up in the air was bad enough. Then he was to put a cold metal object in her vagina simply to get a smear so she didn't have gonorrhea was even worse. I'm certain a few girls decided they didn't want to become beauticians if that was necessary. Others gritted their teeth and let me do the exam.

I certainly didn't like the exam either. These teenagers were usually terrified at the idea of the process. We all survived the exams, some girls more relaxed than others. I never relaxed in that procedure. I thought it was inhumane. And I knew *my* girls wouldn't have either of those venereal diseases. After a few years more experience I realized that many of those girls were no longer virgins, but a boyfriend and a doctor were quite different men. I was delighted when the state dropped that requirement.

*   *   *

In the early years of my practice I took care of many more girls and women than men. Contraception was a chore for women; men only needed to enjoy the act. As I high school boy I worked in the drug store in Scott City and sold condoms, usually to a man. Trying to decide whether a woman requested "Sheiks" (condoms) or "Schicks" (razor blades) I became so frustrated that I simply put the condoms in a sack, charged her fifty cents and fled. As a physician I had to discuss diaphragms, jellies, oral contraceptives and tubal ligations.

Nature is wondrous in finding ways to conceive. A thirty-five year old woman came to see me because her pelvis hurt. Her history showed she had two children in Scott City then had a tubal ligation. After moving to Oakley she had two more children then Jim did a second tubal ligation. After examining her I could find no reason for her pain. This was long before sonograms and scans. I knew her and knew she was rather stoic so I gave her a few pain pills and told her to return in a few days if the pain persisted. It persisted. I again examined her. Again I could fid no cause for her pain. After I told her I could still find no source for her pain she went to an obstetrician/gynecologist at Hays. He called me later and said she had a tubal pregnancy! After two tubal ligations the determined sperm still managed to wend its way to her egg!

Another forty-year old woman came to see me because of abdominal pain. By know I did have the assistance of a sonogram. A year or two she had had a hysterectomy. When I could find no cause for her pain I ordered an abdominal sonogram. The sonogram told us she had a small mass in her pelvis that was bleeding a bit. It also showed that the surgeon had not removed her ovaries. Yes, surgery discovered a tubal pregnancy! This operation cured the mass and removed both ovaries. No future conception in that woman.

*   *   *

I remained a sucker for a girl who needed help. I had grown up and been educated to be a helper. After a while the community had accepted me. My patients knew that I would keep their secrets. I would cooperate with them if I did not believe their health or lives were endangered. I made a distinction between lying and fudging. Carol had many urine pregnancy tests done in the hospital lab. A girl could call me, leave the urine in a bottle in my car and have it tested in the hospital under Carol's name. The girl would then call me at home that evening asking for the results. If positive some girls were terrified; others were somewhat pleased at the results.

One evening I received a call that stumped me. The girl's voice was quavering, almost in tears. "Was it positive?"

"I didn't get any urine for a test this morning."

In a bit stronger voice she started chuckling. "I put the urine in a bottle then wrapped it as a gift. I put in the front seat of your car."

"No. It was not in my car."

We both laughed about someone finding a gift in his/her car, opening the wrapping and discovering a small bottle of urine. She left the bottle in the proper car the next morning.

I assumed that most of these girls with a negative result would not break up with their boyfriends and that they would continue having sex. I talked to the girls who were not pregnant about contraception. A few said they were not going to do that again. Perhaps a very few didn't. I didn't (and don't) have much faith in that approach. Our older son was born while I was in my first year in medical school. Dean was born fifteen months later, when I was in the second year of medical school. After two years of medical school I had not been taught about effective contraception. This was introduced in OB/GYN, a fourth year class. I feared we might have four or five children before I graduated from medical school and internship. I knew that saying "No" or "being careful" was not an appropriate solution to avoiding a pregnancy. I offered the girls who wanted a free exam and a prescription for an oral contraceptive.

Oral contraceptives were first put on the market when I was a fourth year medical student. Kermit Krantz, M.D., was head of the Obstetrics/Gynecology department. He was spearheading a campaign to provide OCs to any woman who wanted, regardless of age or marital status. Many Kansas physicians objected loudly to this project. But, by the time I was interning at Wesley Hospital in Wichita, the number of deliveries at Wesley had been halved. Even with this decline I had delivered about two hundred babies when I left Wichita. In Oakley also the number of deliveries declined markedly. We were quite happy when the OCs became available and I was willing to prescribe them. Abortions later became legal.

In the seventies and eighties there was no good choice when an unmarried teenager became pregnant. Marry the baby's father. Often that marriage lasted only a few years. Have the baby, then give it up for adoption? There were no longer homes for unwed mothers such as the one I trained in at the Salvation Army Hospital in Wichita. Most girls remained home, delivered the infant and then the baby was given away. A third was to have her baby in Oakley and keep the infant. As the late eighties and nineties progressed that became more come. Abortion was also an alternative.

One of those girls who left urine in my car proved to be pregnant. She was seventeen. What was she to do? Could she use her sister's name and have an abortion? However to do this I had to conspire with her. I had to call a physician friend, arrange an appointment for her using her sister's name. Would I do that? After a little hesitation, I made the call. All went well. She enjoyed her senior year without a pregnancy and an infant.

I never liked that part of my practice. I would never have performed an abortion. Arranging an abortion for a girl who saw this as her only way out of that situation appeared to me a bit different. I made these appointments for perhaps two dozen women. Some of them were married women who had older children and, with her husband's support, simply could not face another pregnancy and raising another child. Others were married women who had an affair, then become pregnant. Usually she didn't want her husband to know about the abortion. I made the calls. Rarely the upshot was a divorce. Most requests were from unmarried girls or women. My office records would hold a cryptic (I hoped) note, or no note at all, about those episodes. Some women never returned to my practice. I took care of others for years, perhaps delivering a baby or two after that episode. I was certainly glad when most of the unmarried girls in my practice carried a pregnancy to delivery, married or unmarried.

*   *   *

A fourteen-year-old high school girl made an appointment for a physical exam. She had had a sports physical at the start of the school year. I knew what that meant. She was either pregnant or wanted a prescription for birth control pills. She was one of a quartet of girls who were reputed to be "wild." I knew all of them and liked them. I hoped she was not pregnant. I always entered the exam room with the patient clothed, talked with the patient, and then left the room for her to disrobe and put on a gown.

"Why are you here today?"

"I want to have a prescription for birth control pills."

"OK. Do you know I will do a pelvic exam?" explaining the process.

"OK. Go ahead."

"Are you having intercourse?"

"No."

"Are you planning on having sex?"

"No. I just want to be prepared."

I had not faced that situation. "Do you want to have sex?"

"Not particularly. We (the four girls) just thought we should all be prepared."

We discussed the pros and cons of her going to bed with a boy. She decided not to get the prescription. I told her I would give her the prescription if she asked. But she did ask for her exam, just in case. None of the rest of the quartet had an exam or requested the OCs. Two years late she was steadily dating a boy and asked for the prescription. I cared for all of them for years.

*   *   *

A high school classmate of mine called me and asked me if I would prescribe an oral contraceptive for her sixteen-year old daughter. She told me she thought it was either the pill or a pregnancy. My response was "Yes, if you want me to do this, I will, but she will have to have a physical and Pap smear. Are you sure you want her to take these pills? Will she want to have a vaginal exam?"

She again said, "It's probably that or a pregnancy."

I replied "That choice makes sense to me also. Make her an appointment to see me."

Then she asked me "She is embarrassed by the whole procedure. Can you do the exam without a nurse being in the room?"

I didn't know about that. I had never done a pelvic exam without a female aide being in the room. As a student at KUMC I was used to examining a female in the medicine clinic without a nurse or aide in the exam room; that is all examinations except pelvic exams. Those were performed in the OB/GYN clinic, always chaperoned. There were at least two reasons for that: decrease the girl's embarrassment by having another female in the room and protect the doctor if the patient later made claims about his attitude or actions. My friend said the girl thought she would be less embarrassed if I were alone with her. I was not concerned about her or her mother later saying I had said or done something inappropriate.

The appointed time arrived. My nurse showed her to the door (her mother didn't even drive to the office) and told her I would be in in a few minutes. I entered the room, a bit embarrassed, and told her what I needed to do, then told her I would leave the room and she should put on a gown. Off I went. On my return she was seated on the table, wearing a gown with a sheet over her legs. She seemed fine. I was somewhat more embarrassed. I managed to complete the exam, left the room, returned and gave her my usual OC instructions and a prescription. We were finished.

Later I asked her mother what the girl thought of the whole thing. "She thought you were more embarrassed than she was," she said.

And I thought I had pulled it all off, coolly and calmly.

*   *   *

An older patient of mine approached me one evening and said "My niece, living in Colby, asked me about being put on the pill. She asked me to help her and not tell her mother. Will you give her a prescription?"

I knew the girl; in fact, I had delivered her. "Yes, I will, but she will have to have an exam and a Pap smear. Is she aware of this?"

"Yes, she knows about that. I talked to her about the mechanics. She doesn't want to come to your office. Can you do this somewhere else?"

"Not very well."

"Would you do it in the evening?"

"Yes, I could do that. But I need a nurse or assistant."

"My daughter, Sally, brought the girl to talk to me. You put Sally on the oral contraceptives a few months ago. She said she would bring the girl to you and chaperone the exam if that would work."

After thinking about the exam I said "Sure, we can do that."

And we did. We had no problems, other than leaving an exam room in a mess that evening. The women working in my office occasionally found I had used a room during the evening. They were a wonderful crew to work with.

*   *   *

When I was a teenager I met almost any request from a girl with a "Yes."

During my practice I learned to be a bit more wary of a woman's query. My telephone rang after dinner. A young man asked me if I could come see his wife at their motel room. They were on their way to Denver. I was young and brave (or foolish); I responded, "Yes."

I told Carol where I was going and drove to the Sue-Ann Motel, now the 1st Travel Inn. I stopped at the desk and told the clerk where I was going and expected to spend fifteen minutes or so and come find me if I didn't appear. I entered their room and found two scared kids.

"We were married yesterday and are going to Denver on our honeymoon. Jane has lower abdominal pain, has to urinate every five minutes and has blood in her urine. What is wrong? Do we need to go home?"

I didn't need a urine test or any lab work. "She has honeymoon cystitis. It's an infection in her bladder, an irritation from unaccustomed sexual activity. She wasn't used to that."

I had a urinary analgesic in my bag that would relieve her discomfort. I gave her a couple sulfa pills for her infection and asked her to fill prescriptions for both in the morning. And they could continue on their honeymoon, but avoid sex for a night or two.

"I may never do that again" his response.

I doubt he held to that vow, but perhaps. They were certainly frightened kids the evening I met them. When he asked me what he owed me I said, "The house call is my wedding present to you. Have a good trip."

As I left the motel the clerk asked about the girl's problem. I told him she had an infection and would be well in a few days. I had helped a couple in trouble; I could smile about it, but I saw no reason to tell the story. I saw a few other cases of honeymoon cystitis, but it has been twenty or thirty years since the last one. Perhaps the mores have changed?

*　　*　　*

One evening a young woman called me and asked if I would make a house call to her apartment. As usual I replied that I would; I wanted to care for everyone. I knocked on her door and she quickly opened it. She told me her husband was a truck driver, he was on the road.

"I have a sore breast" she said, and immediately bared both her breasts.

As professionally as I could I obtained the history of her sore breast. Very professionally I examined her painful breast—no redness, no swelling, no heat. "I can't find a problem" was my verdict.

"My belly hurts, too" and she began to unfasten her jeans.

Mumbling an apology I picked up my bag and beat a hasty retreat. The couple moved from Oakley in a short time.

That one was fairly easy. I had never seen her before that evening and didn't see her again. This woman was a widow, ten or fifteen years older than I, a friend. I had been taking care of her for years and wanted to continue to care for her. She phoned and asked me if I would make a call to her home. "Yes, of course I will." So that was what I did.

She opened the door. The light was dim. She was wearing a flowing dressing gown over matching pajamas. There was a bottle of wine and two glasses on the coffee table. I thought she had already had a bit of alcohol. She asked me to sit down and offered me a glass.

I was flattered. Although quite a bit older than I, she was an attractive woman. I liked her. But I certainly was not interested, either as an occasional caller for a drink or as her paramour. Nor did I want to offend her. I refused the wine. "What is the problem you called me about?"

"I twisted my ankle and it hurts."

I examined her ankle. I could see no injury. "Can you walk on it?"

"Yes. But it hurts."

"I'll help you to your bed."

With minimal help she made it to her bed, and then lay down. She had Valium® and Darvon® on her bedside table. I knew she frequently took both of them. I gave her a Darvon® and told her to go to sleep. I said, "I'm leaving. Call me in the morning if your ankle still needs cars and I'll see you at the hospital and X-ray it."

I didn't see her in the morning but I did continue to see her as a patient. Neither of us mentioned the evening. Maybe she had enough to drink that she didn't remember my call. Or maybe she was embarrassed by her call to me. At any rate we remained friends.

Jill was a different matter. I had cared for her throughout her pregnancy and delivered her baby. Now she had come to my office seeking care for her depression. I gave her an antidepressant and told her, as I did many patients, to call me if she needed me. She phoned me at 10:30 or 11:00 one night. I had just delivered a baby at the hospital. As I left the delivery room the nurse told me I had a message. It was from Jill. I called her. "Dr. Ohmart, I'm really down tonight. Can you come see me?"

I was tired. I had to work the next day. But I had told her I would be there if she needed me. "Yes, I'll put my clothes on and drive over."

She was sitting in her living room with her infant on the couch beside her. She started to tell me of her problems, then "Would you like a beer?"

I was still tired but she was a pretty young woman in need. I didn't need a beer but "Yes, I would."

We talked for a couple hours. I had two or three beers. Then I went home. I crawled into bed and told Carol "I think I'm in love."

"You're just in lust" was Carol's response "Go to sleep." We both went to sleep.

Both Carol and I became good friends with Jill. When her house burned Jill and her son lived in our home for about a year. Carol and Jill went to Colby Community College, then to Fort Hays State together. Jill married a young Englishman, with the wedding ceremony in our home. That marriage didn't last long but both Carol and Jill finished degrees at Fort Hays. Neither of us has seen her for years.

*   *   *

Written in May 1991 and published in *American Medical News* (Copyright ©1991 American Medical Association. All rights reserved.) as

Sometimes Caring Can Be More Important Than Curing

She was an eighty-six year old woman. Her heart had been battered almost out of shape by repeated infarctions. Some eighteen months ago the cardiologist she saw in Denver had sent her home, telling her he had done all he could for her. He also told her that she would be lucky to be alive in six months.

She had done fairly well for much longer than he had expected. She was in and out of congestive heart failure and in and out of the hospital. But she lived at home with the aid of one part-time assistant. She was usually able to go to church. One Sunday I met here at a local restaurant; her family had taken her out for dinner to celebrate her birthday. During this time a good doctor-patient relationship became a fast friendship. I came to admire her for her fortitude and acceptance, her never-failing good humor.

During the past few weeks, however, she had become much weaker. The diuretics and unloading agents necessary to keep her out of failure depressed her blood pressure to the point that she could not arise from a chair without help. She had to take so many pills that she claimed that was all she had time to do.

But she remained alert, enjoying her friends and family.

I made frequent house calls. Then her failure worsened to the point that I had to hospitalize her. Once in the hospital she developed pneumonia. I managed to help her past the acute infection and into a swing bed. She asked to go home, but I knew she was not yet well enough. Then, as I have seen so many times, she worsened again, developing pneumonia, uremia and becoming intermittently confused. She asked those of her family who had moved from the community to return for one last visit. Miraculously her sensorium cleared and she conversed coherently with her children and grandchildren, brothers and sisters. Then, after she had seen and talked with them all, she became semi-comatose.

During this time I did the things I had been trained to do, but without much hope. Maintain her electrolyte balance. Increase her diuretics. Wash fluid through her to decrease her BUN and creatinine. Supercillin and other magic bullets for the infection. She hung on, as we all have seen patients do. They asked me how long she had to live, but I was unable to give them any reasonably accurate estimate. Finally her family began to drift away, answering the calls of their families, schools and jobs.

Somehow she began to improve. Probably due more to her tenacity than my medicine her edema cleared. Her BUN and creatinine dropped toward normal. She was able to walk short distances and her sensorium became clearer. And she again started asking to go home. I thought she was asking to go home to live, and replied that she was not well enough. She improved slowly, and continued to ask to go home.

Finally her son caught me in the hall and asked me what my plans for her were. I could hardly respond. I hated to see my friend caught in ping-ponging between nursing home and hospital that so many elderly are, never really well, yet always kept from dying by the miracles of modern medicine. But I knew of no other answer. Then he told me what she had been asking of me for two weeks. "Can I go home to die?"

I told him that I knew of no reason. Why not? Her family could help for a while. We have a hospice staffed with excellent volunteers in our town. And our public health staff is excellent. I did find the courage to explain to him what might happen to her—develop pneumonia, heart failure, etc.—and that the family should decide in advance what to do in those eventualities. I also said that I would always be willing to see her if they needed. Two days later they took her home.

She did well for two or three weeks, then began a gradual decline. She died peacefully one afternoon, comfortable and happy in the thought that she was at home, with her family. Her family was pleased that they had managed to do what their mother wanted. I was relieved that I did not have to see another friend through those last days. The only ones who could be displeased about the situation were the Medicare statisticians who gave our hospital a black mark because one of our Medicare patients died within six months after discharge from the hospital.

Would I do it again? Yes. This was truly a valuable experience for all concerned. The family expressed their love in a mature and caring way. I learned from my involvement—I learned that I did not always understand what my patients wanted. I learned that a family can be a source of remarkable strengths. I again was shown that there is more to medicine than the cure of disease. And most of all I learned that there is more than one way to care for and show love for a friend.

$$* \quad * \quad *$$

Women, even older women, sometimes brought more than a smile to my face. I have chuckled about this pair for many years. Two widow ladies remarried, both seeking my approval prior for their nuptials. I thought this was great. I knew the men involved and they, as well as the ladies, were lonely. I knew everything would go swimmingly. A few days later one of the ladies appeared at my office, almost in tears; she was also quite angry.

"That old goat still wants to have sex. I'm not going to do that!"

My counseling skills weren't up to the task of my changing her mind. The best I could do was a weak "There's nothing wrong with older couples enjoying intimacy."

As she left I thought I had failed at that counseling job. A week later the second lady entered my office. She also was unhappy with her marriage. "I wanted to find a man to have intercourse. I want and need it. And he's impotent and is not interested in attempting to change that!"

Again my counseling was futile. Too bad, I thought, "I wish I could rearrange these couples so that the individuals who still desired intercourse were together and the other individuals were together. I dared not suggest it, however."

The following two episodes have been related to me by patients and I think they are worth sharing by the plain and plainspoken people in care for.

The first involves a farm couple, probably in their late forties to early fifties and was told to me by the wife. She said that she had been sitting on a stool when her husband walked by, patted her on the bottom and said that she "was getting about as broad as the header on a combine." (Fifteen to twenty feet for non-farmers.)

This had hurt a bit, but she said nothing at the time. A few nights later she had her revenge. Her husband was getting a bit amorous, to which her reply was "Honey, ain't no use in firing up a $100,000 machine for a half an ear of corn."

A woman also related the second to me. Her mother had had a mastectomy and gone to live with her daughter and family while she was post-op. The family made no effort to hide the facts of the operation, even from her grandson, who was in the first grade. When he asked her what she had done she said, "I had my tit cut off" and assumed that was the end of it.

She had forgotten about the inquisitiveness of six-year old boys. He came home from school the next day and announced that in his class he had the only grandmother who had a tit cut off. Grandmother was a bit taken aback by this, and certainly not ready for his next statement—"Grandma, can I take you to show and tell with me tomorrow?"

*   *   *

This was never published but named as:

100 Years Of Health

Hazel will celebrate her 100th birthday next month. I had a rare chance to chat with her today at a reception honoring my thirty years of practice in our small rural community. As usual, she told me how important it was to her to have "her doctor" here in Oakley to care for her. As usual, I told her I would starve if all of my patients came to see me as often as she did. I had last seen her at a similar reception five years ago. We may have had an occasional interval encounter in the grocery or hardware store, but she has not been in my office in the interim. Five years ago she told me to hang around in case she needed me. Evidently she didn't.

I do remember taking care of her on two previous occasions, the first about twenty years ago. She called and said that she had fallen and hurt her hip. She got up from the floor, walked to the couch, and then phoned me an hour or so later when her hip continued to hurt. She wanted me to come to her home to see if it was broken. I told her it would be more useful if she called the ambulance and met me at the hospital. She refused. I drove to her home. After a fairly cursory exam I had little doubt that her hip was broken.

I convinced her to let me call an ambulance. At the hospital, X-rays showed a fracture. She allowed me to send her to Hays to see an orthopedist, who pinned it. After an uneventful recovery she returned to her home, where she lived alone.

Several years later her son called me: "Dick, Mom fell at home two days ago. Her left ankle is badly swollen, tender and black-and-blue. She won't walk on it. Could it be broken?"

"It certainly could be," I replied. "Will she come to the hospital?"

She did, and again we found a fracture. I wanted to put a long-leg cast on her, but she would have none of that, especially when she heard what it would do to her independence. She did accept a short-leg cast, but only after I assured her that she would be able to walk short distances with the aid of a walker. I opted for temporary nursing home placement. She overruled me. With her walker, a wheelchair, and one part-time aid to help her, she went home and did well. Within eight weeks her fracture had healed well enough for me to remove her cast. Two months later she was walking without a limp.

Today this indomitable woman offered me a deal. She will hang around for the next twenty years if I will stick around to be "her doctor." I again told her that I didn't think she often needed a doctor, but she said she wanted me around anyway. So we sealed the deal. Darned if I don't think she has more chance of making 120 years than I do 79!

*   *   *

Published in *American Medical News*, Nov 28, 1994 (Copyright ©1994 American Medical Association. All rights reserved.)

Learning To Live, and Die, With Grace and Strength

"I may not be here that long."

That was Hazel's reply to my telling her I was going to be gone for a few days and would see her on my return, in about a week.

"I know that," I replied. "And I'm sorry." She continued, saying that she had lived over 100 years and had enjoyed a good life. She realized that she couldn't live forever and was ready to go. Since she had chosen to have no surgery for a colon-obstructing carcinoma, I couldn't even wish her anything different. I was the one whose voice broke, however. The old man had to leave the room and allow my associates to conclude that morning's visit. That was the last time I saw Hazel alive.

My absence was mandated by plans my two brothers and I had made at the time of our Dad's funeral, three months before, to meet at his home this week to empty and clean it preparatory to selling it. Dad also had died of cancer. He died quietly one morning in March, alone and in private, as I am certain he wanted. He had spent the prior two days saying his good-byes, either in person or by telephone. He had told me, the eldest, what to do with the bills, insurance papers, etc. that he had been unable to complete. He had spent the afternoon before his death with Mother, holding her hand. She later told me that all he had said was "I'm sorry." He, too, was ready to die, although he did not voice that thought

My wife's aunt, Virginia, died last fall, at the age of 92. I had seen her only a few weeks before her death, when we all knew it was inevitable. She was her usual gracious self, apologizing from her hospital bed for the fact that she had only water to offer us. She told us that she did not expect us to make another trip from Kansas to California after her death, which her sister, 87 years old and legally blind, could handle the memorial service and cremation they had planned. That was what was done!

Another friend/patient, knowing she was dying of lung cancer, elected to remain at home and die of pneumonia, rather than prolong an existence that did not allow her to do anything she liked to do.

Where do these people get their strength? Why am I saddened more by their impending deaths than they appear to be? Is it only my selfish desire to keep them with me for the support they have given me that makes me mourn their deaths so deeply? Will I be that gracious when my turn comes?

Two weeks ago my wife Carol and I visited her Aunt Edna in California. This was the second time we had seen her since Virginia's death, and she appeared stronger than ever. She goes to the Oakland A's baseball games, the San Francisco Opera, and out with friends, just as she always did. She remains one of the most up beat, optimistic people I know. When a friend asked her at dinner what the source of her strength was she replied very simply, "I believe in God and that He will tell me what to do."

On my return home and to my practice I had a visit from another 80-plus year old woman, one of my regular patients. She is a widow, has seen one of her sons die, and has a fair amount of arthritic pain. But she is also up beat. So much so that I believe I gain more from visiting with her than she does from seeing me. She broached the subject by mentioning the fact that there seemed to be a lot more cancer around than in the past. Two of her friends, both much younger than she, have terminal malignancies. When I asked her how she managed to stay in such good spirits in spite of seeing all this, she replied "I have much to be thankful for."

While others had problems that were insoluble, hers were fairly minor. She would simply continue to do what she could to make her life pleasant and would accept whatever the future might bring.

Later that week I had a visit from another self-described "stubborn old woman." She did not want to come to my office because she was afraid I might put her in the hospital. At age 94 she told me that if she was going to die she wanted to die at home. She was in mild heart failure, so I simply prescribed a little Lasix® (her only medicine) and asked her to return if things worsened or return in ten days regardless. I also gave her my standard lecture, one I find myself using more frequently than I used to, on the idea that sometimes coming to see me at the onset of symptoms might prevent a later hospitalization. She guessed this might be so, but I'm not sure I convinced her of the fact. She too has an inner strength that I envy. She ascribes it to stubbornness and independence, traits that she does possess in abundance.

My mother, confined to a nursing home for the past five years because of Parkinsonism and severe osteoarthritis in her legs, has become much more alert mentally and physically stronger in the three months since Dad's death. She first told me that I would have to take care of her financial affairs. I thought that would be easy. The next time I saw her I realized that what she meant was that I would have to do the legwork, as she might not be physically able, but she was certainly going to make the decisions. Especially after she caught me in a math error!

Where does this strength come from? I have not yet asked her, but I will.

We have recently celebrated the D-Day 50-year anniversary. Time and again I watched on TV as the survivors (many highly decorated) of that operation said, "I was just an American boy, just doing my job. I was not a hero. Some other GI was the real hero."

It appears to me that those men, now in their 70s and 80s, all had the strength to "do my job," whatever they may have seen it to be. I am not at all certain that I now have, or would have had, that strength.

I am 58 years old. I have lived a comparatively comfortable, middle-class American life. My wife and I have reared three children, have four grandchildren, and what is termed in contemporary terms as a "good support system." Yet I doubt that I have the strength or fortitude displayed by any of the above individuals, or many others of their generation. As I observe the members of my generation I am not sure that I see anyone (or at least many) with those traits. Why? Did our parents, who were forced to fight their way through the Depression, gain strength that they have denied us by trying to provide a "better life" for us and protect us from similar catastrophes? Did World Wars I and II provide cohesive, strengthening forces that those of us who barely remember the second war, and remember too well the Korean Conflict and the Viet Nam quagmire have not experienced? Is American life truly too much a life of ease (at least for those with whom I associate and practice) to allow us the opportunity to become hardened by fire? Has the loss of family cohesiveness and the religion I was taught as a youth led to a sense of rootlessness and loss of guidance previously looked to as a source of strength?

The above questions could be, and have been, debated by minds better honed than mine to answer such imponderables. And no decisions have been reached, at least of which I am aware. I choose to believe that I, and everyone else, have within himself the seed of that strength. I have not been called upon to force that seed to burst into sudden bloom under the stress of warfare, strife or economic disaster. I have not lived long enough for the seed to mature spontaneously to fruition. But through the assistance of my patients who continue to teach me while I "treat" them, through the continued observation of others around me and through the deaths of my father and friends, I am slowly learning and growing. Perhaps, when my turn comes, I will be able to display the strength and graciousness, the class, of those who have preceded and instructed me.

*   *   *

I wrote this in August 1991. It tells of a mistake I and a student made, and my response. It was published in *American Medical News* (Copyright ©1991 American Medical Association. All rights reserved.) as

Powerful Bond With Patient Grows Out of Tragic Outcome.

"I'm mad as Hell at you!"

Those were the words that greeted me as I entered the room. I hadn't known what to expect, but that was a stronger reaction than I was prepared for. My first impulse was to bolt from the room. I restrained myself, assured myself that the tough old broad did not have a gun or other weapon, and took a deep breath.

"I can't blame you very much," I replied. And, in truth, I couldn't. A few months before she had driven her second husband forty-five miles to see me because of his epigastric pain. The senior medical student I had with me had done most of his history and physical. I knew the patient as an ex-drinker who had had many acid-peptic problems, and believed his present problem to be related. After a cursory exam I gave him a prescription for some Zantac® and started them on their way home, with my parting advice to "Let me know if things don't get better in a few days."

I heard sooner than a few days. They had gone only a few miles from our town before he suffered a cardiac arrest while in their car. She drove on to the closest town, trying to give him CPR with one hand while driving with the other. Of course, there was little to be done on her arrival. Not happy over my diagnostic triumph I comforted myself with the knowledge that it could be extremely difficult to differentiate between the two conditions. I couldn't hospitalize everyone I saw with low chest or upper abdominal pain to observe them for a possible heart attack. Yet I knew that, had I ordered an EKG, I might have made the correct diagnosis and kept him here in the hospital. But I had been in practice long enough to know that everything is clearer in hindsight and I did not mope long over the episode. I did like his wife very much, however, and hated to lose her as a patient, as I felt certain I would.

This was the first time I had seen her since then. My appointment book had said "talk," which usually meant something other than the run-of-the-mill office visit. It certainly was! One of the reasons I had liked her so much was her courage; another was her honesty. Both were shining forth this day. While I would have hidden and said nothing, she would have none of that. She wanted to know what I really had thought when I sent them on their way. I told her that I had believed it was his ulcer acting up again. "Could it have been his heart?" she asked.

"Yes, it could have," I lacked another response. I couldn't match her courage; the least I could do was match her honesty.

"Why didn't you get an EKG?"

"I didn't think there was enough question to get one."

"Would it have made any difference?"

"I don't know."

"Well, I am mad at you."

"That's understandable, but I can't change anything now."

"I know that, but we have been friends for a long time, and I still want you for my doctor. The only way I know to get over my anger is to face it with you."

So face it we did. Again we became fast friends. Over the years she shared her fears and joys with me. We tried to handle her weight problem, her hypertension and her diabetes. She asked my opinion on changes in her personal life, as well. (Not always did she follow my advice, though.) I liked to see her name on my appointment book, because she always had an interesting story and I could temporarily lift my guard and tell her what I really thought without fear of offending her. I wish I had taken time to meet her outside of my office, but didn't, much to my loss.

She also had chronic complaints of epigastric pain, usually relieved by antacids or her Tagamet®. She had been X-rayed regularly. Then her pain no longer was relieved as easily. I scheduled her for an EGD. There, staring me in the face, was an obvious carcinoma of the stomach. Biopsies proved me correct. After some discussion I referred her to our nearest surgeon, ninety miles away.

"I won't let him operate if you're not there" she told me.

"That's silly, he's an excellent surgeon."

She already knew this as he had removed her gallbladder in the past, as well as working on various members of her family. She was adamant.

"You're my friend. We've been through a lot together."

She was right, and I needed to go to Hays anyway, to see my ophthalmologist. So the surgery was scheduled and we both went to Hays. The operation was simple, in spite of her obesity, and all seemed to go well. There was no sign of metastatic disease, and I drove home congratulating myself on having done well for her this time, at least. However, all was not to go that easily. For whatever reason, she developed renal failure and was transferred to a tertiary center where dialysis was available. Septicemia complicated her uremia. She spent almost two months in the ICU there, and then died. Her daughters said that she welcomed death after all the discomforts of her last days, and I know she would not have been afraid to face the end. I am sorry that I could not face it with her, to have helped her through that final experience.

I tried to tell her, some time before the last episode, how much I had learned from her—honesty, courage, strength in adversity, and most of all, that sometimes facing a bad situation squarely can make even the bleakest experience a valuable lesson. She scoffed at me, what could she, an uneducated farm wife/beautician thirty years my senior have to teach me? A lot, much more than she ever knew, was, and is, my answer.

*　　*　　*

The dry words in an obituary recall vivid memories of my forty-six years in Oakley. Elizabeth's obituary recalled reminiscences of my entire career in Oakley. The obituary was in the paper of May 6, 2009, although she died April 19. It states she died after a long illness. I hope it was not Alzheimer's, as I found her wit and conversation a pleasure. The story of her family, intertwined with my life, forms a chronicle of an old doctor's life.

I first met her and her husband when I was a preceptee in Oakley in 1961. Ernie had caught his arm in a grain augur, ending up with severe lacerations of his hand and arm. Jim and I, although there was not much that I did, repaired the mangled extremity. He spent a few days in the hospital. I saw him at Jim's office once or twice; then I was gone, completing my education. We became friends but I thought I would never see either of them again. Ernie and Elizabeth were tough farm stock, the kind of people I had grown up with in Scott City. These were the kind of people I wanted to care for once I became a physician.

After earning my degree and finishing an internship in Wichita I decided to return to Oakley to practice. Jim had taken care of Ernie and Elizabeth and their family for years. I occasionally saw one of them if Jim were too busy to see them or absent. I met her sisters, her brother who was in the nursing home for years, and her children. After Jim's death they continued to see me. Attempting to be Jim's replacement I had an idea that I was a surgeon, as Jim had been. I performed two operations as a solo surgeon. One was on her daughter. The pathology report on my abdominal incision stated it was "normal thyroid tissue." I knew I had been nowhere near her neck! Perhaps I was not destined to be a surgeon. The surgery on her went well, in spite of the pathology report. Always enjoying obstetrics I had the pleasure of delivering many of her grandchildren.

I cared for one of Elizabeth's sisters as she aged, then died. I always was glad to see them and made time to chat with them. I certainly enjoyed it. I hope they, too, enjoyed those chats. Elizabeth knew that I was doing a bit of writing. She asked me, somewhat shocked at her temerity, if I would be interested in reading a few of the stories she had written. I said I would.

She brought the stories to my office and I read them. "Yes, I certainly enjoyed your stories."

It was not an exaggeration. Most of them were about growing up and living on a farm in Northwest Kansas. She had lived a full life and her stories spoke of her strength and caring.

Elizabeth's sister, Freda, brought her husband to Jim. We decided he had appendicitis and Jim did an appendectomy. Romeo had not only appendicitis; his appendix had ruptured and he had peritonitis. He spent several days in the hospital, while we treated him with the few antibiotics available at that time. Romeo later had pneumonia, then carcinoma of the prostate. This again gave me an opportunity to learn the strength of that family. I cared for Freda after her breast cancer.

I delivered all of one of Freda's daughter's babies. The last, twins, graduated this May in Oakley. My service in that family's life is completed. For forty-eight years I have been a part of their lives. I have learned of strength, caring, humility and honesty through their joys and sadness. Those younger than I now have their own lives elsewhere, away from Oakley. Those older than I have died. Occasionally I see one of my contemporaries and chat a bit. This was the life I dreamed of as a student, the life I lived as a rural physician. I hope the young physicians are blessed as I have been.

Chapter 7

Teaching Students; Students Teaching Me

Male Medical Students Only

Jim's first medical student had been sent to Oakley in 1951, the first year of the preceptor program. KUMC continued to send students to Jim. I arrived in Oakley as a brash, inexperienced fourth-year medical student in January 1961. When I began my practice with Jim, I also spent time as a mentor, especially in Jim's absence. I enjoyed my experiences with the students and I hope they enjoyed the time they spent with me. I learned something from most of the students who spent time in Oakley.

In the 1960s and 1970s the medical students who precepteed in Oakley were male, many of them married and fathers. Most of their wives were teachers, nurses or working in other fields to support their husbands while they attained their MD degrees. Few wives could spend a month in Oakley. If a wife did accompany her husband to Oakley, Jim rented a small apartment where the student and his family lived. If he came alone, as when I precepteed in Oakley, the student lived with Jim, eating and sleeping in Jim's home. At that time the preceptorship was to show a student how a small town doctor lived, as well as practiced medicine. The ultimate goal of the preceptor program was to entice new physicians to settle in a rural area. This worked on me, but I doubt that it had that effect on many young doctors.

*　　*　　*

The community was used to having "young doctors" spend four to six weeks with Jim. Those Oakley residents felt a bit of pride that their community and their doctor had been chosen to have students sent to Oakley for part of their education. After Jim's death I was asked to serve as a preceptor. I was delighted! I had enjoyed the time I had spent with Jim's preceptees and I saw no reason to doubt I would continue to enjoy teaching. As the preceptor, however, a couple of unpleasant tasks befell me; I had to grade the students and had to criticize them. I never liked either but learned to criticize gently and, probably, grade much too easily.

In January of 1972 I received my first medical student after Jim's death. Where to house the students became a problem. Fortunately the first student was married. The apartment Jim had maintained was open so I rented it. It was inexpensive to rent, but it wasn't much of an apartment. It had a kitchen, a bedroom and not much more. Paula and Carol had provided pots, pans, dishes, etc. from their castaways. I don't know where linens were found. Five medical students spent a month in that apartment in 1972. Fortunately each of them brought a wife with him. Two had small children. The couples were young and looking forward to a doctor's life. Carol and I thought they could suffer a bit on the trail to luxury.

The number of medical students assigned to Oakley dropped to a trickle. I had two in 1973, one each in 1974 and 1975 and none in 1977 or 1978. In 1975 I accepted my first physician assistant student from Wichita State University (WSU). None of those brought a spouse or child to Oakley. No longer did I maintain the apartment. If needed, I rented a room and the student ate at the hospital. In 1976 when we opened the new hospital the students stayed at the hospital, sleeping in an unoccupied room.

With two new doctors planning to practice in Oakley an office complex was added to the northwest corner of the hospital, where New Frontiers now has their offices. As well as doctors' offices we designed a two-bedroom apartment for the students in the basement. I remember only one problem in that arrangement. We simply expected the students to act as adults. We threw the students together, regardless of gender, race or religion. One male PA student, when found he was to share an apartment (although not the bedroom) with a pretty female medical student, refused and returned to Wichita. Most of them became friends.

*   *   *

In my office the receptionist was to ask the patient if it was all right to be seen by a student. Rarely did a patient decline; many rather enjoyed the attention of a student who usually spent more time in talking with and examining a patient than I. The student took a history, examined the patient, then left. The student would return to my office and discuss the patient with me. Together we returned to the exam room and talked to the patient, where the student might demonstrate his/her salient findings on the patient. Then we outlined our plan of attack for that patient's problem, usually medication/treatment but occasionally tests such as X-rays or blood tests.

If a complex or serious problem was diagnosed I would ask the patient to return to be certain that the illness or injury was alleviated. If I did not need to see the patient again and it was more than a simple cold or sore throat, I might ask a patient to return and see the student at no charge so the student could see the results of our treatment.

During the time I was alone I, from time to time, asked a student to take care of a patient alone in an office visit, usually during a flu epidemic or if an emergency had set our schedule back by hours. My receptionist would ask the patient if the student could see the patient and prescribe the necessary medications. If a problem arose the student would talk to me or, if necessary, I, too, would see the patient. This routine worked well within our office. No one complained to me about this approach. There may have been patients who simply went to another doctor but I knew of none such.

The students were often asked (or forced) to be first responders in the ER. After examining the patient he/she was to call me, then I would go to the ER if needed, or ask the student to take care of the problem if appropriate. One evening a new student and his wife were having dinner with Carol and me at home. Gladys, the nurse at the old hospital, called and said a tourist had appeared at the ER and had some chest pain. Gladys said he was in no distress; he was a fairly young man. I asked Tom to go to the hospital, talk to him and call me—my usual approach. No phone call. I said, "This is a slow, cautious man. Undoubtedly he's thoroughly examining him."

I waited a while longer. Still no call. "Carol, I'll call the hospital and see what's going on."

No one answered the phone. "Carol, now I'm concerned about Tom. I'll go see what's happening and you keep Doris here. We'll be home when we're done."

I found Tom, Gladys and the aide (the entire hospital staff) in the ER, trying to resuscitate the tourist. He had a heart attack; his heart had stopped. The three of them had been doing all that could have been done, not much at that time, although we did have a defibrillator which they had been using. Years later we all learned the Advanced Cardiac Life Support protocols, but there was nothing anyone could do that night. I walked to our patient's car and told his wife "Your husband had a heart attack. The nurse and the young doctor did everything that could be done. He did not survive."

Back at home I said "Tom, I'm sorry you were caught in this situation, especially on your first night in Oakley. Both of us learned something tonight. You do everything you can but occasionally things turn out badly. I learned that even a young man can have a heart attack. I should not have sent you to the hospital alone following that call."

Having learned from that experience I usually responded to chest pain by going to the ER, even though the chest pain was usually muscular pain, an upset stomach, or perhaps an attack of gall bladder pain. Later we had an ambulance with two-way radio communication to the hospital and I carried a pager. I was always summoned to the ER for true emergencies, even though many of those proved to be inconsequential.

*   *   *

New Students, Male and Female, MD and PA

The first female medical students to come to Oakley were married. Both wife and husband were medical students, coming to Oakley together. One couple spent the month of August 1965, the other in December 1966. Linda Duston was the first single female student to arrive in Oakley. She arrived in April 1970. Linda was engaged to a doctor practicing in Holton, Kansas. She married him and they have practiced together for many years. Gradually the number of female students rose until thirty-five or forty per cent of the students in Oakley were women. I continue to spend a few days at KUMC every fall interviewing KUMC applicants and now half of the applicants are women.

The first physician assistant student I accepted was Dennis Elliott, who returned to work with me after his graduation in 1975. He worked with me for three years. Those PA students had graduated from high school followed by at least two years of college. That was followed by a year of basic science at WSU. The last year of PA training was basically an apprenticeship with various physicians. Then they graduated. In the early years many of the male PA students were military-trained medics. Dennis had spent four years at Kansas State University, then joined the Navy and trained as a medic. He had then served a year or so in Vietnam during that war. Most of the female PA students had been nurses or medical techs before they entered PA training. All of these PA students were adults who had held jobs, experiences denied most medical students. At that time most medical students, including me, had spent their lives as students, even though they often were parents. I hope most medical students became adults after they entered practice and had to earn a living, although I know of a few whom never lost their student ethos.

*   *   *

When I was a student in Oakley Jim introduced me as Dr. Ohmart to his patients. And most patients called me an intern and called me "Doctor," not "Mister," Ohmart. I continued to use the title for the medical students; although not exactly correct I felt it was appropriate. The title doctor was never used to address a PA student. I introduced Dennis as "Dennis, the physician assistant who works with me." He spent a year or so correcting patients who called him "Doctor Dennis." He finally realized patients were never going to abandon the title so Dennis abandoned his efforts.

PA students were always introduced as Mister, Miss or simply using a first name. It never occurred to me that the PA students might have objected to my introducing a medical student as "doctor," followed by my introducing the PA student as "Miss." One of those adult young women finally inquired if I actually meant to denigrate the PA students. "You call a medical student Doctor Brown. You call me Judy. I have a bachelor's degree. I'm going to be a PA. I think you should have a title for me!"

I could find no appropriate title for her so I began introducing all students as Miss or Mister with a first name only. No one complained about the change.

*   *   *

Students Educate the Community

Rarely was I busy but, if so, Carol might then take a young man to dinner. Occasionally a friend would ask her "Who is this? Is it your brother?"

Carol, who had no brother, awaited a chance to answer that question affirmatively when we had a black student. But no one asked. We both thought it was a lesson for Oakley residents that a happily married couple could have single friends outside of the marriage.

I tried to educate our patients, but didn't always succeed. When I was in high school in Scott City the school announced sports physicals to be held in the dressing room at the field house; one evening only, for boys. (No girl sports.) We were told to strip down to our shorts and line up. Then it was my turn. Basically the examiner applied his stethoscope to my chest then checked me for a hernia. That was the exam! When I joined Jim he was used to the same procedure, but also looked at the boys' ears and throats, still in the football locker room. The boys' responses to these physicals ranged from extreme shyness to a totally nude boy proudly prancing around the locker room. Both in Scott City and Oakley coaches assisted us and the exams were free. It was our contribution to our patients and the school.

After a year or two we decided it was too loud to hear heart beats so we began to do the exams at our office building in the evening. We were still assisted by the coaches and still free. But the boys remained dressed in the lobby, disrobing before entering an exam room. As the school began to provide girl's sports the same procedure was followed with two exceptions. There was one evening for boys, one for girls. The girls retained their bra and panties, and they were given gowns to wear if they desired. Most did! We went to Monument and Grinnell and did school physicals in their gyms. There we were examining fifth and sixth grade students. I postulated the Ohmart Theorum: the girl's heart rate was inversely proportional to the girls' breast size. It usually held true.

The building housed our offices as well as Bill Funk, the dentist. One evening a gold crown disappeared. I think we simply asked more coaches to supervise, but continued the exams. We always tried to schedule the school exams when we had a student. After Jim died it was almost a necessity to have the assistance of a student or two. If alone, even a brief five-minute exam would have taken me much of the night to complete the exams. After I moved my practice to the Center Street office this routine was continued.

In August we would announce two evenings for school sports physicals, one for boys, one for girls. We would charge each student five dollars and the money would be returned to their schools—Oakley, Grinnell or Wheatland schools. Those who missed the evening physicals would have to schedule their own exams and pay the usual office call charge. We had much assistance from the coaches and teachers and this appeared to me to work well. Many of the girls realized they could wear a two-piece swimming suit and didn't have to disrobe at all. The high school students all wanted an examiner of the same gender as the student. Often I managed that but there were more girls to examine than a female student might manage. Many had to be examined by old Doc Ohmart although they should have been used to seeing me.

There was a problem for those students if he or she missed the opportunity to come to the evening exams. They had to make an appointment at my office for their exams. I was usually booked up two weeks or so in advance. The students had to have their exams signed before they could practice. I asked my reception to say "I will schedule an exam for you. But you will probably be examined by a student."

The boys always asked whether the student was male of female. They didn't like the idea of having some young woman inspect their testicles and groin. If it was a female student most of the boys complained, but underwent the exam. A few boys complained hard enough that the woman examiner would do most of the exam, and then I would arrive and check him for a hernia. Mothers and the female high school students said, "I have always been cared for by a male. What is the problem? That a boy has to be examined by a woman? It would be good for the boys to see a female doctor!"

I agreed, but few of the boys agreed.

*   *   *

Not only I, but also Carol and our kids enjoyed the students in Oakley. We often had dinners with the students and their families. We went to school activities, first to see my children, later the kids we had seen at the office. We went to the movies, the balloon fests, any activity the students might enjoy. But my favorite activity was taking an attractive young woman out to dinner, especially after my children were grown and Carol was often visiting grandchildren in Texas. I then, alone, had the undivided attention of the young woman I escorted to dinner.

I always had a silent chuckle when I escorted a single woman to dinner, a ball game or a movie. I would have thought that, after years of having students in my practice, Oakley residents would have become accustomed to Carol being gone and my escorting a young woman. But more than once I caught someone looking at us, trying to decide whom I was taking to dinner or a ball game. A few brash souls asked me who the young woman was.

The Wichita PA program sent Oakley an attractive young black woman. Her first rotation had gone poorly. Lauren was from Baltimore. She was shy. Most of the rotations were in small Kansas towns with few blacks. She was considering dropping out of the program. She was sent to me to encourage her to complete her training. We got along well. I don't think anyone denigrated her ethnicity. She was doing well in her assignments.

That fall Carol was running for the Kansas House of Representatives. Some friends had scheduled a nut fry in a pasture south of Oakley as a fundraiser. The bulls had been castrated that afternoon. We took Lauren to the pasture that evening. Alcohol flowed freely. She didn't drink. Ranching, Kansas sports, hunting—these were all the men spoke about. She had little to add to the conversation. She was sitting on the ground alone and someone laid a half-gallon jug of bourbon beside her. I quickly snapped a picture of Lauren with the jug. I was certain she was ready to leave Oakley, but she hung in there.

A few days later one of the men at the pasture party had a small cut on his arm. I looked at it and asked Lauren to suture it. During that time she chatted with him. As he left he told me he thought she would make a great PA. Saturday evening Carol, Lauren, another student and I were at dinner at the country club. I received a phone call "A boy in the ER has a little cut on his leg."

Dinner was about to be served. I knew I could repair it in a flash, much more quickly than a student could. "Wash it up, lay out some 4-0 silk suture and I'll be there in a few minutes."

I drove to the hospital, sutured the laceration and sped back. My party was just sitting down to eat. But Lauren was not there! Looking around I spied a group of cattlemen who had attended the Saturday afternoon cattle auction. There was Lauren, surrounded by the cattlemen. One of the men there was the man whose arm she had repaired.

Walking over I said, "Lauren, your dinner is ready. Are you ready to go?"

"Yes, I guess so" was her reply.

She said the group had walked in and her patient had recognized her. He had simply picked her up, chair and all, moving her to his group and introduced her to the entire group as the wonderful girl who had sewn up his arm.

I was afraid that, after six weeks in Oakley, she was certain that she would not complete her training. As she left she assured me that she had a wonderful time in Oakley and was going to continue her work. Later she asked me for a recommendation to Johns Hopkins Hospital where she worked for some time.

*   *   *

Another black woman, this time from Wichita, was sent to me. Her parents brought her to Oakley and wanted to meet me. She had spent two years in California at college before her PA training. She had driven herself to California. Why her parents wanted to meet me I had no idea. Perhaps they thought Western Kansas still was inhabited by wild Indians, or, at least, wild cowboys. After meeting and speaking with me they returned to Wichita. She had attended Southeast High in Wichita, with predominantly white students. She told me she had been a cheerleader, their "token black."

She was an excellent student and enjoyed the Oakley community. She went to the Balloon Fest in September, getting a ride in a balloon, although I remembered her father's admonition that I take care of his daughter. That evening she and a white male medical student attended a dance following the balloon fest. She was the only black person there but enjoyed dancing with the men. The medical student told me one of the local men at the dance was enthralled by her. I teased her a bit and she said, "He had a bit too much to drink, I think. He asked me to marry him."

She said she laid her arm beside his and asked him if she thought that would work. She told me he said "You can milk my cows. Those old cows don't care."

*   *   *

Students Teach Me

I learned from almost every student. My lessons were not always of a medical nature. My most memorable medical student was Beth, a petite blond. She arrived in Oakley on a Sunday. Wednesday afternoon we were driving to Colby for the Circuit Course meeting (These were six meetings a year, where faculty members from KUMC spent a week touring, giving daily lectures to doctors out in the state.) when this angelic girl said, "What does anyone do in Oakley other than eat, drink or f***?"

I was forty-five years old, a college graduate, a practicing physician and had spent twenty some years in Oakley. I had certainly heard, and probably used, the word more than once. But I was astonished to hear that utterance emanate from this attractive student and use it so nonchalantly. She didn't know me. I was her instructor. Didn't these kids have any respect for their elders? She obviously was intelligent; she was a fourth-year medical student. I was flabbergasted. My stammered response was "I don't know."

I never became accustomed to the words that flowed from sweet young things. But I was never again shocked by such words. I rarely criticized. These students taught me to use such Anglo-Saxon words as "pee," "fart" and "shit" to our patients since they express normal bodily functions that all would understand. But to this day I believe a professional should use professional language if speaking to a professional.

Beth spent two months in Oakley and we became good friends. Towards the end of her rotation we were driving from the hospital to the office and I told her we were going to remove a skin cancer from a man's arm. Usually I removed the lesion, and then watched as the student sutured it. She asked, "May I do the complete procedure?"

I paused only a moment and replied "Sure, if you give me a big sweet smile."

She looked at me and said tartly "How about if you let me do it because I'm a damn good doctor?"

She removed the lesion, doing it well. And I had been put in my place. Never again did I respond with such a sexist response. Aloud at least.

*   *   *

I had a morning routine that I religiously followed six days of the week. I awakened at 6:00, showered and shaved, not awakening Carol. Leisurely I read the morning paper while eating cereal or toast with a glass of milk. Coffee was delayed until after making rounds at the hospital, for a fifteen minute coffee break about 9:00. I arrived at the nurses' desk at 7:30, expecting the student(s) to meet me at the desk. The nurses would report to us any significant events during the night.

That morning the nurses had smiles on their faces. The students were almost giggling. There, on the desk where I would lay the hospital charts, was a nicely laid out Kleenex. The expression on my face brought gales of laughter, not just from the students but the nurses as well. I even had to smile. For months, or perhaps years, the first thing I did after seating myself at the nurse's desk was to pick up a Kleenex and clean my glasses. I continued the routine but I often smiled about the habits of the old man.

*   *   *

The PA student with me had been sent to me specifically because I was a kind, gentle instructor. For some reason many physicians failed to instill self-confidence in their children. She was quite bright but her father was a physician and she had no self-confidence. She had failed a rotation or two, had been sent to a class on self-esteem and then sent to me because I was not a tyrant. We walked into the ICU where Jack had recently had a heart attack. I started explaining to him about cholesterol.

"Jack, there is a good cholesterol and a bad cholesterol. One actually reduces the risk of a heart attack. The low-density lipoprotein (LDL) is the

124

good cholesterol. That's the one you want. The high-density cholesterol (HDL) is the bad cholesterol. It's the one you don't want."

She listened to my little lecture, then interrupted me and said "Dr. Ohmart, you have them backwards. LDL is the bad cholesterol. HDL is the good cholesterol."

"Are you certain?" I asked.

"Yes, I'm sure about that!"

Jack looked at me. The nurse looked at me. I laughed and said, "If she's positive, I made a mistake. I've been confused on that more than once."

We completed rounds, and then I looked at a book where the cholesterols were listed. Yes, she was correct. "You don't need any more self-confidence. You just corrected your instructor in front of a patient and a nurse. I think you're cured!"

*   *   *

It was her last night in Oakley. I asked her to see a young woman in the ER complaining of an earache. "She has a perforated ear drum. She told me her husband slapped the side of her head causing the perforation. How do we treat this?"

"Nancy, it's easy. Tell her to keep water out of that ear and don't let her husband hit her ear again. It will heal itself. I need to see her in a week or so to be sure it has healed."

Nancy was going to protect her patient. "Dr. Ohmart, promise me that you will talk to her about her rights, that there is an organization that will help her and keep her husband from abusing her again."

"OK, Nancy, I'll do that. Go to bed and I'll tell you goodbye in the morning."

Next morning she met me and again ordered me to talk to her patient about that evening. A week later the patient walked into my exam room. Her ear was healed. Holding to my promise I said "Judy, you don't have to put up with this stuff. If you need help you can call CASA, or I'll call them for you."

"Oh, Doctor Ohmart" she replied, "Sam and I have a scuffle and then we have wonderful sex. He just got a bit carried away."

So much for my intervention.

*   *   *

It was past noon, a cold and windy winter day, the kind of day no one wanted to be outside. I was driving home for lunch on Second Street. I had just passed a woman walking along the road, heading west as I was. I knew her; she walked for exercise but this was an especially nasty day. Peering into my rear view mirror I was wondering, "Should I offer Ruth a ride?"

I heard the shriek of the train! "Oh shit! Carol will be so mad at me!" was my only thought.

The train and I collided! It picked my pickup up, throwing it into the deep ditch south of the street. I slid across the seat, ripping my CB radio off the dash and splintering the upper right windshield with my head. I clambered out, inspecting my wrecked pickup. Then the ambulance screamed up. "Doc, what happened? Are you hurt? Lie down and let us take you to the hospital!"

"I'm OK. I'm not going to the hospital! I'm the doctor. There is no other doctor in Oakley. I'm not hurt. Just let me go home and tell Susan that I'm OK. Susan is due to come to my office to work that afternoon. If I don't see her she'll be frantic. Carol is in Texas."

The railroad agent added his pleas for me to go to the hospital. But I was adamant. "I'm not going to any hospital!"

I knew there were two excellent students at the hospital having lunch, a medical student, Greg, and Kelsey, a PA student. I knew if I were hurt they could take care of me but my only apparent injuries were a few skinned knuckles, a skinned knee and a headache. Later I learned that the students had been at the nurses' desk and heard that the ambulance had been sent to where someone had been hit by a train. They said they were certainly glad Dr. O was here to take care of the accident. "How dumb can one be to hit a train?"

Then they heard the radio say Dr. O had been the driver who had been hit by the train. They were terrified at the idea of treating their preceptor, or attempting to resuscitate him. Neither the students nor I have forgotten that accident.

Susan had eaten lunch at home then driven to Second Street to drive to my office in town. But she couldn't get past where the train had hit a pickup. She could see that it had been my pickup. The ambulance was gone. She had driven by the hospital and knew the ambulance had not been at the hospital. "Dad's at the undertakers!"

Someone took me home and I called Susan at my office and told her I was not hurt. Then I ate lunch and went back to the office to work that afternoon. A few days later I got a bill for the damages done to the train engine. My response was that if I would pay for the damages to their engine they could pay for the damages to my pickup and my back. I heard no more about that.

*   *   *

Carol and I had season tickets to the theater in Denver. We usually spent the weekend, leaving Oakley Friday evening, attending a play Saturday afternoon and driving home Sunday afternoon. Winter weather rarely prevented our excursions. Rod, the hospital administrator, and I thought I should have one weekend a month free. We usually tried to hire a *locum tenens* who would cover Oakley while I was gone. This weekend Carol and I wanted to see the play in Denver. Rod couldn't find a *locum*. There were two students in Oakley, a girl from KUMC and a PA student, a nurse who had spent several years as a cardiac ICU nurse at Wesley before beginning PA training.

There were no patients in the hospital. I knew the young women could handle any minor emergencies. I told the EMS and the nurses at the hospital that there would be no doctor in Oakley that weekend. Carol and I headed for Denver Friday evening. This was before the cell phone era. When we entered our Denver apartment our answer phone was blinking. The call was from the Logan County Hospital nurse.

"Dr. Ohmart, one of the patients in the long term care beds is in trouble. I think he had a heart attack. He is not in any pain. The students and I have moved him to an acute care bed, got an EKG and started oxygen on him."

"You've done all there is to do for this eighty-seven year old man. He's had a couple of strokes and is often confused. I'll drive home, but it will take four hours to get there. Call his children and let them know about the situation. Just do whatever you think is best."

Carol and I drove home. At the Goodland rest stop all cars were shunted to stop. A throng of uniformed armed men were inspecting all of the cars. It included Kansas, Colorado, Nebraska and Wyoming officers.

After being inspected we were then released, arriving at Oakley about 3:00 AM. I dropped Carol off at our house then drove to the hospital. Our patient had died. His family had arrived, seen dad alive, but unconscious, and then sat with him until he died. The family was not upset. They had left the hospital before my arrival. The nurse/PA student had seen death before. The medical student had not. I spoke with both of the young women, apologizing for the incident. I called the mortician and he took the body away. Our patient's death was unfortunate but not unexpected. I was sorry I had been away, but the girls had handled the situation well.

"Are you both OK?"

Both replied in the affirmative. Carol and I had a couple hours of sleep then drove back to Denver for the play and dinner. We stopped at Goodland for coffee and found a pair of Kansas Wildlife and Parks officers there. I inquired about the stop. They said that once or twice a year they set up a road block looking for hunters without licenses, illegal game or too many animals bagged.

*   *   *

Students in Oakley, particularly medical students, approached death as a foe, wanting to do everything possible to delay or prevent a death. They had all been taught CPR; many had observed, or taken part in, a resuscitation. Most of those deaths had resulted from trauma, accidents or cardiac deaths. I, too, knew the routine we all followed in CPR. But there was, and is, another form of death, the demise that comes to someone with terminal cancer or another inevitable conclusion. These young physicians wanted to resuscitate everyone. I tried to explain that prolonging an inevitable death for a day or two might cause pain and suffering, not only to our patient, but also to the survivor's family members. I wanted to discuss this in advance as we had no time for questions in an actual CPR.

Students queried me. "He wants to see his daughter before he dies. She will be here tomorrow," a student might say.

"That might be reason enough to attempt a resuscitation."

Another student might say, "I need the knowledge and experience in a code."

My response might be "You can do that at KUMC, not in Oakley. I know you need that experience, but these are my friends. I won't prolong his dying just for your experience. Death is the end of life. All of us will reach that point."

Perhaps, as a young physician, I too would have prolonged dying as long as possible. But I doubt it. CPR was just becoming a part of medical care. We were all thrilled that a life could be saved. There was a reason to work as long as possible on a young, previously healthy patient. But in most instances dead was dead. In Oakley we didn't have to make decisions about a brain dead man nor whether removing a ventilator was proper care. These patients were usually transferred from Oakley long before such decisions had to be considered.

The advent of living wills rarely played a part in such decisions in Oakley. My dying patients were usually elderly, with a long life behind them. Others, younger, had terminal malignancies. I had spoken with these patients and their loved ones about dying long before that point had been reached. I knew what he desired. Rarely, long absent children might question my decisions. Usually, after explaining the situation, we reached a consensus—the Oakley family, those from other communities and me. Usually a student would be included in the discussion as an observer; that was a part of his education.

*   *   *

As the years passed the medical students were less likely to approach medicine as I had. More of the students were women, women who wanted a husband and children. The men also wanted more family time. None of them wanted to devote their lives to medicine as I had been trained. I did not then, and do not now, regret my life.

My enjoyment of my practice grew. I was caring for my friends. More medical help arrived in Oakley and I was able to have a bit more free time. By then I was habituated to working hard.

"I don't want to work as hard as you do, Dr. Ohmart. Do I have to?" was a common question.

"No, you don't. I did not plan on a career as the only doctor in a small town. I was thrown into that situation. I considered leaving Oakley, going into a residency in internal medicine or psychiatry. But I decided against leaving."

"I love my practice and my life. I'll try to convince you that medicine is fun, not a chore. I hope you find it a profession, not a job. I hope, whatever path you choose in medicine, you find it rewarding and enjoyable."

I learned something of my self in exchanges such as that. I also hope the students learned from my mini-lectures.

Chapter 8

Kidney Stones, Broken Bones

Sticks and stones may break my bones, but words will never hurt me

Kidney Stones Hurt!

Stones may not easily break one's bones but they can certainly cause a lot of pain. My first encounter with a patient having a kidney stone was shortly after I began practice in Oakley. A grizzled farmer entered the emergency room one morning, asking for a doctor. The nurse at the hospital called us and said the patient was in severe pain. Jim sent me to the ER as he was busy and I often had time to spare. When I entered the hospital he was walking around the small room. As he walked he told his story.

He had been driving his tractor when an excruciating pain hit him in his right low back. He was half a mile from his pickup; he rode his tractor to his pickup at a speed of six or eight miles an hour. "That was a damn long ride!" he said.

There he had to get in his pickup and drive the thirty miles to Oakley. The pickup was somewhat faster than his tractor. Nor did he worry about the speed limit! In the ER he couldn't stand still. He couldn't lie down for me to examine him. But his story indicated he had a kidney stone. He did manage to pee in a bottle. His urine specimen had blood in it. That was all I needed! I ordered a nurse to get fifteen milligrams of morphine for me and managed to convince him to lie still long enough for me to give him the intravenous analgesic. Almost instantaneously he ceased writhing, smiled and said, "I know why kids like that stuff. It's great!"

* * *

I had long ago learned that a patient with a kidney stone was always looked askance in an ER, usually seen as a drug addict trying to get narcotics. Transients off I-70 often stopped in Oakley, thinking that a rural hospital would be an easy mark. And we probably were. But I tried to detect obvious frauds. In the Oakley ER if a patient with severe pain presented at the hospital he/she was quickly seen, offered pain relief, then concerned about diagnosing the problem. Oakley residents were rarely a problem. After a few years I knew most of them by sight. I believed them. If it sounded like a kidney stone he/she was given a shot for pain, then getting a urinalysis, an X-ray of the abdomen, and, hopefully, seeing blood in the urine and a stone on the film. After having relieved my patient's pain I then sent him home, with instructions to strain his urine for the offending stone. If the pain returned he was either to call me or go to the hospital where the nurse would call me and repeat the analgesic.

After two or three episodes of this the patient might remain in the hospital, especially if he lived a long way from Oakley. If the stone were large, or if he were impatient, he might be referred to a urologist, Salina in my earlier years, later to Hays when a urologist established a practice there. There the offending stone could be removed surgically.

Azalea was my all time fraud. Her daughter was the new science teacher in Winona. They were getting moved into their home and her daughter was inventorying her supplies for the coming year. They came to the ER in the evening, saying Azalea had a kidney stone, a problem she frequently faced. She was in pain. She appeared to me to be a sweet old lady, maybe 70 years old. Her daughter was now a resident in the area.

She did have blood in her urine; the X-ray showed no stone, but she said she had uric acid stones, which rarely showed up on an X-ray. I gave her a shot of morphine. She was happy and they went home to Winona, saying, "You're such a sweet, kind man. I'm delighted to find such a good doctor in Oakley."

The next morning she was back with her pain. Again I gave her a shot. After two or three more episodes of pain I insisted she go to a urologist in

Salina. She didn't like that idea. "I've had these before. It will pass and I won't have any trouble until the next episode."

But I insisted, "You have to see a urologist."

I was beginning to doubt her story. I certainly had control of the situation because I told her I would not give her narcotics if this persisted. I phoned a urologist in Salina and he said he would see her the next day. I gave her a shot that evening and agreed to give her a last injection in Oakley as she started her ride to Salina. The morphine would last three or four hours; the drive would take about three hours. I gave her the morphine in the morning and off she went.

"I was rid of her whether or not she was a fraud," I thought. "If she has another episode I will cross that bridge when it comes."

A couple hours later a nurse at one of the Hays hospitals called me and told me Azalea was in their ER, asking for narcotics for her kidney stone. Doubting her even more, I told the nurse it might be a fraud but she might be telling the truth. I asked her to give her the morphine, thinking again that she would be out of my hair (and Hays') for the time being at least. I would face the women and Azalea's stones after they returned, if the urologist said her story was true.

That afternoon a nurse from Salina telephoned. She had not shown up in their office, or at either of the Salina hospitals. Had I sent her on as planned? "Yes. They left Oakley this morning. The nurse at the Hays hospital had given her another injection of morphine and sent them on to Salina. Undoubtedly she was a phony, wanting narcotics. Sorry to have troubled you, but I'm glad you don't have to fuss with her."

I thought I would not hear from her again, even though she would be a Winona resident. Certainly I would never again give her a narcotic! Two days later the Winona superintendent called me and asked about the couple. I told him my story, but his was worse. They had loaded up all the microscopes and anything else they could carry and disappeared. I think neither of us heard of them again.

*   *   *

Alan Adams joined me in practice the summer of 1981. As Jim Marchbanks before me, I immediately left for a vacation, spending a couple weeks in California. Shortly after our return Carol moved Susan to Manhattan for college. Carol drove home with flank pain—pain so severe she had to stop beside the road, unable to drive. After subsiding a bit she drove on, only stopped again by the pain. In that stop and go fashion she arrived in Oakley, where she headed for the hospital. My new associate had to care for the old man's wife.

Alan's initial task was to relieve Carol's pain. After two doses of morphine did not diminish her pain Alan ordered a third. The nurse questioned the young doctor's third shot. "Doctor, that's a lot of morphine."

Carol loved his reply. "Give her that stuff until she stops hurting!"

An X-ray showed a large kidney stone in her left ureter. At that time the only choices were waiting for her to pass it or send Carol to the urologist in Hays to remove the stone. Neither Alan nor I thought she would pass that large a stone, so Carol was given another shot of morphine and we headed east for Hays, retracing the path she had just followed home from Manhattan. But now I was driving and Carol was having little pain. She was merely vomiting, a common side effect of morphine.

The next morning the urologist tried to remove the stone through her bladder. He couldn't manage that. There was now a lithotriptor, a device that pulverizes kidney stones. Carol could sit in a water-filled tub with ultrasound waves passing through the water, Carol and to the stone where the lithotriptor would break up the stone. This would create stone fragments small enough to be passed in her urine. This machine was so innovative that several northwestern Kansas hospitals shared the machine. It was mounted in a van and would spend a few days in one hospital, then move on to the next. Hays' turn was two or three weeks down the road. None of us thought waiting would be a good idea, so the urologist opted for an abdominal incision and removed the stone. A few days in the hospital and Carol was home, not very perky but pain free. A year or two later Carol's dad called and asked her what a kidney stone felt like. Yes, he also had a stone!

*　　*　　*

Those Sticks Break, Too

Broken bones were frequent in Oakley, then as now. Most were in kids, falling, climbing or in sports. The elderly also came in for their share of fractures because of weakened bones or loss of balance, or both.

The simple, comparatively easy, fractures I cared for in Oakley. Fractures in automobile accidents were often more severe, accompanied by other injuries. The more difficult cases were splinted, bandaged and transferred. There was no ambulance in Oakley during my early years. These patients had to be driven by parents or friends, first to our hospital then to a referral hospital if needed. Later they were transferred by an ambulance and finally by air, if the patient warranted.

I was covering for Jim, the month before my internship, a year before I moved to Oakley. The nurse at the hospital phoned me and said she had a boy with a broken arm in the ER. I told her "I hope it isn't broken, I've never set a bone."

One glance at the boy's arm was all I needed to determine he had a Colles' fracture. A Colles' is a break in the bones just above the wrist, leaving an unmistakable crook, described as a "silver fork" deformity. An X-ray confirmed the fracture. I knew how to reduce it. I had seen the residents at KUMC do it. All I had to do was bend the bones a bit further than the broken bones had been, pull them down separating the breaks, and then bend them back into normal alignment. Put a cast from his hand to above his elbow and I was done.

At KUMC and Wesley there were always anesthetists on call to assist with painful procedures. I had no such help. I was in a panic! What should I do? Maybe I should send the boy to an orthopedist in Hays or to Quinter where Jim had asked Drs. Gunter and Hiesterman to assist me if I had problems. "I definitely have a problem!"

Dr. Sekevac walked by and I asked him to look at the boy's broken arm. He said he'd take care of it. Gordon looked at the boy's arm, lifted it and suddenly bent it back and yanked on it. A quick scream from the boy and his arm was in place. All I had to do was put a cast on it.

Kids' Colles' fractures were, and probably still are, quite common. A running child tripping or stumbling and falling forward will catch himself with his hands. That catch will protect his face but sometimes cause a Colles' fracture. I learned to give the kid an analgesic rather than reduce it cold turkey. I used a number of approaches, a barbiturate, a narcotic, Valium®, an inhaled anesthetic, injected a local anesthetic into the area around the break, but the best was probably ketamine. It was injectable, acted quickly, had a wide margin of safety and the child remembered nothing of the reduction.

One of Dale's friends, a six or seven year-old girl, fell and broke her arm. I reduced the break, put a cast on her arm and again X-rayed her arm. It looked fine. Four weeks later I removed the cast. The reduction had slipped and the deformity had recurred. Now her bones had knit. I knew that a child's bones would remodel themselves as she grew. A bend would be outgrown. A twist would not remold. Once a girl started making estrogen her bones would cease to grow and remodel. She had no twist in her arm. Just a crook and a lump. She was a few years from puberty and estrogen. I said, "Larry, as she grows her arm will remold itself. As a teenager it will look the same as her other arm,"

"Doc, I hope you know what you are doing. I'll haunt you forever if Cindy has a crooked arm!"

I took care of her for years. Once in a while she would fall, hurt her arm and we would X-ray her again. As I had told Larry her arm gradually lost the lump and crook in that arm. Eventually an X-ray of that arm showed no sign of her old break. I used that set of films to show parents if their child had a bit of a deformity. "Give him a little time and he'll be as good as new."

I took care of two kids who sustained bilateral fractures of their wrists. If one had a cast on each arm, holding their elbows at ninety degrees was incapacitating. You couldn't feed yourself, dress yourself or care for yourself. Fortunately both of them had a minor fracture of one wrist. I put a cast from the hand to above the elbow on one arm, a cast immobilizing only the wrist of the other. He could use the fingers on that hand and move his elbow.

Colles' fractures were common in another age group—older women. The older women were prone to the fracture because of osteoporosis. They usually didn't have much of a deformity; their broken ends were simply jammed together—impacted. At KUMC I was taught to leave those alone, let the ends knit. Their bones didn't remodel; their estrogen had taken care of that years ago. It usually left a lump or a bit of a bow. These women usually had normal function of their hands; maybe her forearm was a little shorter or a little bend just above her wrist. Later orthopedists decided to operate on those fractures, insert a plate or screws, in the bone. Her hand and arm didn't work any better; it just looked more normal. I remember only one patient who chose surgery. She was a tourist who thought this old country doctor didn't know what he was doing. She opted to have me transfer her to an orthopedist in Hays. I don't know what her outcome was. Two friends who opted for the surgery had months of trouble with their arms, repeat operations, etc. The newer approaches were not always the better.

*   *   *

I drove home from a Kansas City meeting with a painful thrombosed hemorrhoid. It had developed as I drove to KC. Carol and the boys were planning to ride the train to KC and spend a day or two in Kansas City before driving home. On my drive to Kansas City my rectum began to hurt. I realized what was causing the pain, a clot in a hemorrhoidal vein. I knew what to do about it. Incise (open with a scalpel) the vein and let the clot out. That released the spasm around the vessel and the pain was relieved. At the conference I spoke with the director of the meeting and he said he would handle it. He took me to the medicine clinic and one of the residents looked at my hemorrhoid and said, "I spent several years in general practice. All I need to do is get a scalpel and open the hemorrhoid."

Sounded simple! But we were in the medical clinic. No such instruments were to be found there. Scalpels belonged in the surgery clinic. They paged the gastrointestinal department head. He looked at me and said it wasn't a surgical problem. All I had to do was sit in a hot tub and soak. Eventually that would relieve the problem. I found a few detective stories and spent the next three days soaking, missing the entire conference. Carol and the boys arrived and I told her my travails. "I now know why family practice was my specialty choice. I could use the best treatments, not constrained by specialty lines."

We drove home, Carol driving and me trying to discover a method of sitting on my painful rear. I knew Jim would incise the hemorrhoid and relieve my pain. But when I called Jim he was at the hospital, taking care of Linda, with a broken leg. "Dick, I'm glad you're home. I need an anesthetic to set this girl's leg. Will you put her to sleep?"

"Of course" was my reply. Off to sleep she went. Jim set her leg, put a cast on it and we waited as she awakened. Her parents took her home, and then I told Jim of my problem. We went to our clinic where he removed my clot.

*   *   *

My family and I had few problems with health, but most of our problems seemed to be related to broken bones. When Susan was two years old I was carrying her down from a bleacher at Ahearn Fieldhouse in Manhattan, after we watched Susan's Aunt Barb in a college rodeo. Susan was asleep in my arms and I couldn't see where I was walking. I missed the last step, stumbled and fell. Trying to avoid falling on Susan I caught myself with my elbows. I hurt my right shoulder. Although it hurt I could use my arm as long as I didn't have to lift that hand and arm. I stuck my thumb in my belt to support that arm and Sunday Carol drove us home to Oakley.

Jim had surgery scheduled Monday morning and I was the anesthetist. I thought I could manage that since I didn't have to lift my arm. Monday morning Jim and the nurses watched as their anesthetist entered the hospital with his arm in a sling! "What happened? Can you do this? Why didn't you call us and cancel the surgery?"

"I can do this with no problem. All I have to do is stand up and use my hand at waist-level. I can squeeze the bag with no problem at all. I'll be fine." That was correct. We had no problems.

Then Jim had my shoulder X-rayed. It showed I had broken the head of my humerus. I was in a sling for three or four weeks. I had no problems at the office. I think I even delivered a baby during the time I was wearing a sling.

The following Wednesday afternoon I was home reading when the phone rang. "Dr. Ohmart, your son had a bicycle accident and he is screaming that he broke his leg. He won't let us move him out of the street."

There was no ambulance or EMTs or they would have picked Dale up, beating everyone else to the accident scene. I told Carol "Dale just has broken bones on his mind because of my break. Take the car and pick up Dale and the bike and bring him home."

Off she went. A bit later she called from the hospital. "Dick, I think it's broken! When I picked him up his lower leg bent in the middle of it. It isn't supposed to do that, is it?"

No, it wasn't. After I arrived and had his leg X-rayed I saw that he had broken his tibia and fibula in the mid-shafts. "Dale, you're leg is broken. I'll call Jim and have him put a cast on you."

"No, I want you to do it!"

With the nurses' help we moved Dale to a cart and wheeled him to the ER. There I, with a sling on my arm, and a nurse put Dale's cast on, running from his foot to his groin. Dale spent the summer in a cast. I was finished with my sling in two or three weeks.

*   *   *

The femur, the largest, heaviest bone in man, seemed to be one of the most commonly fractured bones. At least I remember many of them. An easy fall didn't break that bone. Many of them occurred in automobile accidents. A high school boy stopped along the highway to help a woman and another car hit him. A horse threw its rider, and then rolled on him. Mother fell on her infant, fracturing his femur. Several were pedestrians hit by cars.

It was simple to care for an adult who sustained a femoral fracture. We had a number of Hare traction splints. This splint had a ring that was lodged against the pelvis of the fractured leg. Two rods ran down the sides of the broken leg where canvas was attached to the rods, forming a sling that supported the broken bone. Traction to the foot was used to straighten the break and hold it in place, relieving pain. The patient could be transferred to an orthopedist who would surgically repair the break with either inserting a rod inside the bone (intramedullary rod) or using a plate and screws.

I was taught that orthopedists did not use a surgical approach to most fractures in children. Their fear was that the bone might not grow as the other did, or might develop an infection in the bone. As newer and better antibiotics were developed the risk of infection declined but I still took care of the children in Oakley. I saw Jim take care of bilateral femoral fractures in a one and one-half year old with skin traction. We simply ran tape down the sides of his legs, leaving an open stirrup below his feet. We then wrapped elastic bandages around his legs to hold the tape in place. The boy was placed on his back with both legs held skyward. Using two pulleys at ninety-degree angles allowed weights going down, pulling his feet up.

I took care of an infant whose mother had tripped on a step and fallen on him, fracturing his femur. We used skin traction in his crib at the hospital. His mother was still nursing him and continued to nurse while he was in the hospital. After two or three weeks his fracture had a heavy callus. Someone made a board on which the infant could lie with traction on his foot. He could go home and his parents could care for him there.

One summer I had nine adolescents with femoral fractures in the old hospital. They were spread out in the summer so we never had nine at the same time. We certainly didn't have enough frames, splints, pulleys and ropes to care for them at once. Rod Bates, although the administrator, was of immense help in assembling the bed, frame and traction equipment. We became quite adept at setting up that apparatus. Of course we had no ambulance. Someone brought him (almost always a male) to the hospital in a car. It was not extremely painful to move a kid to the table to X-ray him if, usually I, held traction on his foot/ankle.

Rod also was an X-ray technician. Between us, we usually reduced the fracture in the process of moving and X-raying his femur. We then transferred him to a cart, then to a bed. The femoral traction was set up to flex his hip a bit. We then placed his lower leg in a hammock, several inches above his mattress, with his leg parallel to the mattress. A pin was then inserted through his tibial tubercle where a rope from his knee was to hold his femur at about thirty degrees. The rope was then passed through a pulley over a bar at the foot of his bed, hanging toward the floor with weights on it. To avoid a foot drop he wore a sneaker during the day, holding his ankle at ninety degrees. He would be hospitalized for four to six weeks, and then was placed in a hip spica. This was a cast which went around his waist covering his hip, leg and foot. He was then on crutches for another six to eight weeks.

I don't remember any femoral fractures during the last ten or fifteen years in my practice in Oakley. Perhaps there was not such a fracture. Perhaps I simply don't remember. Or perhaps we transferred such patients to an orthopedist. Keeping a patient in the hospital in traction for a month or so was extremely expensive for the parents and the hospital, any hospital. The orthopedists could insert a rod, plate or screws on a femoral fracture, keep him in the hospital for a few days then send the boy home, letting his parents take care of him. This certainly saved money in the hospital; I'm not certain the boy's care was better. It depended on his family.

*   *   *

Marilyn was rushed to our ER after an automobile accident. Her older brother had been killed. Another brother had a broken femur. Perhaps another sibling had a broken arm. But Marilyn was unconscious. She had no laceration on her head. She obviously had a broken arm and fractured femur; we knew how to manage those. But what, if anything, could we do for her closed head injury? X-rays showed a skull fracture. Actually the break looked as if her skull had been cracked like an egg; a line in her calvarium encircled her skull just above her ears. It appeared as if the pressure inside her skull had lifted the top of her cranium one-quarter of an inch above the lower. It looked to me that her fracture had allowed her brain to expand as it swelled, causing less damage to her brain than being compressed in an unfractured skull. Regardless, she was unconscious. Forty years ago no one had more to offer to a patient with this injury than we did.

We put a cast on her arm. We put her femur in traction. I consulted a neurosurgeon who said he had nothing more to offer us. We waited. And waited. The staff fed, bathed and exercised Marilyn. She didn't respond, even with some of the painful things we had to do to her. We waited for a month or so. Then she opened her eyes. No other response. One morning she said "Mommy." All of us were elated! Later I walked into her room and she said "Dr. Ohmart."

I was in tears. The night nurses had spent hours teaching her to speak my name. She progressed slowly, but steadily. Her leg was put in a cast (her arm had healed) and she was sent home with her parents. She was in the fourth grade and resumed school. Progress was slow, but she was gaining. I saw her occasionally as she grew up. She graduated from high school. She was married. Then I lost track of her.

The summer of 2007 the photography department chair asked me to judge the photography in the Gove County Fair. After judging, I wandered around the exhibits. There was Marilyn! She had a couple of children with her, and an older child was showing an animal. I was delighted to see her! She, as always, was shy but spoke about her children, her life. Neither of us mentioned her months in the Logan County Hospital. But I, at least, knew that, as she walked away, I was watching a miracle.

Chapter 9

I Practiced In a Wilderness

I noted in the 2000 census that Logan County has a population of three persons per square mile, 3046 people in the county. Years ago, in applying for a Medicare program, I learned that the government considered a population density of six per square mile as a wilderness. I've always thought of Oakley as a delightful rural community. It certainly is not urban, but I have enjoyed my life there. Carol, having grown up in the San Francisco Bay area, did not always relish our life in Oakley as much as I did. Nevertheless, we both have lived in a wilderness for more than fifty years. Most people would not think of Western Kansas as a wilderness. A wilderness should be forested, dotted with lakes and small cottages. Instead it is a dry land, almost a desert, where farmers pray for rain or irrigate to raise their crops. Our annual rainfall is about twenty inches. Ten inches of annual rainfall is considered a desert. The wind can blow for days on end, until it feels as if the wind has leached all the moisture out of both plants and inhabitants. A harsh, unforgiving land, but one where Carol and I made our home. Our wilderness, or at least my wilderness.

I relished some of the astonishment found by tourists who, wandering in this wilderness, hoped to find medical assistance. What they found was a rural physician, competent but one who lived his life in Western Kansas. One evening I had been helping Susan work with her horses, wearing jeans and boots, with an aroma of horse manure surrounding me. I was called to the hospital to look at a kid whose family had been spending the night in Oakley. I was used to going to the hospital dressed however

I was and I saw no need to clean up to come see some sick kid at 9:00 at night. I drove to the hospital, walked into the ER and introduced myself, washing my hands.

"I'm Doctor Ohmart. What's the problem?"

"Hello. I'm John Brown. My boy has a little cut on his head. He fell at the pool this evening."

Mrs. Brown sniffed, sniffed a second time and said "That smell is making me sick. Won't it make Jimmy sick, too?"

"I don't think so. I'll hurry as fast as I can."

She left the room. I cleaned and sutured his minor cut. Off they went. Mr. Brown thanked me. I heard Mrs. Brown say as she left "Are you sure he's a doctor and not a veterinarian?"

*   *   *

Rattlesnakes

My first experience with a snakebite was when I entered the hospital one morning to visit our patients. There I found a man Jim had cared for the evening before. This man had stepped out of his house onto his porch. Barefooted, he had stepped on a rattler and been bitten. Jim told me that morning "I thought he might die last night. I'm glad he was close to town. The snake must have injected his poison into a large vein to make him that sick that fast."

He was in the hospital for a few days then went home.

My second experience was to be one of the most trying episode in my medical career. I was mowing my yard Sunday afternoon. Peggy drove up to my yard "Dr. O, didn't you hear the phone?"

Carol and our kids were in Scott City. We had an outside bell in the backyard but I was mowing the front so didn't hear it. "What do you need?"

"A young man came into the ER saying he had been bitten by a rattlesnake while climbing Lone Butte. He put a tourniquet on his arm and drove to town."

Lone Butte is about a forty-five minute drive from Oakley. He had to walk (or run, although running was not the thing he should have done) to his car, then drive to Oakley. Now he was in our hospital. With only Jim's prior snakebite to remember I thought he might be dying. I stopped my mower, clambered into my car and sped to the hospital.

A brief history was all I needed. "Are you certain it was a rattlesnake?"

"Yes!" And the poison was already discoloring his forearm, the site of the bite. A nasty blue-purple, the swollen skin surrounded two small puncture wounds.

"I've been trained as a medic. I'm on leave just prior to being shipped to Viet Nam. I put a tourniquet around my arm and drove to Oakley."

He had applied an arterial tourniquet, as he had been trained, a tourniquet to prevent massive bleeding from military wounds. A tight tourniquet applied for an hour would damage his arm because of lack of oxygen below the tourniquet. I loosened, but did not remove, his tourniquet. I knew that we had at least one unit of antivenin in the hospital. I quickly scanned the directions. First, skin test the man to be certain he was not allergic to the horse serum the antivenin had been prepared in. That meant waiting fifteen minutes to determine that he had no untoward reaction to the horse serum. Then inject half the unit around the bite, then the rest intramuscularly above where the arm had been bitten. While I waited I ran to our office and looked at my *Current Therapy.*

This was the bible for physicians who needed a fairly quick answer to a treatment problem. This cookbook was printed annually, which I religiously purchased but rarely used. In it the writer said to give the antivenin as quickly as possible. Then I should immerse his arm in ice water. Use tap water only. Don't use saline as that might lower the water temperature sufficiently to freeze the tissue in his arm. The idea was that the cold would slow down the action of the poison, allowing him to absorb the toxins, not damaging his tissues as badly as if the toxin were absorbed rapidly. The book suggested a variety of ways to cool his arm, none of which we had in Oakley.

While I was injecting the antivenin into my patient, I sent Peggy to my home to get a wash tub I had in my garage. She returned with the tub, cleaned it thoroughly and filled it with tap water. She then put ice in it and immersed my patient's arm in the solution. Although he said it was cold it also relieved his pain. Then we waited.

I had asked him about my transferring him to a larger hospital but he asked to stay here. "I have relatives in Oakley; I was here to see them. Please let me stay here where I can see them."

I had read the up-to-date treatment for a rattlesnake bite. While I had no water cooler to use on his arm I thought the ice water would do the job. We had no warming blanket to cover the rest of him, which the book recommended. But it was August in Western Kansas, we had no air conditioning and his room was on the west side of the hospital. The room would be unpleasantly warm. He should do fine. So I kept him in Oakley.

The next morning his arm looked much the same. And it continued to look about the same, perhaps a bit worse. After two or three days I attempted to remove his arm from the water. He screamed in pain "Leave my arm in the water!"

He adamantly refused my offers to transfer him to another hospital. Finally I insisted he be transferred to Fitzsimmons Hospital, the army hospital in Denver. I wasn't pleased about the transfer—I wondered what would become of him. I always wanted to see the results of my treatments. But I had no further ideas for his future care.

I later learned that the doctors had to amputate his hand and forearm. This led to my first malpractice suit. I had done everything I could in an emergency. I had read and followed the newest information on snakebites to the best of my ability. But I should have transferred him to Fitzsimmons that evening, regardless of his wishes. Then, and throughout my career, I perhaps was too willing to cooperate with a patient's requests.

I cared for ten or twelve snakebitten patients, all doing well. After that experience I learned to use several units of antitoxin, all intravenously, in a snake bitten patient. The package insert had been changed. I had followed the instructions on the package insert in Oakley. Now the directions in the package said to use up to ten or twelve units of antivenin depending on the degree of envenomation. I never used the ice again. The next year the section on snakebites had been removed and replaced with a section on handling drug overdoses. I handled those with better results.

*　　*　　*

In the early years of my practice there were no pagers. In Wichita a physician could check out, or in, to a service where the physicians on call would leave the phone number where they could be reached. Those physicians not on call would not be located by the service. In Oakley I usually called the hospital and said, "I'll be at . . ." leaving a phone number or location. (I was given a T-shirt from the staff at the hospital, which bore the inscription "I'll be at . . .") One afternoon I was in the dentist's chair. I was alone in Oakley at the time, no other physician, no student or assistant.

The nurse phoned saying "I have a seven or eight year old boy in the ER who says he was bitten by a rattlesnake."

I had learned that those calls did not require the same urgency as a heart attack or car accident, but I asked Bill to let me walk to the hospital and see what was up. This was an easy walk to the hospital, except for interrupting Bill's work on my mouth.

The boy's father said "We just moved to a farm east of Oakley and there are a lot of big weeds in the corrals. My boys were playing in the weeds when one of them screamed and said a rattlesnake had bitten him. Neither of them saw the snake. Something just stung or bit his leg. The bite was about ten or fifteen minutes ago."

To further complicate the boy's history, Dad had warned them repeatedly that there might be rattlers in the weeds. I looked at his leg. I could see one puncture wound in the calf of his leg. There was no swelling, no discoloration, and no sign of a second fang puncture. And the boy said, "It flew away after it bit me."

I thought it was most likely a bee or wasp sting. But I kept the boy in the hospital. (In the old days I could do that simply to observe a patient and his insurance would pay for it.) I returned to the dentist and had my dental work completed, then again visited the boy. No change. It was county fair time so I went to the rodeo that evening. There one of the riders injured his shoulder. Off to the hospital we went, X-rayed his shoulder and put a sling on his fractured clavicle.

I then again went to see the boy. His leg was now swollen and turning purple. "I don't think your attacker flew away. I think you were bitten by a rattler, even if only one fang hit you."

The new antivenin package insert spoke of degrees of envenomation; grade 0 to maybe 4. Zero was a bite but no envenomation. The grade 4 was the most severe, signs of systemic poisoning within minutes. "I don't think our boy received a large amount of the venom or his signs would have appeared sooner. But I remember my first bite. I don't want to undertreat this boy. And developing serum sickness does not depend on the amount of antivenin injected. It's an all or none reaction. I'll give him three or four units of antivenin."

His leg turned a deeper purple and became more swollen, but he had no real problems. Several days later he came to my office complaining of hives and a red, itching skin. He, of course, had serum sickness.

I treated more snakebites. We always kept a plentiful supply of antivenin in our hospital. If other hospitals ran short of the antivenin they would call and ask us to borrow from our stock in Oakley. Other physicians knew that I had treated a number of bites and I was often asked my advice. I had become the snakebite expert of Western Kansas, although somewhat against my volition. The lessons of the first bite and following suit have remained forever in my mind.

I probably took care of a dozen more rattlesnake bites, all within the first few years of my practice. I don't know whether the snakes became less aggressive or whether my neighbors became more careful, but I didn't see one in the last fifteen or twenty years of my career. All of the other snakebite cases survived with no lasting ill effects. None had a severe reaction to the horse serum but they all developed serum sickness, a delayed allergic reaction to horse serum. Antihistamines and steroids cured their rashes and itches. One tourist climbing Castle Rock, south of Quinter, after being bitten drove by Quinter, thinking it too small to have a physician in town. It took him over an hour to get to Oakley and he did well. A three or four year old girl was bitten near an irrigation well. She got lots of antivenin because the instructions said the smaller the patient the more antivenin was needed. She also did well.

*　*　*

An Ambulance Comes to Oakley

I-70 was being constructed when I moved to Oakley. It barely nicked the corner of Logan County but the US Department of Transportation stated that all counties in which an interstate highway ran had to have an ambulance service. This was in the early 1960s. The ambulances at that time were little more than a mode of transport, having a "scoop and run" approach. Little medical assistance was provided on an ambulance. Don

Hall, our undertaker, believed that his station wagon, having served to transport sick and injured to the hospital for years, was adequate. More than one patient asked me, while riding with him, if Don was headed for the hospital or his mortuary. The expense of an ambulance and a staff to man it was considerable. Jim died. Don died. And we still had no ambulance.

One evening Dennis was on call. He called me and said "A young man headed northeast out of the high school parking lot ran into a pickup at Eight Street. He's badly injured. I need you and I've called Koster (now the mortician) to come pick him up."

I found my victim lying in the south ditch. Nine o'clock at night; it was dark. The lights from the surrounding vehicles showed a seriously injured young man. I kneeled over him in the ditch. The grass was strewn with sandburs but I didn't feel them. A cursory exam disclosed that both legs were broken. His left arm had an open fracture with some of the bone missing. He had a head injury. And he was bleeding profusely. I could not determine if there were any abdominal injuries. I think he was unconscious but I'm not certain.

"Dennis, go to the hospital and get an IV setup and fluids, bandages and a stretcher! Come back and help me start the IV, cover him and we'll get him on the stretcher!"

With only the lights from the cars and flashlights we managed to start an IV and start some fluids. We attempted to staunch some of the bleeding, rub some of the burrs off him and splint his extremities. We then placed him on a stretcher and put him in the mortician's station wagon. Then they headed for Hays. Dennis and I picked the burrs from our legs and picked up some of our mess. We found a fragment of his radius on the ground. I don't remember whether we thought they might be able to use that bone in Hays or not, but we had not sent the bone fragment with our patient. After months the boy was back in school at Fort Hays.

Neither Logan County expense nor a lack of personnel led to any hindrance in purchasing and staffing an ambulance in Oakley. By now trained EMTs (Emergency Medical Technicians) rode the ambulance, doing much more than picking up and transporting a victim to a hospital. We had learned how important such a vehicle was. Now there are two ambulances in Oakley and one in Winona. I'm sure they have saved lives, have carried many patients to the hospital and comforted friends and relatives of the sick and injured. And I never again had to work in a ditch to save a life.

*　　*　　*

I helped train the EMT staff. Many of them were nurses or other hospital personnel. Others were teachers, firemen or other Oakley volunteers. We developed an excellent EMT Service. Then I had some questions about the service. I wrote this in 1989; never submitted for publication.

Whatever Happened To Minor Accidents?

It was county fair time and I should have known better. But I was tired, so I went to bed, even if it was only 9:30. Besides, last night was the rodeo and my services had not been requested. Tonight was demolition derby night. Surely no one would be hurt. Off to slumberland I went, only to be violently recalled by the telephone. Sure enough, the ambulance had dropped a young lady at our hospital ER. As the only physician in town, that meant a hospital call for me.

Arriving at the hospital I found an apparently intoxicated young woman strapped to a backboard, neck braced with a cervical support. All but her mouth was immobilized, and that was working overtime, not always sensibly, and rarely repeatable. History revealed that she had been perched atop a four-foot rail fence, can of beer in her hand, enjoying the jousting of our modern knights. Excited when her champion knocked another car from the derby, she fell off, landing on her back.

Only a few years ago she would have arisen, supported by her friends if necessary, dusted her jeans off, grabbed another beer and clambered back on the fence. No longer! We now have ambulances and EMTs. They both were at the demo derby in case anyone was hurt. Spotting the ambulance, my patient's friends called to them. The EMTs, true to their training, made no diagnosis. The patient complained that her back hurt and that was enough. Out came the backboard and accompanying paraphernalia, and onto it went our heroine. Next stop the hospital and old Doc Ohmart!

What were my choices when confronted by an apparently inebriated girl, strapped to a backboard, who said her back and neck hurt? What would you do? Beep went the pager of the X-ray tech. Buzz went the machine. Click! Click! Out came the films from the developer. C-spine. T-spine. L-spine. All normal, as I would have been willing to bet. (But not certain enough to bet my malpractice insurance on it and send her away without the X-rays.) By this time she was more-or-less sober and quite apologetic. Home she went with her boyfriend; she missed seeing him win the demolition derby. I missed 2 hours of sleep. She was stuck with a $350 bill for ambulance, hospital and doctor services.

We have an excellent group of EMTs here in our small town. I certainly do not mean to denigrate or make fun of them. They are not physicians. They have certain protocols to follow. Back complaints or injuries mean a backboard. Head or neck trauma means immobilize the neck. Chest pain calls for oxygen and a cardiac monitor. Certainly these precautions can be valuable. They do save lives and prevent tragic consequences. But, once applied, only God and the doctor have the authority to remove these encumbrances. Since I have no direct line to the Almighty, that means I have to go to the hospital, evaluate the patient, order necessary tests and then make the decision whether or not to strip the patient of his/her protection. That means many unnecessary trips for me, trips that once would have been considered not only unneeded but also ludicrous.

Consider another young lady, this one brought in from a local bar shortly after 11:00 PM. She was a girl I know, and I believed her story. She had worked all day with little food, going to the bar for dinner, not drinks. She had had nothing to drink, but slumped to the floor while standing talking to a friend. She awakened almost before she hit the floor. A simple faint? That's what she thought. However someone had already notified the ambulance. Another bystander kept her on the floor until their arrival. In their usual style, our EMTs strapped her down, tied her up and hauled her off to our hospital. There she said that she had always fainted easily, and that this was typical of her fainting episodes. She denied any pain or disability. Since I knew her, I did a brief neurological exam, stood her to see that she could, indeed, stand and walk, and sent her off with her friends to get something to eat. No X-rays, so her bill was much less. But it still cost her more than her day's wages.

I have learned what to do to head off many of these "emergency" ambulance runs. I go to as many of the local high school football games as possible, because I find myself at the hospital seeing players that I could have examined on the field if I don't attend. Attendance is *de riguer* at rodeos, hot air balloon launches, etc. Fortunately I enjoy attending most of these activities. I am an avid photographer, interested in recording life in Oakley. Our small town offers little in the way of entertainment, so I am glad to attend and photograph what there is. But I continue to see "injuries" brought to the hospital by ambulance that I would have told my own kids to shake off and get back to their activity.

Now no one wants to take that responsibility. Coaches, teachers and other supervisors are taught that it is better to be safe than sorry, to err by being overly cautious rather than missing an injury. Parents and friends are hesitant to challenge an "authority." EMTs, as I have mentioned, are not trained to diagnose, but to protect and safely transport the injured. So, for want of anyone to call an injury minor, many uninjured people end up at the hospital. This not only adds unnecessary hospital calls to my already busy schedule; it adds untold dollars to local medical bills. I can not even begin to estimate the dollars this sort of "protection" must add to the medical expenses of the country as a whole. Simply because no one wants to assume the responsibility to term an injury minor.

Is it all unnecessary? Of course not. Yesterday I saw a young man with a halo supporting his cervical fractures. He owes the fact that he is not sporting a more ephemeral halo and wings to our EMTs. He was involved in an auto accident about six weeks ago, suffering a scalp laceration. Conscious at the scene, he had no complaints of neck pain. Our well-trained EMTs immobilized his neck anyway. I glanced at him in the ER, asked the senior medical student working with me to repair his laceration and turned my attention to patients who appeared to be more seriously injured.

The student soon approached me to say that he thought we should X-ray his patient's cervical spine. The patient said that his neck had started hurting a lot as he lay on the cot, and his left hand was starting to tingle. X-rays revealed fractures of C4, C5 and C6. I immediately arranged for him to be airlifted the 250 miles to our nearest neurosurgeon. When he called me to let me know what he had found, the neurosurgeon said, "It is sure nice to get someone before he's already a tragedy. Be sure to compliment your EMTs." I did this, but I probably will continue to tease them about putting cervical collars on everyone they bring in who has a neck.

And, C-collars or not, I certainly prefer to care for minor injuries rather than serious ones.

*   *   *

Blizzards On the Prairie

Even though Logan County is nearly a desert, we sometimes have more moisture than we need. Usually it comes as rain when we want to plant or harvest crops. Occasionally it comes as a blizzard. I often had problems with the snow and ice in Oakley. More than one mother-to-be, hearing of a coming snow storm, called me and asked if I would deliver her here if she couldn't get to her doctor in Colby, Quinter or Hays. I always acquiesced but was never called on for such an emergency. One instance I was unable to get to the old hospital to deliver one of my own patients. My patient had phoned and said she was in labor. I met her at the hospital, examined her that evening and thought she was either not in labor, or perhaps very early labor. A blizzard had been forecasted and she lived in Grinnell so we kept her in the hospital. I went home. When the call from the hospital came I couldn't get out of our Park View addition.

Our first house at 615 East Sixth had only two exits from the Park View addition. Usually I left our home driving west on Sixth Street, by Saint Joseph Church, then south to the hospital. That street, north of what was then Higgason's greenhouse (southeast of Saint Joseph's), was always blocked if there was a bit of snow and wind. Our other exit was driving north to Eighth Street, and then turning west to Center Street. There was a major problem in that route; Eighth Street was elevated, there was a three or four foot ditch on the south side of the street, always quickly filling with snow. Rarely could I get up to Eighth Street. I was effectively snowbound until the city cleared Sixth Street.

Our new home, then the most northwestern home in Oakley, was a different matter. Our garage doors were on the north side of our home. We had a concrete basketball court north of our house and garage so Dean could play ball. A driveway led from the slab to Elm Street, some forty feet. Wind from the north always drifted over the garage doors and/or the driveway. One morning Jill, then living with us, and I were outside looking at the snow; my cars snowed in inside the garage, Jill's car buried on the slab. We were laughing, hoping that no one needed a doctor because it would take me a long time to get to the (old) hospital. I was in no hurry and was dreading using the shovel. It would be a major undertaking.

Carol shouted to us "Jill, you have a phone call."

"Me? Who would call me after a storm?"

The telephone system still used operators to make phone calls. Jill was one of the operators. And the chief operator was calling Jill to come to work. "I can't get to work! I can hardly get out of the house!"

Her response was "You get out of the house to the street. I've called the fire department. They have a van with chains on that they use for emergencies. They'll be there in ten minutes!"

"A telephone operator is more important than the doctor," Jill laughed at me.

Off she went with the firemen. Thirty minutes later my phone rang again. The hospital was on the line and said someone had fallen and cut her head. I was needed there. I knew what to do—call the fire department and ask for their assistance.

* * *

Another storm. Another story. This was later, when we had the new hospital. The nurse called me "Doctor, the highway patrolman just brought in a man with a broken leg."

"What am I supposed to do? I can't drive to the hospital. Someone would have to come in and X-ray his leg. And we can't move him to an orthopedist in Hays. The roads are closed. Just put him in a bed."

"He's in a lot of pain. You could splint his leg. And Jerry Chaput has said he will use his snowmobile to take you to the hospital."

"Give him 15 milligrams of morphine and I'll get dressed and watch for Jerry." A few minutes later Jerry showed up. I slogged to the street, straddled his snowmobile and off we roared. Someone was there to do X-rays. Yes, his femur was broken. We splinted his leg and put him to bed. Two days later we were able to transfer him to Hays to an orthopedist.

* * *

The nurse at the hospital paged me one afternoon. Bill had walked in and said his chest hurt. I drove to the hospital and asked Bill's story. "Doc,

I shoveled the snow off my walk, then started on the driveway. Then my chest started to hurt. The more I shoveled the more it hurt. So I walked to the hospital."

The walk was five blocks in the snow! An EKG showed an acute myocardial infarction. Treatment in Oakley then was to place him in the ICU, treat him with TPA, a drug to dissolve the clot in his artery, and later transfer him to a cardiologist to study his coronary arteries. All went well. Bill was transferred to the care of a cardiologist where he required one or more bypasses in his coronary arteries. He did well for years. A walk in the snow was never an appropriate treatment for an acute MI, but this didn't appear to have caused Bill any problems.

*   *   *

The forecast was for snow, perhaps a blizzard. I wanted to go to Denver for a continuing education meeting in Denver. Dennis could cover Oakley. I would be in Denver before the snow hit. It probably wouldn't be as bad as forecast. I drove to Denver Wednesday for the three-day meeting. I stayed at a motel northeast of Stapleton Airport, a motel where Carol and I frequently stayed. The meeting was in downtown Denver but I was familiar with Denver and had no qualms about those arrangements.

Thursday morning I drove to the meeting. About the middle of the afternoon an announcement was made that if anyone hoped to leave the hotel where the meeting was held he should leave now. The storm had arrived! I left Denver and drove to my motel. There I hunkered down for the snow. There was a restaurant in the motel, so I had food. It was warm. If I didn't get to the meeting I would just have to miss it.

It snowed. And it snowed. And the wind blew. Friday I could not get out of the motel. I always took a book with me. I loved to read so I had a chance to catch up on that. By Saturday I was tired of reading. I was stir crazy! And I still couldn't get away from the motel. I called a friend and she managed to drive to the motel and take me to her home. We spent Saturday evening and Sunday talking, playing cards and visiting with her daughter. Monday she took me to the motel and we shoveled my car out of the drift so I could get away from the motel. But I-70 was still drifted closed. And remained that way for a week. Tuesday I drove south to Pueblo, then to Garden City and north to Oakley. The long way around, but I got home.

Carol had her own stories to tell of the blizzard. Dale, leaving KU for spring break, had been told I-70 was closed. He couldn't get west of Hays. He phoned Carol who made arrangements for Dale to stay with a friend of Carol's in Hays. The snow and wind hit Oakley. That evening she heard a knock on her door. A young couple stood at Carol's door, cold and bewildered. They had been told the Methodist Church, southeast of our home, would be open for stranded travelers. They were given directions but they had driven west on Eighth Street past the church, past our home and gotten stuck west of our home. Fortunately they walked back east and found our home. If they had walked west they might very well have walked to their deaths. They spent two or three nights with Carol.

The next morning Carol received another phone call. A tiny voice said, "I'm a friend of Dale's at KU. Two of us were driving home to St. Francis when they took us off I-70 at Oakley. We had to stay at the truck stop. All night! We're scared. Can you get us and take us to your house?"

Carol phoned Dennis. He had a jeep, which he thought could get him to the truck stop and pick up the girls. He did, then drove back to town and got food for all Carol's guests. By the time I got home the girls had left for St. Francis. The couple had driven east, giving up their planned trip to Colorado.

It was days before travel from Oakley to Denver on I-70 was opened. In digging out the underpasses they found a man frozen in his car. He had stopped to park in the underpass and been buried. Truly a wilderness.

*   *   *

I later bought a four-wheel drive Ram Charger. With all that power and four wheels I was ready to go when winter came. There was the snow. There were the drifts. I was certain I was prepared. Roaring into a drift north of the hospital I again needed help. I was stuck! After this lesson I was more cautious about snow; there were drifts too large to attack. But I no longer needed to ask someone to take me to the hospital.

I also learned that if I left the Ram Charger in the garage or on the slab I could not get through the snow on the driveway. If a bad storm was coming I parked the Ram Charger on Elm Street. There the wind would always blow the snow away, either in front of or in back of my car. One or the other would be clear and I could drive onto Elm, then to the hospital, where Second Street was usually blown free.

A January storm was coming, but the ground was already icy. I was preparing to move my Ram Charger Saturday afternoon. I stepped on the icy running board, slipped and hit my head on the concrete. After moving the Ram Charger I went in and told Carol that I now knew what someone meant when he told me he saw stars. Carol asked me what I would do if one of my patients came to see me with that accident. I said "I might send him to Colby for a CT scan. But it would be twenty miles in a blizzard. The drive is more dangerous than the possibility of an injury to his brain."

I was the doctor; I didn't think I had been hurt. I watched the Super Bowl and worked Monday. On Tuesday my subdural hematoma drove me to another physician in Oakley. Blizzard or not she sent me to Colby for a CT scan which revealed the subdural hematoma. I was then flown to a neurosurgeon in Denver to remove it. I had found I was not the indestructible old doc I had believed I was. I had become a patient while oblivious to my injury. The surgeon told Carol I would be back to work in a week. Wednesday morning I had a stroke.

After spending months in a hospital Carol told me this story. I was no longer going to practice medicine.

PART II

ARTICLES WRITTEN BY DOCTOR OHMART

Chapter 10

Dr. O Begins To Write

I always loved to read. After having earned a degree in English at the University of Kansas including a couple of classes in writing I thought "I can write as well as some of the articles I read. I should write." I unearthed a bit of time so I started writing. These five essays were written in the eighties, none of which were published.

Romeo

Romeo. Never was a man more inappropriately named. A lean and slow-speaking farmer, he was hardly a Shakespearean character. Instead he could have stepped from the pages of a Faulkner novel. His life, too, could only be viewed as a Faulknerian saga, tragic yet heroic, in a mold that the citizens of Yoknapatawpha County would easily have understood.

I remember when I first met him. My partner hospitalized him. Not for any dramatic disease, but for a disease of teen-agers, appendicitis. True to his destiny, this man could not suffer even a child's disease in routine fashion. His inflamed appendix ruptured, leading to peritonitis, a frequently fatal disease in those days before super-antibiotics. Peritonitis was followed by a wound infection of gigantic proportion. More as a testimony to his strength than to his medical care, he survived.

My next memory is of another illness, again not a routine problem, but a pneumonia which did not respond to the antibiotics of the era. A chest X-ray revealed an abscess, cavity or similar void in his right lung. Was it lung cancer? We did not know and could not decide in our rural hospital. To the state university school of medicine he went.

After all the –oscopies were performed they still had no answer. The next logical step was a thoracotomy. This proved the lesion to be non-malignant, but the illness was extremely debilitating. He gradually regained his strength and was able to resume farming. But he had been ill and unable to work through most of the financially good times on the farm. Although his wife and daughters tried, they were unable to fully take advantage of those few years. The three girls all did manage to graduate from college. And the lessons of patience and endurance they learned at home were undoubtedly of more value than many of their college courses.

But the Furies were not yet through with Romeo. He next presented to my office with an unusual type of pain, scattered throughout many bones and joints. A bone scan revealed multiple metastatic lesions, and an exploring finger encountered an unyielding prostate. This was followed by all of the indignities to which modern medicine often subjects those for whom it purports to care. An orchiectomy bought him some comparatively comfortable months. Chemotherapy, although it made him extremely sick and uncomfortable, bought more time. Time enough for him to see his farm go the way of the sale. Time enough for him to see his last daughter married. Lots of time in which to suffer. And time enough to teach me valuable lessons.

During that time Romeo taught me of the heroism and dignity of man. He was always aware of his impending demise. He knew that his family needed him. Maybe he also knew how much I needed him. He died slowly, but courageously. Although he was forced to spend much time in the hospital he never became a complaining patient. I am sure he suffered untold extremes of pain, but all he would say was "Doc, you got any stronger pain medicine?"

He always had a smile for me, a young doctor unsure how to react to my dying friend. He was a man for whom I cared deeply. He was also a man around whom I was quite uncomfortable, because my Medicine, my god, had failed him. His God, and his strength, were greater than mine. He ultimately died, but not unmourned, and not unremembered. And certainly not without making a greater contribution to my life than he had ever suspected. From Romeo, not Shakespeare's youthful lover but a more tragic figure, I learned humility and compassion. I learned that a man may always control his destiny, even if that destiny is ultimately reduced to how one faces death.

*   *   *

A Fable of Cautious Love

Once there was a small teddy bear. He was a teddy bear very smart in the ways of the scrolls, and very persevering. He lumbered along in his young teddy bear way, persevering and getting smarter in the ways of the scrolls until the ancient bears, all very stuffy and proud of the young teddy, sent him to the bear university so that he might learn still more and become more akin to them. He was a success at the university, learning much more and becoming ever a stuffier bear like the bear-ancients. One of the lessons he learned well was that he had a fair amount of ability. Another lesson he absorbed was that he had an almost unmatched capacity to persevere. He also discovered that he was smarter than the average bear. While at the university he made a few friends, mostly among bears of similar gender and predisposition. He always felt very uncomfortable in the company of little

161

girl bears, and most of them paid him scant attention. He vaguely sensed that something was missing from his life, but, not being sure of what it was, he kept on persevering, certain that all things come to talented bears that persevere.

Then one day he returned home for a visit. There he met an amazing creature. It was obviously female and intrigued him no end. It was small and cute and cuddly, somewhat like the female bears he had met, but it did not act like any female he had ever seen. All his smarts and perseverance had not prepared him for this being. But the little creature seemed to like him, so he hung around. He also looked in all his books trying to discover what this thing might be, but he could find nothing quite like it. It was fuzzy, like a bear, but sometimes prickly, instead of soft. It moved in a funny way, raising its head to look, and then suddenly dashing off in some other direction, perhaps not the same way it had looked. It had many talents, a beautiful voice, a lot of smarts and something else, something that he had not encountered before.

This creature was gentle and loving! Not snippy and brittle like the female bears he had known. He was intrigued by this creature and kept poking at it until he fell in love with it. She also fell in love with him. They set up housekeeping and had three children, all different and rather strange mixtures of the two parents. During the time of rearing of these three offspring, the little female creature transformed. She changed from the chrysalis she had been and became a beautiful butterfly. The teddy bear was proud of this transformation, but afraid of it as well. He had never seen anything so beautiful or that moved so quickly. Her smile or touch brought great joy to his little bear heart, but brought a fear as well. What could such a glittering, flittering butterfly possibly see in a plodding, persevering bear? Would she not be attracted to another glittering creature and leave him for an exciting life with someone more similar to her? But all he knew was to plod along behind her as she flittered.

He learned much this way. Sometimes, when he felt secure, he helped her flitter, and even lumbered along only slightly behind her. Other times, when he felt insecure or threatened, he would pin the poor butterfly down with his paw. Occasionally only a word or two would be so weighty that she was constrained by them. For she was a fragile and delicate creature. But, as in the ways of both butterflies and bears, she kept flittering and he kept plodding. He thought it was a life with more ups and downs than the average bear led, but he had known since cub-hood that he had more talent and perseverance than the average bear. And besides she was so bright, and warm, and cuddly. And she taught him so much. He could tolerate a few ups and downs.

Then, one day after the three offspring had become mature creatures and left their den, he awakened to the fact that their relationship had become comfortable! He relished this, as he had always liked to be comfortable in his bearish way, and he felt secure. He no longer worried about "What if she leaves me?" because he believed she no longer would. Once more, plodding and perseverance had overcome all obstacles and the love of that creature he had cherished for years was assured. He no longer had to be on guard, or worried about her being swept away. He had achieved bear heaven—comfort. Assured of her love, he did not cultivate her as he once had. Immersed in his work (for, after all, the bear elders had instructed him well in the ways of the bear world), he did not realize that his precious butterfly was flittering away, that what he had felt as comfort and security, was stifling her. She was not leaving him for another creature; she had learned too much for that. But the glitter and the sparkle that were an essential part of her were fading. He had not nourished the warmth and love that had first attracted him to her, and they were waning, as was her spirit.

Too late, he realized that it was ordained that a bear and a butterfly could only meet as their paths crossed in time. They were so different that what one found nourishing, the other would find stifling. It had always been thus and would forever more be so. But he was a very stubborn bear, one who knew that he had many talents and excelled at persevering. So he told himself that he would persevere, and perhaps, someday, he would again bask in the love of the glittering, flittering butterfly.

*   *   *

Cookbook Medicine? Only If Best For My Patient!

She walked into the reception, a smile on her face, with not a sign of a limp. Striding up to me, my 94-year old friend said that she wanted me to hang around to take care of her if she broke her leg again in twenty-five years. Figuring that she was as likely to be around in 25 years as I was, I agreed.

No one would have guessed that this woman had sustained a broken left ankle only four months before the reception. She had been a widow for eight years, living alone during that time. She was alert and capable, driving, playing cards and doing her own housekeeping, lawn work, etc. She had not bothered to phone her son until the day after she fell, then only asking him to get her a wheelchair. He insisted that he take her to the hospital where I could examine her and X-ray her ankle. The X-rays revealed a bimalleolar fracture of her right ankle, with several millimeters of displacement. She absolutely refused my suggestion that she be taken ninety miles to see an orthopedist for an open reduction and fixation. I was not very anxious to put her in a long-leg cast, as I was afraid that this approach would immobilize her to the extent that she would never get back on her feet. I finally decided to attempt a closed reduction and put her in a short leg cast, hoping that would hold the reduction and allow her to retain some mobility. The reduction was easily accomplished, as was the cast application.

Now what was I to do? She had the answer to that, too. She was convinced that she could not walk on her leg, but she would not learn to use crutches. Instead she would rent a wheelchair, hire someone to help her and just stay home. She did that quite successfully, as evidenced by her appearance at the reception.

I knew throughout the course of her care that I was not following an approved approach to her break. Yet I also knew that the usual approach might not be best for her. I used my best medical judgment, tempered with caring for Hazel, to treat her as best I could. Fortunately time proved me correct in this instance.

Several years ago one of our fine high school athletes didn't rise after the last play of our last football game. My on-field examination of his knee showed me the most flexible medial collateral ligament that I had ever encountered. X-rays at the hospital, however, told a different tale. His ligaments were intact. Instead he had a fracture of the medial femoral condyle, allowing a square of bone to swing out when I stressed it. The boy, a senior, was defending state champion in his wrestling weight. His first question, of course, was "When can I wrestle?"

After positioning the fragments normally I applied a full leg cast. The orthopedist I phoned said that this was the best way to treat the fracture, but that wrestling this year was out of the question. Chris and his parents simply did not accept that. He continued to work out with the wrestling team while wearing his cast. By the end of wrestling season he threatened to take his cast off himself if I didn't. So I took it off. He wrestled in the regional tournament wearing a brace. He advanced to the semifinals, mostly on upper body strength and guts. As this is not a fairy tale, his weak leg finally caught up with him and he did not qualify for the state tournament. But he was able to say that he had tried. I do not know whether I could have kept him from wrestling or not. But

I was glad that I had allowed him to try, whatever the professional or financial risk to me. His risk had certainly been explained to him and his parents.

Elva would be dead now if we had followed the instructions sent home with him. He had had a gastrectomy for carcinoma of the stomach several years ago. Because he had seven positive nodes out of twelve showing the cancer, he was placed on a monthly chemotherapy regimen. The chemo depressed his white cell count, the cells that helped prevent infections. His first course was followed by a severe pneumonia. Following his recovery from this the oncologist recommended a reduced, but still rather drastic, dose of chemotherapy. This course was followed by an even more severe bout with pneumonia, one that nearly proved fatal. Following a long discussion with both Elva and his wife, we decided to give him no more chemotherapy, only what medicines were necessary to keep him comfortable until his death.

Today, several years later, he is still alive and shows no evidence of his original malignancy. Yet we disregarded the advice of the oncologist who had seen him. The oncologist stated that there was no alternative but to follow the protocol for gastric carcinoma with positive nodes. While I am sure that Elva, in his long-term survival, represents an unusual case. He exemplifies a growing number of patients who return to me on extremely rigorous chemotherapeutic regimens because that is what the experts say should be done. Many of them are aware that the chemo is not curative, and may prefer a shorter, but perhaps more comfortable, life without the side effects of chemotherapy. Yet their desires, and those of their families, have had scant attention paid to them in the referral hospitals. The recipe books must be followed, for whatever reason.

I certainly don't mean to imply that I am always correct and the "cookbook" approach incorrect. Many times I will begin a course of treatment, only to decide that I should lean more to the standard. I will then simply move in that direction. This, to me, is the art of medicine—initiating the treatment that seems most appropriate, closely monitoring my results, and continuing or changing my therapy as the patient's condition indicates. This was the case with a seven-year old boy with bilateral Colles' fractures. The right one was not badly displaced and we tried and tried to leave him with one free arm, just so he could care for himself at school. But he was too active and it hurt too much, so he temporarily wore two long-arm casts, and friends zipped his pants.

Every year that I practice, however, it becomes harder for me to use my judgment and experience to individualize my approach to patients. I am sure all of you have noted the same problem. Hospital regulations, Medicare regulations, legal proscriptions—they all contribute to this difficulty. They combine to take much of the challenge, enjoyment and personal reward from medicine. There is always that sneaking little fear, "What if things don't turn out right this time? How can I defend my choice of therapy in court?"

I am not happy with that thought, but I don't know how to escape it. I simply continue to care for my patients as best I can. I hate to sound like an old fogy mourning for days long past, but I can't help but wish there were some way to practice as I did twenty-five years ago. Since there doesn't appear to be any way to roll back the clock, however, I will continue to resist formulary medicine when I think it to be in the best interests of my patients, accepting whatever risk is involved and hoping that things turn out for the best, both my patient and myself.

*   *   *

This was written in August 1988. It was in response to innumerable questions about cholesterol. I don't think it was ever published.

Doc, Do I Have Cholesterol?

"Doctor, what about this cholesterol business? Do you suppose I have any?" This has become one of the most common questions asked of me. It's almost as if cholesterol is to be equated with herpes or measles, something unalterably bad, something no one would want, or at best something to be endured and remedied if possible. Everyone knows that "having cholesterol" is equivalent to asking for a heart attack before fifty, or, if that is avoided, a stroke before sixty. Is it really all that bad? What is cholesterol anyway? How do I know if I have it? And am I really doomed to an early disability or death if I do have it?

Of course not. As with most problems in medicine, that of cholesterol is not a simple "do I have it or not" proposition. Cholesterol itself is a white, waxy substance. It is found in all cells of animal origin, although the amount varies greatly depending on the type of cell. Each of us needs a certain amount of cholesterol for it is important in many structures. It is the chemical base of many hormones, including those that make us man and woman, and who would want to give that up? In fact, it is so important to us that each of us manufactures cholesterol in our liver. If we ate no cholesterol at all we would still produce what we need, and perhaps make too much. The other side of cholesterol is that it is found in, and may be responsible for, the plaques that narrow arteries throughout the body. This is especially true in the coronary arteries (those supplying the heart muscle itself with blood). The higher your cholesterol the faster these plaques develop. So a certain amount is necessary, but too much may be harmful. That is part of what has made it such a difficult problem to come to grips with and solve, if indeed we have it solved at present.

Further complicating the situation is that a "normal cholesterol" was, until a few months ago, considered to be anything less than 280 milligrams of cholesterol per deciliter (mg/dl) of blood. This was based on the average value of serum cholesterols obtained on large numbers of supposedly healthy people. But doctors and others have known for many years that this "normal" value might not represent the optimum value. Many societies with a lower rate of atherosclerosis and coronary heart disease than ours have been shown to have significantly lower average cholesterol values. It has long been known that the Japanese, who eat much less beef and more fish than we do, have a lower incidence of atherosclerosis than we do. They also have a lower average cholesterol value. However Japanese-Americans, eating a "normal American diet," lose this advantage. Their cholesterol rises to that of the average American, and their rate of heart disease also rises. But factors such as stress, exercise (or lack thereof), smoking, diabetes, gender and many others have been shown to play some part in the development of coronary artery disease (CAD), further complicating the picture.

A start was made toward resolving the confusion surrounding the cholesterol issue when the Adult Treatment Panel of the National Cholesterol Education Program published their guidelines concerning ideal adult cholesterol levels. This was in October 1987. Although temporarily adding to this confusion (A man with a level of 265 mg/dl whom I had told was "normal" in September 1987 was now [August 1988], by definition in the high cholesterol, high-risk group, although his cholesterol had not changed.), this should ultimately clarify the problem and our approach to it. We at least have some guidelines for which to strive. These cholesterol levels are:

- Desirable: less than 200 mg/dl
- Borderline: 200-239 mg/dl
- High: 240 mg/dl and above.

Although certainly not a death sentence, a cholesterol level over 240 mg/dl honors its possessor with about twice the risk of developing coronary heart disease as someone with a level below 200.

So, now that we know that some cholesterol is needed but that too much is harmful, what do we do? The first step is to get your cholesterol tested. This is quite easily done, and, for screening purposes, does not even need to be fasting. Your family doctor can do it, many public health departments do it and there are health fairs or hospital PR programs in many communities, shopping malls, etc. where you can have it tested. If your screening test is below 200 mg/dl, great! You passed and may continue as you have been doing, no need to worry about cholesterol. If your level is above 200 you haven't failed yet, so don't plan on cashing in your life insurance. The test needs to be repeated, this time after a 12-14 hour fast. This test should include a triglyceride level and an HDL (high-density lipoprotein) level. Both of these are carriers of cholesterol and allow calculation of the LDL (low-density lipoprotein) fraction of cholesterol. This LDL fraction appears to be most closely related to the development of coronary artery disease and should ideally be below 130 mg/dl. For some strange reason the HDL fraction seems to be a "good" form of cholesterol, in that higher levels of this fraction seem in some way to protect against the development of CAD. If this "lipid profile" reveals an elevation in the LDL fraction of your cholesterol, then you need to begin a cholesterol-modifying program.

This may not be as formidable as it sounds. It is estimated that every 1% reduction in cholesterol is accompanied by a 2% reduction in coronary risk, so even moderate cholesterol reduction is helpful. Regular exercise appears to raise the level of the protective HDL. Weight loss, if you are overweight, helps to lower cholesterol. Age and gender both influence cholesterol levels, but we can do little about changing either of those. That leaves us with dietary changes as the foundation for cholesterol modification. Surprisingly, the primary dietary factor is not the amount of cholesterol we eat. The amount of saturated fat we eat is the major dietary determinant of our serum cholesterol. The term saturated is a chemical term, referring to the number of hydrogen ions bound to the fatty acid in relation to the number of binding sites. The fewer hydrogen ions, the less saturated the fatty acid. In general the saturated fats are solids and the unsaturated fats are oils, but palm oil, coconut oil and palm kernel oil all contain a high percentage of saturated fatty acids, more than do tuna and chicken fat, for instance. The cocoa fat found in chocolate is also high in saturated fatty acids. It is thus possible to eat something containing no cholesterol and only vegetable fats (most non-dairy creamers, for instance, contain coconut and palm oils), and be eating incorrectly if you are trying to eat a cholesterol-lowering diet.

O.K. My cholesterol is 250, my LDL is 160. What do I do? What can I eat? Assuming you are not overweight and already exercising, that leaves diet modification. Fortunately the danger in an elevated cholesterol is not an acute one. You have some time to learn what to eat and what to avoid. The basic modifications are:

- Eat less total fat. Try to keep this below 30% of your calories initially. If further tests show insufficient lowering of your cholesterol, try to decrease the total fat to less than 20% of your total calories.
- Eat less saturated fat. This can be done by simply decreasing your total fat intake, decreasing the saturated fats that you eat and by substituting unsaturated fats for saturated fats.
- Eat less cholesterol.
- Eat more complex carbohydrates (starch and fiber). These usually are plant products and contain no cholesterol and little fat.

In general this means avoiding eggs, dairy fat and animal fats. After 3-6 months of a low fat diet you should have a repeat cholesterol (this alone is adequate for most follow-up exams). If your cholesterol remains higher than you desire, either a stricter diet, medications, or both may be prescribed. The modified diet remains the foundation of treatment, however.

How do I know what to eat? There are a number of good guides available. The Public Health Service has a number of excellent pamphlets available, as does the American Heart Association. There are a number of cookbooks with excellent menus and recipes, ranging from the *American Heart Association Cookbook* to *Can You Trust A Slim Santa Claus?* Learn to read the labels on the foods that you buy, especially the processed foods. Many communities have educational programs through community colleges, county extension programs, hospitals, etc. Take your time and learn the new eating patterns. This is not a do it and forget it problem. If you wish to maintain an improved cholesterol level you will probably need to remain on the modified diet for the rest of your life. However, if you lower that 250 mg/dl cholesterol to 200 mg/dl and maintain it there, you have decreased your risk of coronary artery disease by 100%, down to that of the general population. Now be sure to use your seat belt and drive carefully!

*   *   *

Dr. Goodheart

I have been awakening with a recurring dream for the past few weeks. Not a nightmare, exactly, but yet rather disturbing. It occurs after a particularly frustrating day at my office, especially if I have seen an inordinate number of "crocks" during the day. In the dream I am again a young physician, just finishing my residency and eager to attack illness in the real world. I am on my first employment interview.

The unobtrusive sign above the door said "Dr. Goodheart's Malady of the Month Clinic." I checked the address again. Yes, this was really the place. Not exactly what I had expected in a clinic name, but catchy and certainly one to be remembered.

I was amazed as I walked into the reception room. No TV set with today's soap opera or blaring rock music in this office. Instead there were, faintly, the strains of "Daphnis and Chloe." The windows were draped and the lighting subdued. The chairs were soft and comfortable and only two were occupied, both by well-dressed, attractive young women. I realized immediately that I had entered the reception room of a successful doctor, one who truly cared for his patients.

I was just finishing my residency and this was my first job interview. Even my nervousness was calmed by the relaxing ambiance of the room. I walked to the receptionist's desk and introduced myself. "Hello. I'm Dr. Newman."

"Oh yes. Dr. Goodheart is expecting you," she replied, with a smile and a tone in her voice that relieved me of the rest of my pre-interview jitters. "Just a minute. He'll see you as soon as he has finished with his present patient."

Within minutes a tall, gray-haired man ushered another attractive young woman to the receptionist's desk. "Mrs. Smith needs to have the usual lab-work done and another appointment scheduled with me after it's completed. There is no charge for this visit."

Then he turned to me. "You must be Dr. Newman", he said with a smile. "I'm Stanley Goodheart. Please come with me."

I followed him through a carpeted corridor and into an office the likes of which I had never seen. Warm but soft lighting, quiet music, pleasing lithographs on the walls—it was a room designed to subtly announce that the man I was seeing was a warm and caring, successful physician. A far cry from the tiled concrete floors and painted walls of the hospital at which I was training.

"Let me tell you a little about my practice and philosophy", he said, and I settled back to listen. "I have been here a little over twenty-five years. When I came I was prepared to care for individuals and families, managing the illnesses that I could and referring the others to the appropriate specialists. I did a good job of that. But as time went on I realized that there was a large group of people I was not helping. Most of these were young women with a multitude of problems."

"Sure, I would relieve her present complaint, but within a few days or weeks she would return with another, usually non-specific, complaint. I realized that I was providing only symptomatic relief, if even that. In an effort to do more I undertook some library research."

"I remembered that, during my internship, the ER nurses there had given a lot of Methedrine® and Plebex® (methamphetamine and B-vitamins) shots for one or two of the local physicians. And the young women getting the injections all swore that they felt much better after the shot. So starting with that treatment in mind, I found a diagnosis, that of 'Tired Young Housewife Syndrome'. A little more reading yielded the diagnoses of 'the Vapors' and 'Neurocirculatory Asthenia'. And hypothyroidism was certainly in vogue a few years ago when our only diagnostic tool was the BMR. Low blood pressure was also a common diagnosis in this group of women for a few years."

I had heard of none of these diagnoses other than hypothyroidism, and, being a well-trained young doctor, I knew of that entity as a condition easily diagnosed by a thyroid profile, but rarely found. I wondered where all this was leading. But Dr. Goodheart's manner was charming and his story was interesting, if not yet obvious. So I continued to listen.

"I remembered the man I joined in practice. He had treated many young women with various mixtures of amphetamines and barbiturates and how they all felt better and got a lot more done. Nor did they seem to become addicted to those low doses. And I realized that there was a large group of people, mostly working women with children at home, who suffered from this condition, call it what you will. That is why I founded my clinic, 'Dr. Goodheart's Malady of the Month Clinic.' My success in helping these women cope with the problems they face has been spectacular, if I do say so myself. My patients all feel much better. They refer their friends and neighbors to me so I have an almost unending supply of patients. Because these people really do feel better and function better I am professionally satisfied. And I make more money than I have time to spend. That is why I am looking for an associate."

My head was whirling, but I heard him say something about following him to see how the clinic worked. As he rose, so did I, and we walked to a back room staffed with three women answering telephones.

"Doctor Goodheart's Health Center.

Bring us your trouble,

We'll burst it like a bubble."

"Like my little rhyme?" Doctor Goodheart asked. "It's surprising how many patients tell me they felt better the moment they heard it. Listen to what the operator says next."

"Yes, this is the office you were told about. I think we can help you. Tell me a little about your problem . . . You're tired all the time . . . Sleep sixteen hours a day . . . Irritable, scream at the kids . . . Can't get the job done at work . . . Can't seem to concentrate anymore? Yes, that does sound like this month's special, the chronic fatigue syndrome. And that is something that Dr. Goodheart and his aides have been having good results with. Let me schedule an initial appointment with Dr. Goodheart for you . . . Cost . . . The initial interview and physical exam is free. Then if Dr. Goodheart thinks he can help you he'll order some lab work to exclude problems other than the chronic fatigue syndrome. He will want to see you again to go over the results of the tests with you and establish a schedule for therapy . . . Oh, yes; there are numerous things that can be done to help you. Nutrition Therapy. Exercise programs. Vitamin Therapy. Relaxation techniques. Biofeedback. Yoga . . . O.K. You're down for next Tuesday, the 15th, at 10:00. Don't forget to bring your insurance information."

"Dr. Goodheart's Health Center.

Bring us your trouble . . ."

I turned to Dr. Goodheart, confused by what I had seen and heard. "If you don't charge for the visit and physical how do you afford all of this?"

"Ahh, my boy," he replied. "The patients are charged for the rest of our services. The initial visit is a confidence-builder, bait, if you're a fisherman. Let me show you the rest of my plant."

After a whirlwind tour of his high-tech lab ("All we send out are our EBV antibody titers"), bio-feedback room, exercise room, and viewing two individual and one group therapy session we arrived back at his office.

"I can tell that you are a bit overwhelmed", he said. "Here, have some juice, sit back and relax and I'll tell you a bit more about my practice. Almost all of my patients have the same diagnosis; they are a self-selected and self-referred group. Most of them have seen several other doctors and been told 'It's all in your head', a phrase we never use here. They are happy to have a 'real' diagnosis and therapy encouraging them to be more active. And they truly feel better! Most of them have good coverage by medical insurance. I rarely see a Welfare patient. They are too occupied with where the next meal is coming from to worry about being fatigued. I also rarely see a Medicare patient—they all expect to be tired at that age. I bill the patient. She is expected to pay me and collect from her insurance. So I have eliminated one of the major hassles of most medical practice, third-party payers."

"Where did the clinic name come from? I went through specializing in hypoglycemia, systemic yeast infection, mitral valve prolapse, chronic EBV infection and the chronic fatigue syndrome. I couldn't change the sign over the door and on my stationary quickly enough. I thought about Dr. Goodheart's Women's Clinic, but that smacks too much of abortion and birth control and I didn't want any of those messy right-to-lifers demonstrating in front of my office. So I finally chose 'Dr. Goodheart's Malady of the Month Clinic.' Has a nice ring, don't you think? It really doesn't matter what we name it; we're dealing with the same population of women, regardless. And my treatments work as well, no matter what the disease name is. Everyone feels better after completing one of my regimens."

I started to rise, completely befuddled. "Is this truly what the practice of medicine is? He certainly seems sincere. And the women to whom I spoke all attested to his care and their improvement".

"Just a minute, my boy," Dr. Goodheart said. "I judge people quickly and accurately. I think you're the man for whom I have been looking. I have an offer for you that no one else will beat. I'll pay you $180,000 for your first year here, with a percentage of charges for lab work you generate on top of that. You'll work a forty-hour week, no nights on call. You will have six weeks vacation/CME time off. And most of all, you will have the satisfaction of truly helping a segment of our population that is attractive, clean and pleasant to work with. They badly need care and have difficulty finding appropriate care. What better opportunity to practice here could a new physician ask for?"

I continued to rise, my mind whirling. "Was it for this I had spent hours studying Lyme Disease, JRA and the various hepatitides? Does disease have to be manifest by objective signs, improper lines on an EKG, unwanted spots on X-rays or lab results more than two standard deviations from the norm? Was the practice of medicine only a matter of telling people what they wanted to hear, rather than informing them that they had no true 'disease' and hence no pills would cure them. Yet one of my most respected professors of medicine had defined disease as 'the lack of ease' and stated that our primary goal as physicians was to remedy this, if possible. That certainly was what Dr. Goodheart was doing."

"I need some time to consider this," I mumbled. "May I let you know in a couple of weeks?"

"Certainly, my boy," Dr. Goodheart exuded in his most paternalistic manner. "I wouldn't want you to make a mistake in a decision such as this. Take all the time you want."

I awaken, only to find that I still face that decision. Is the "science" of medicine the only way to approach a patient? If I can not see a problem/answer on a lab sheet or X-ray does it not exist? Is Dr. Goodheart a fraud, or is he using the "art" of medicine to provide ease for troubled people? I know there is a large group of very uncomfortable individuals out there, looking for some sort of relief. How is the best way to approach them? How can all of us bearing the title "physician" best offer them surcease? And how am I to decide what is right for me? Little wonder that this dream recurs. It certainly represents my deep frustration with the minimal relief I often have to offer. This phantom physician may be offering me an end to those frustrations, if I can and will incorporate some of his techniques into my practice. Perhaps, in the interest of sleeping better, I will do that.

*   *   *

Prairie Wedding

After writing various essays it occurred to me that I might attempt to get a few of my little treatises published. I submitted "Prairie Wedding" to *Medical Economics*. The editor there wrote me a note, thanking me for the article and saying she liked it very much, but that it was not suitable for them. She suggested two or three other magazines that might accept it. After another couple rejections it was published in the *Journal of the American Medical Association* in 1989, my first published essay. I'm certain that if this had not been accepted I would never have submitted another. "Prairie Wedding" was later translated and printed in the Japanese edition of the *JAMA*.

The AMA did not allow me to use this essay in my book, so I will say a bit about it. In it I attended a wedding at the bride's parents' farm home. I had delivered the groom; I had cared for the bride for years. The site was a well-kept farmstead, similar to many others in northwest Kansas. It exemplified life on the high plains, and the hard work and perseverance necessary to survive there. The afternoon was hot and windy but the bridal party and the guests were used to both. As one lady, dressed for a church wedding, said, "We'll all look the same, windblown and dusty." I think the setting and the weather both were designed for this couple.

As I looked at the guests I saw them as my patients and my friends, individuals with malignancies, neurological problems, and other acute and chronic diseases. I saw children who were frustrated by the problems of dealing with elderly parents in an environment that does not treat the elderly gently, either financially or physically. But I was proud of the strength of those at the wedding. I hoped that I, also having grown up in the high plains, might cope as well as my friends were coping.

And then I thought—"These people are my patients . . . No, not just my patients. They are my people and my friends. I am part of them and they are part of me. This is medicine as I dreamed of it in medical school. I am doing what I dreamed of and trained for, what I enjoy most, helping my friends when I am needed. If only all physicians could have this experience before becoming entrapped by the technology of contemporary medicine, perhaps many of the problems apparently existing in physician-patient relationships would disappear."

*   *   *

I was now a published author. I had little spare time but I enjoyed writing. My next published essay was written after Dr. Alan Adams left Oakley, leaving me again the single physician in Oakley. With Carol's assistance, this was written and published in *Medical Economics* in July 1990

When My Partner Left, I Made My Patients My Partners

My first reactions were shock and anger when Alan, my partner of five years, told me that he would be leaving in two months. How could he do that to me? I had been the only physician in our rural county of 3600 for ten years before he came, and I certainly didn't relish the thought of repeating that experience. That had imposed major strains on my marriage, interfered with the way I wanted to raise my children and stressed my sanity almost to the breaking point. After I calmed down and discussed the situation with Alan, I agreed that it appeared to be his best move. Our economically depressed rural area, with the population both decreasing in numbers and increasing in age, did not seem to be the best place for a young doctor with two small children to plan on spending a lifetime. I, too, had been getting the recruiters' brochures and occasionally listening to a phone call. He could work fewer hours and make more money almost anywhere he chose to go. Who could blame him for leaving?

Next I needed to sit down with my wife, Carol, tell her of Alan's decision and try to plan our course. Fortunately our marriage had become solid enough that I knew I could count on her for advice and help. That has proven invaluable. Our kids were grown and married, so child rearing no longer posed a problem. That left only my sanity to save. The obvious first consideration was that we, too, leave Oakley. I had considered retiring from Family Practice and doing locum tenens work for some time. There were also many ER and salaried positions open. But I thought I had been my own boss for long enough (26 years) that I would not relish working for someone else. Carol and I had both grown up in Scott City, forty-five miles south of Oakley, and our parents, all in their late seventies or eighties, still live there. Someday they might well need our care. Two of our three children also live in Northwest Kansas. Both of us liked the area and did not want to get too far from our families. So it looked as if we would be staying in Oakley.

That still left the question of how to preserve my sanity. Carol said she did not want the experience of caring for a husband who was either mentally or physically ill. I could not blame her too much. We both remembered the never-ending on-call status, with the attendant night and weekend interruptions that had caused most of the stress in my prior solo practice. We needed some way to decrease the number of unnecessary telephone calls. Since having a physician-partner had led to about a 50% reduction in those calls we decided, at her suggestion, to make my (now our) patients partners in their own care.

This was not as great a change as might first be supposed. Three of our parents had been teachers and we had absorbed many of their values regarding both formal and informal education. Even before Alan joined me I had believed that an educated patient made fewer unnecessary demands on me. My efforts at teaching, however, had been sporadic and unfocused, usually consisting of what I remembered to say in the exam room and handing out a few pamphlets if they were handy. I had, at one time, purchased a VCR and half-dozen tapes and installed them in a back room. After six months of occasional use they languished there forevermore. Alan, too, had believed patient education to be important, but our attempts at this had also been episodic and not too fruitful. Neither of us actually wanted to take the initiative and devote the needed time to developing our education services. Now I was forced to invest that time.

Carol had not been idle as I frantically tried to handle my earlier practice. She had obtained a Masters in Communications with a special interest in humor from a comparatively near-by university. She had also developed a large list of mistakes she thought many doctors made in dealing with their patients, most of which she believed ultimately cost the doctors more in time than they saved. These ranged from the generic, such as issuing unexplained commands (e.g., "Take these and you'll feel better.") to the specific, such as playing pop music or soap operas in a waiting room. She was willing to become my first partner and help design a practice healthier for both the physician and the patients. We took an oft-postponed trip to see some friends in England, returned just before Memorial Day, Alan's last day, and spent the weekend reorganizing what we now considered our practice.

Our first step was to give the practice a name, "Partners In Health." The hardest part of that was the telephone. As our receptionist learned to answer "Partners In Health" patients thought they had the wrong number. Because of this one of our early projects was writing a newsletter, which we intend to print on a more-or-less monthly schedule. In it we explained that I had decided, because of the sudden growth in my patient load, to institute a number of modifications in the way I approached patient care.

One of these changes was to make better use of Carol's knowledge and talents, making her a partner in the practice. Another was to utilize more effectively the skills of the women employed in the office—they, too, would be considered partners in our healthcare endeavor. They were to provide warmth and care, not merely to be employees putting in their hours and anxiously waiting to get that last patient out of the office. The third and most important change was to make each patient (I don't like the word, but can find no better one.) a partner in his/her care, accepting as much responsibility for his or her health as appropriate. This is not as radical as it might sound, as our rural population, particularly the elderly, is still not far from the frontier traditions of independence and self help.

Our hope was, and is, that with time and increasing knowledge, each individual will assume a larger part of his own care, learning how to obtain symptomatic relief for minor complaints, and how to differentiate those from the symptoms of problems requiring my attention. We also hoped to help each of our patients educate himself about prevention of illness, through encouraging better health habits, decreasing tobacco and alcohol consumption, etc. We believed this will make our patients feel more responsible for themselves, truly partners in their own care.

As I said, Carol and I spent the Memorial Day weekend reorganizing the office, physically as well as attitudinally (we hoped). Our first requirement was to better utilize the space in our building. Because there is so much questionable "health" information available, we wanted a room in which to display hand-selected health related items. To this end we moved the office manager/bookkeeper's computer and files back to what had been Alan's office. With only a little extra effort we wired her computer into the big one at the receptionist's desk. Nightly our computers whir, updating the one in back with the day's transactions. Not only does this give the bookkeeper an up-to-date record of our accounts; it serves as an additional backup in case something should happen to the data on the front computer. In the former front office Carol has installed a small shop where she stocks books and audiotapes on diet, health, humor and self-care. We also have several small audiotape players that patients can use to listen to individual tapes. This room is open to anyone to shop in, not just waiting patients, and provides a source for items not previously available in Oakley.

No more does the latest soap opera, or a new rock tune, blare from the waiting room TV set. (In fact we no longer want to call it a "waiting room"——perhaps a relaxation room. We're not sure yet.) We put a VCR on line with the TV set and play educational videotapes, trying to gear them somewhat to the people expected to be in the room. So far we have tapes on infant care, growth and development, nutrition, first aid and pregnancy. We still maintain the VCR in the back for tapes on delivery, breast self-examination and other subjects that we did not feel appropriate for general viewing. We can show videotapes consisting simply of relaxing music and abstract and/ or pastoral scenes. We have a cassette deck, so that the TV does not need to be on all the time. The tapes we play are usually classical or "New Age" music chosen for their relaxing and soothing qualities. (Our receptionist says they relax at least one person into sleep daily.) Many patients have commented on the improved atmosphere. These tapes are also for sale, if patients want them to use at home. We have not used subliminal tapes in the waiting room as we're dubious about the propriety of that, but we do sell subliminal tapes designed to encourage weight loss, relaxation and the development of self-esteem.

This has involved quite a change in the way our staff approaches patients. Carol and I had been discussing some of these changes for years. Then after one long weekend we said to the staff, "Let's change our entire attitude." They have responded admirably. We take a half-hour every Monday afternoon for a staff meeting to discuss problems, offer suggestions and retell amusing episodes. The office atmosphere is markedly lighter, and I think there is a greater sense of working as a team. I did not expect nor achieve miraculous changes, but the staff is slowly responding.

I am trying to take more time with each patient (although at times this seems almost self-defeating). During this time I briefly explain the problem, what to watch for and why, or why not, that visit was necessary. The patients appear to appreciate this, as they see it as saving them money. I see it as ultimately saving me time. So we are both happy with this approach. We have put new patient education brochures in racks along the hall walls and in the waiting room, and the brochures disappear regularly. Carol has designated to herself the task of keeping the magazines in the waiting room up-to-date and appropriate. We are enclosing many single-sheet patient educational items in plastic sheet-holders and putting them in loose-leaf notebooks in the waiting room. Our receptionist can easily remove these and make a copy or two if a patient requests. I believe that our "waiting room" has become a much more comfortable place to sit out the inevitable delays, and our patients confirm this. Their blood pressures also confirm it. I have no statistics, but I have a distinct impression that blood pressures are a bit lower after 15 minutes spent listening to calming music than the latest rock tune.

A lot of things have changed in the nine months since we started, especially considering that I have had to carry a heavy patient load and do my part of redesigning the office in the evenings and on weekends. I have noted a marked decrease in the number of phone calls I get at home. I do get as many or more phone calls at the office as I did, but they are more to the point, and usually prevent an office call, thus saving me time and our patients' money. More patients are researching their own problems and discussing them with me, often offering suggestions about their care. (Sometimes making me do some research of my own).

For example I see a man with severe postural hypotension. He has been to innumerable doctors and had all the scans, monitors and procedures imaginable. He still has syncopal episodes secondary to his hypotension. Several weeks ago I hospitalized him after one of these episodes which had left him with a mild neurological deficit. During this hospitalization his wife asked if he could have the Shy-Drager syndrome. I had to tell her that I had heard the name, but didn't remember what it was. A little research disclosed that, indeed, he could suffer from the syndrome. I had, however, already tried one of the recommended medicines, pseudoephedrine, with minimal results. Nor did the second recommended medicine, ergotrate, relieve his symptoms. Then she came up with the use of indomethacin as a suggestion. I could not find any references to its use, but we did try it. While not a 100% cure, he is at home and able to sit up and walk short distances, better than he could do without it.

She did my research for me, saving me time and helping her husband.

Of more direct benefit to me was the response of our community to the recent influenza epidemic. I was among the first in Oakley to contract this (thanks to the fact that I had neglected to get a flu shot—a fact of which my wife dearly loves to remind me). Fortunately I got sick just before the New Years' weekend. I skipped out on the office on Friday and Saturday, then had Sunday and Monday to recover. By Tuesday I could stagger through routine office hours, but not much more. Our December-January newsletter had contained an article about influenza, its symptoms and how to treat them, and how to differentiate influenza from more serious illnesses. In the two months since then many people have proudly told me that they didn't have to bother me because they had read the newsletter. They were pleased to be partners in their own care!

Of course, the idea has drawbacks, also. Encouraging our patients to read about their illnesses and suggest approaches to their care has led to a number of phone calls about medicines and techniques that I am unwilling to try. One woman, in particular, calls me once a week to report on her mild, diet-controlled diabetes and her blood pressure, and tell me what "they" have said. This is surely more than I need to hear from her, but she feels better for the calls, and they are not much bother to me.

We plan on doing more. Carol has done nutrient analysis of foods and meals for a chef, with whom she has written two books on low-fat, low-salt cooking. She hopes to establish a program in which our patients can bring their favorite recipes in for analysis, and perhaps aid them in substituting more healthful foods in their cooking. She has considered offering evening classes on nutrition and diet as well. We believe quite strongly in the value of humor in maintaining one's health and as an adjunct in healing. Carol has presented seminars on this subject to groups as diverse as RNs and the Kansas

Cosmetology Society. We hope to utilize this approach, perhaps also through evening classes. She is working with the staff to help them realize that, although we may deal with serious problems, we do not have to be overly somber in our approach. As mentioned above, we plan on publishing a monthly newsletter, detailing more of our plans, and including recipes, jokes, information and asking for more patient suggestions.

As this is a somewhat new approach for our community, there has been some concern about the old ways of care. I have tried to reassure our patients that acute illnesses will be treated in much the same manner as in the past; we will not try to laugh away a strap throat or appendicitis. Even chronic illnesses will be managed much the same as in the past. However, in those chronic illnesses that have proven so difficult and frustrating to control, such as osteoarthritis, obesity, hypertension and chronic pain syndromes, we believe that humor, nutrition, relaxation and patient education may well be as effective, if not more so, than many of the standard medications. They certainly have less potential for harm. We also hope that this approach will give me more time for my own humor and relaxation. To this end we have established "Partners in Health" as a community health service, offering all of our patients a more active voice in their care. We have already achieved one of our goals: I am enjoying my practice more than I have for years. I believe the rest of the approaches will work much as we anticipate, to the benefit of all concerned.

*   *   *

The Older Generation Leaves

After the deaths of several members of my family I wrote about those deaths. The first of these was Charles Socolofsky, my father-in-law, in 1990.

When Did You Grow Old, Charles?

I hardly recognized the man in the coffin. Surely that gaunt, almost frail, figure was not the hearty farmer/rancher I remembered. But it was. My father-in-law died in May. He was seventy-seven years old, but his death was unexpected. I had been close to Charles, both geographically and emotionally, and had seen him frequently. The body in the coffin did not much resemble the man I loved. What had happened to the man who, when I was a young buck of twenty-two and helping him on the farm, could scoop more milo in an hour than I in a day? Or the man of sixty-six, who, with my twenty-three year old son Dean, dug a path through a snow drift in Denver to get into a garage? Even last Christmas his booming laughter and exuberance remained the same as always, although Dean did say that his pitch game was off. When did he disappear? Had this shadow in the coffin lived within that body I remember as so strong?

Today I have been looking at some pictures he saved. There are pictures of my wife Carol and me with infants, with school-age kids and with high school and college kids. Occasionally there is a picture of Charles. That is the Charles I remember, laughing, holding a horse, and teaching a grandchild with love and with humor. He ages, but he never looks old. I do not find an answer in his pictures.

Charles was always a teacher, and he left me with many lessons. One was to look within myself for the answer to a question such as this, if no obvious answer presented. Perhaps the answer does lie within me. Somehow we view those we love, especially parents, as always in the prime of life. As long as Charles was alive I was a young man, even though fifty-four years old. I am not so young today, and I will be even less young following the death of my own father. There is a protection in being the younger generation and I have lost part of that protection. Now I understand why so many people say to me when a parent dies "I didn't realize he was so sick." or "How could this happen? He has always been so strong." But when did he get so old and frail, this man who had always been my friend and teacher. Does he have further lessons for me?

I have known for some time that it was much easier for me to counsel my patients about raising their children after I had gone through the same experiences. Somehow reading about sleep lost with a fussy infant, worry over a troubled teen, or the despair that can come with the breakup of a long-term romance is not the same as having experienced those times with your own child. I have laughed with my patients and cried with my patients through the child-rearing years. As an older man I will now cry, and yes, laugh with them through the parent-losing years. Now I know what it means to lose a loved one. Not that I like it, but Charles, ever the teacher, has taught me his last lesson.

But I still don't understand, "When did you grow old, Charles? I never realized."

*   *   *

I wrote this in May 1991, after Charles' death. I expressed these thoughts about death during a short vacation in the Napa Valley of California. It was never published.

Death, What Is It? What Does It Mean?

I thought I had my feelings and beliefs about death under control. I had seen a number of people die, young and old, friends and strangers. I knew what happened. I knew what it meant. Or I thought I did. As has happened many times in the past, I never understood what was going on until it happened to me. Not that I died, but a death happened.

Almost exactly one year ago my father-in-law died. It was the first death in my immediate family. And I learned that I did have neither my feelings nor my beliefs about death as well thought out and well-ordered as I had believed. I have not been able to handle death at all well since that time. I choke up and cry when I try to talk to my friends and patients about a death. I fight death and feel a personal defeat whenever a patient dies, whether his death was expected and reasonable or unexpected and unreasonable. (Or what I deem reasonable/unreasonable.)

Why the change? Is it that I now know what it is like to lose someone important in my life? Is it that I am more acutely aware of the pain and changes death brings to the living? Is it that I hate to admit defeat, having lost someone with no chance to fight for him? Or is it that I feel I had a chance to fight for him and wasn't successful? Or am I only more aware of my own mortality?

I have no answer. I only know that in Donne's words "each man's sorrow [is] my own." I don't mind shedding tears, but weeping interferes with my work. I don't know how to handle that sorrow, or where to turn for help. My intellect, always my aid and comforter, stands in my way. I am too proud to turn to the local psychologists and psychiatrists; I think I know as much as they. Religion is scant solace. My turning that way would upset Carol, and again my knowledge and skepticism stand in my way. I am not certain that I have friends to discuss this with, because I am the one who should have all the answers. Yet I don't have this answer.

I don't even know if I need help. My experience and education tell me that time will do much to heal the loss I feel and my response to that loss. But I have two living parents and a mother-in-law. If I feel as I have for the past year after each of their deaths I may not have enough time to heal my pain.

So far I have numbed my pain with the best narcotic I know, work. But I see that that will only be partially effective. I was beginning to make mistakes, let things slide by, etc. before leaving on this vacation. I can not hide in providing shoddy care, or I will only feel worse. I truly do not know where to turn.

I have always prided myself on my ability to take care of myself. What little help I have needed from outside myself has been provided by Carol. Now she, too, is almost overwhelmed with our situation and not able to offer me much help. I am not sure that I can handle the present situation by myself. I am paralyzed by my inability to admit that and ask help, plus a lack of faith in the traditional givers of such help. I can readily see why the Catholic Church has regarded Pride as the deadliest of sins.

Yet I know that I could decide to ask for help, and do it immediately, and with few if any regrets. It is making that decision that is the sticking point. I don't want to admit that I need help and seek such help until I am sure that I actually need that help. If I can avoid it I don't want to admit my need. Certainly doesn't make much sense to me, and probably would make less sense to anyone else. Or maybe this is a stage everyone goes through prior to asking for help. How do I know? And maybe I have simply been dwelling on this until I have built this fear into a bogeyman in my head. Maybe it truly does not exist. Today I think that is correct, but today I am in the Napa Valley, California, far removed from family decisions and the practice of medicine.

I have no end to this, nor have I reached a decision. As not to decide is to decide, I will probably continue to do exactly as I have been, unless things worsen on my return to Western Kansas.

*   *   *

Both of my parents died in 1994. I wrote this to be printed in Dad's funeral bulletin; he died March 5, 1994.

This morning I heard the honk of geese. Looking up I saw the flock heading north. I cried, for the first time since his death. And I realized something of what Dad had left me. Dad was a teacher, not only by profession, but by nature. He left his boys those teaching skills. He taught us of his loves—the outdoors, sports and people. He taught us of the beauty of the prairies, the birds and the flowers. He was gentle, and he left us his gentleness. He was strong, and he left us his strength. He was possessed of a dignity based on his own sense of self, his desire to be independent and to impose on no one. During his illness he insisted on being treated as a person, and he responded in kind. He respected all people and was in turn respected. Above all, Dad was a kind and caring man. These traits are his legacy to us. We will miss him very much.

*   *   *

These were written for *Dialogue With Your Doctor*.

As most of you know by now, my father died March 5. Mother, my brothers and I certainly appreciate the cards, memorials and other condolences you have offered. I don't suppose anyone is ever ready to lose a parent, yet as such things go, Dad's death was not bad. He was diagnosed as having lung cancer that had spread to his liver in November. Always a fighter he opted for chemotherapy and a 10% chance of remission. I don't know whether the chemo helped him or not, but he didn't last long. He did, however, live alone and take care of himself until some six to eight weeks before his death. He appeared to have no appreciable pain at any time.

He was an ex-teacher and coach, who had become an insurance agent. I realize now how many of the qualities I like in myself I owe to him. Without my knowing it he taught me many a lesson, lessons about caring for people, not getting discouraged when things get tough and remaining true to myself and my beliefs. It is too bad that it required a serious illness, followed by his death, to make me aware of how much he had given me. But I did have an opportunity before he died to tell him of my appreciation for his legacy to me and of my love for him. Many are not given that chance. I hope I can continue to give to you what he has given me.

*   *   *

I also wrote of my father's death, published in *American Medical News*, Oct 10, 1994 (Copyright ©1994 American Medical Association. All rights reserved.) as

A Cold, Western Kansas Day, and Signs Of Rebirth

"I don't like what's happening to me, Dick."

"I don't either, Dad, but I don't know anything to do about it."

"I don't think there is. I'll just have to accept it."

With tears in my voice I thanked my dad for all he had given me. Not cars, money, or other such. Dad had been a teacher and insurance agent and he and Mom had never been well off. He had, instead, given me a much more valuable endowment, the heritage that has made me a successful physician. This includes the strength to bear the loads, both physical and emotional, that a small-town family physician is expected to carry. They also include his own sense of the innate value of every individual, regardless of social or financial status; Dad's joy in the simple, such as bird-watching; his enjoyment of the outdoors and his never-ending love of people.

I repeated my thanks and stumbled out the door to my car. I did not see him alive again. On the drive home my thoughts returned to the past Christmas season. Everyone around me was dying. Those of you who practice medicine will be familiar with the circumstances; I am sure you have noted the same phenomenon. There are times when all my patients are basically healthy, just sick and hospitalized. Then there are other times when everyone in the hospital is terminally ill, or nearly so. This was one of the latter. Further stress was added by the fact that the patients were my friends, individuals whom I had known and cared for for years.

Ernie had been battling lung cancer for six months. His main complaint at present was that he couldn't eat and was losing weight and strength. I hoped to be able to get him home to the care of his wife and family sometime before Christmas. Hard work and a large dollop of luck accomplished this.

Betty had recently been hospitalized here, then in Wichita, with cardiomyopathy and profound congestive heart failure. She had been home only a day or two before developing pneumonia and reappearing at our hospital. She was afebrile and went home on the 24th. I thought she might do well.

I didn't have such hopes for Lucille. For two years she had valiantly battled a carcinoma of the colon that had metastasized to her liver and elsewhere. Her oncologist had told her that there was nothing more he could offer her; that she should come home and enjoys her two delightful granddaughters. She was in my care because of sepsis and I knew that she would not be dismissed before Christmas. My hospital patients were not encouraging.

It was no better at home. Preparations there were harried. My mother had been diagnosed as having breast cancer in the spring of 1993. When a mastectomy revealed positive axillary nodes neither her surgeon nor I felt that she would tolerate chemotherapy. My father had completed his first course of chemotherapy for cancer of the lung, metastatic to his liver, in early December. He was to return for his second course just after the New Year. All of their children, grandchildren and great-grandchildren were gathering at our house, for what we knew would be the last Christmas we would all be together. While happy and peaceful on the surface, the season was not bringing the joyous reunions of past Christmases.

Christmas Day dawned bright and clear, not even cold. My first phone call from the hospital was to tell me that I had a young woman in labor, certainly fitting for the day.

I went to the hospital to check her. All was well. Lucille received her IV antibiotics and went home to be with her family. Before I left the hospital, however, Betty's husband called. She was weak and short of breath. Could I see her? Of course I could see her. X-rays revealed some worsening of her CHF, and she was febrile again. I admitted her and went home for dinner. I could not get cancer off my mind, but tried hard to enter into the Christmas mood, as were the other members of my family.

Evening rounds disclosed that Lucille had enjoyed her day at home immensely. The OB was doing fine, although her labor was quite desultory. Betty was feeling better. My parents had both seemed stronger and more alert than for some time. Our customary family games produced the usual laughter, not apparently forced. Mother had reverted to her old self and directed us in getting the family pictures she wanted, brooking no interference. Our parents presented us each with a gift none of us had anticipated. Dad had taken the material to the nursing home where Mom lived and for a year they had been making a memory book for each child and grandchild. Mine contained things ranging from my baptismal certificate to the celebration in Oakley of my thirtieth year of practice there, just the summer before. Many tears were shed, but mostly in private. All in all, not a bad day given the circumstances.

I returned to the hospital at 3:30 AM on the 26th, expecting an easy delivery. It was not to be so. With some Pitocin® augmentation her contractions picked up. I was in the middle of a low forceps delivery when Betty coded. I was the only doctor in town. The only nurse in the hospital was assisting me in the delivery, as was a physician's assistant student who had remained with us over Christmas. I sent both of them down to the code, while I did what I could to further speed up the delivery. Before I finished they had returned, saying that Betty was again breathing and had a sinus rhythm. We then delivered a healthy, 8 1/2-pound boy, the best present of all.

Betty was airlifted to Wichita, where she died on New Year's Day. Ernie returned on New Year's Eve, with a raging pneumonia. He died on January 5th. Lucille lived another month or so, and then died in a referral hospital, fighting gamely to the end. My parents returned to their hometown, 45 miles from me, Dad to complete his chemo, Mom back in the nursing home. Both of them probably handled their illnesses better than I have.

Now it has ended. I spent Thursday afternoon with Dad. That evening he called my two brothers to say "Good-bye." Friday the home where Mom resides took her to see him. She later told me all he could do was hold her hand and say, "I'm sorry." I'm sure he was. After almost fifty-nine years of marriage he was sorry to leave her, especially because she was dependent on him for so many things that he would no longer be able to provide. Sorry that he was the first to die; no one had expected that. And sorry that he could not continue to offer her his love, as he had for all those years.

I received a phone call from the nurse on duty at his hospital early Saturday morning. He was much weaker. Before I could dress and leave she called back with the news that he had died. Dad, a very private and orderly person, had died much as he had lived. He said his farewells, apologized for not being able to complete the most important task of his life, and died in peace and privacy.

We buried him March 8, 1994. It was a cold, Western Kansas spring day. But that morning, as I left for the church, I heard the honking of a flock of geese, northward bound. Meadowlarks sang for the graveside service. Dad taught me to know and appreciate these signs of spring and rebirth. It was only fitting that they should offer me solace at his death and help provide the strength needed to return to my practice, where my patients continue to depend on me for the strength and caring he gave me and taught me to offer others.

*   *   *

These were my thoughts on my mother's death in *Dialogue With Your Doctor*.

Once again I would like to offer my thoughts about a parent to you. Since this is occasioned by the death of my second parent I think I can assure you that it will not happen again. My mother was born July 29, 1911, the third daughter of a minister in the Church of the Brethren, whom I remember as a kindly, but stern, man. I remember Mother as an intense, intelligent and ambitious woman. She must have displayed these traits even as a girl, for she graduated from McPherson College with a degree in chemistry in 1934, definitely a woman ahead of her time. My father was a classmate and they were married in 1935.

I am certain that living through the depression left a permanent mark on them, as it did on many of you. She cared deeply for her three sons, but this love was not often expressed in words. With those words she tended to our education, discussing things with us, arguing with us, and correcting us if necessary (rarely). She did not like to be wrong, and not often could we prove her so, but all of her children persisted in our attempts. She imbued all of us with a lifelong love of learning. Many of the traits that have made me a successful doctor have come to me as her legacy. As I have grown older I have become more aware of what she has given me. I have also realized how much influence Mother had on all of us, most of the time without our being aware of it. She once told me she would have liked her three boys to be a doctor, a teacher and a minister. She got two out of three, the minister turned out to be an engineer. But I doubt that she was really happy with that 67% success rate. She expected a great deal of us and I'm certain she expected the same of herself. I have much to thank her for.

It is a strange feeling to now find myself the eldest member of my family, and it's a feeling that I don't particularly care for. I'm certain that many of you have experienced it as well. Not exactly an expectation that I will be the next to die, but the sense that there is no longer a generation between me and whatever lies over that divide. Somehow I have lost a protection, something that insulated me from the thoughts of my own mortality. Perhaps, with time, these feelings will fade in intensity. Or I will simply come to accept them as part of an ever-learning, ever-changing me. I miss both of my parents; I would like them as they used to be, as many of you knew them when they came to Oakley to watch their grandchildren in school activities. Their losses, and my new position, have generated many new feelings and ideas within me. It will be extremely interesting to see where these lead me.

*　　*　　*

Carol's mother's death on September 27, 1999 was somewhat different than any of the others. She was eighty-seven when she died and had been a semi-invalid for two or three years. Her younger daughter, Barbara, had lived with her in Scott City for several years. Had Barb not been willing to care for her mother, either Carol would have had to care for her or have convinced (or have tried to convince) her to move to a nursing home. She would not have gone willingly to a home. I'm not certain we could have managed that. She was tough, truly from the pioneer stock she came. Barb saved the day. Caroline had failed during the last few years of her life and her death was no surprise. And I, while not immune to family deaths, was more experienced during the deaths of my parents. But she was the last of my parents and parents-in-law. Carol and I are now the old folks, a description we don't relish.

*　　*　　*

This was a letter I wrote to *American Medical News* in 1991. I was dismayed at how the writers had managed to finagle a DNR (do not resuscitate) order from an elderly Christian woman. To me, both then and now (2010), believe that a physician convincing a patient that heaven would be better than life on earth is not a physician's task.

LETTERS/ADL
AMERICAN MEDICAL NEWS
515 N. STATE ST.
CHICAGO, ILL 60610

Dear Sirs:

"Helping a patient decide to let go?" "Ethics Committee?" I am appalled at the article by Dr. Misbin. I am not black, female nor particularly religious, but if the tricking of an elderly woman into what appears to me to be an equivocal acquiescence to a DNR order represents the way medical ethics is now taught, give me my old teachers of medicine. They taught me to respect my patients and their beliefs without using any such high-sounding words as "ethics."

In my almost thirty years of practice I have learned only too well that our patients die, all of them, some quickly and some after a prolonged and painful illness. I, too, help patients and their families make DNR decisions. But I try to be honest with them. I was taught, and continually relearn through experience, that the best way to approach a dying (or any other) patient is with compassion, kindness and respect.

It does not seem to me that Dr. Misbin shows any of the three of these in his approach to Mrs. Jones. Rather, it appears that he regards her as a challenge, a chance to show that he can succeed where her attending and even a kindred soul (another black woman) could not. (Why he thought a third-year medical student who did not know the patient was a logical choice to approach her about this decision is beyond me, even if she was black and female.) It further appears that he takes advantage of a simple woman's simple religious beliefs to get a questionable "Yes" to the DNR order.

Both he and her attending also appear to laugh, not only at the patient, but also at their success in using something we almighty doctors know is only hokum to achieve their ends. I'm sure the bookkeepers and DRG-minders in their hospital were delighted. I'm not sure the other patients should be too pleased by this approach. Perhaps this is state of the art "Medical Ethics" and "Quality Care" in Florida. If it is, give me the wilds of Western Kansas and a six-gun when my turn comes and I'll care for myself.

Yours,
Richard V. Ohmart, M.D.

*   *   *

Published in *American Medical News*, in 1991 (Copyright ©1991 American Medical Association. All rights reserved.) as

For Old Style Doctor, Medicine is His Life, Not Merely a Job

ANACHRONISM—"Anything that is or seems to be out of its proper time in history"

Am I an anachronism? I'm not certain, but judging from my correspondence of late I just may be.

I am a fifty-four year old physician, Fellow of the American Academy of Family Practice, Board Certified in Family Practice. I am also the only physician in a rural community of 3000 souls. This makes me on call virtually all the time. The people who comprise my patient load are my neighbors and my friends. There exists between us a mutual respect that has been carefully nurtured throughout the 27 years I have practiced here. I have built this practice and I love it. I don't believe I am a martyr. My practice is not, of course, perfect. Some days are quite long; calls interrupt my personal activities, etc. The most frustrating problems concern government and third party regulations and restrictions. All those are usually fairly minor hassles compared to the joys of my practice, however. This is medicine as I envisioned it as a youth. Yet it does not seem to be medicine as most physicians in training now anticipate it.

It seems to me that an era in American medicine is passing. Perhaps the type of medicine I enjoy can only be practiced in a rural community which history has almost passed by. Our small farmers hang on by the skin of their teeth. The small retail businesses depend on those who are not easily mobile. They purchase locally rather than go to nearby, cheaper Target or Wal-Mart stores. I try to practice up-to-date medicine in a solo rural practice.

Perhaps we are all anachronisms. I recently received a letter from the fine young physician who had joined me after he finished a Family Practice residency. The son of a small town physician, he came to Oakley expecting to care for his friends as he had seen his father do. He found, however, that the never-ending call, low payments and third party interference did not let him do that. He had less time to spend with his family than he desired. About a year and a half ago he left Oakley for an Emergency Room job. I could not blame him for leaving then and I cannot now. He did what was right for his family and his own future. In his letter he mentions some of the irritations we all face in our practices, then goes on to say, " . . . the sad thing is that I (and many other physicians) cope by having a job rather than a profession."

I would have to agree that most of the medical students for whom I serve as preceptor are also looking for a good job, rather than a profession. Eight-hour days with little night call, shared responsibilities, and good wages—these are the qualities that they seek after their residencies. There is certainly nothing wrong with any of this, but it seems to me that they are missing the great heritage of medicine by reducing our profession to a job. They cannot be blamed, however. They see medicine as it now exists, constrained and limited by regulations promulgated by those interested in "quality of care" and "cost-effective medicine" (Are they the same thing, or mutually exclusive?)

I feel sorry for them, for most of them will not have the thrill of seeing the boy he delivered and whose broken arm he fixed last year score this year's winning touchdown. She will miss seeing the kid from the wrong side of the tracks get a scholarship and a college degree, or deliver a baby for a young woman she also delivered. They will miss many of the rewards of medicine. But they have other rewards, rewards that I have never had. Most of all, they have time for themselves.

There is certainly no moral value attached to either of these choices, one is not "good" and the other "bad." But I, too, think it is sad that few young physicians will know the pleasures, yes and heartbreaks, of a practice such as mine. I'm too old to change my style of practice, and I'm not sure I would if I could. I enjoy my life/practice (they are one and the same) in Oakley too much. I will continue to try to live with the new order, even as I mourn the passing of the old. When I can no longer reconcile the two I will give up the profession I love, either for retirement or a job.

*   *   *

This was written in September, 1990 and published in *American Medical News* (Copyright ©1990 American Medical Association. All rights reserved.) as

I'm Living My Dream, But the Costs Are Mounting

Years ago, longer than I care to think, I argued with my best friend and high school classmate about our futures. Both of us wanted to be doctors, but within those dreams our ambitions varied widely. He thought that specialization was the only way to practice medicine, and he went on to get a Ph.D. in steroid biochemistry as he completed an OB/GYN residency. I was sure that a family practice in a small town, much like the one we were growing up in, was the way I wanted to practice medicine. I have now been practicing as I dreamed for twenty-six years. However, reality is finally intruding and I am not sure whether I have been lucky or not.

I finished high school in a rural Western Kansas town, then attended the University of Kansas, both as an undergraduate and for my medical education. I was married as a senior in college and my wife presented me with a boy during each of my first two years in medical school. I completed a rotating internship at Wesley Medical Center in Wichita, as this was before the establishment of Family Practice residencies. We then moved to Oakley, Ks in the summer of 1963, where I joined an established physician in family (or as it was then called, general) practice. I was as proud as anyone could be that I was actually a doctor and able to practice as I had dreamed. Our third child, a girl, was born shortly after we moved to Oakley. I joined the AAFP, and became Board Certified when the American Board of Family Practice was established. I was on top of the world, ready to do battle with all that might threaten my flock.

How things have changed in twenty-six years! I still love my practice. The people whom I serve are not just my patients, they are my friends, individuals with whom I have spent one half of my life, and I would have it no other way. Yet the practice of medicine is not as much fun as it once was. The man I joined in practice when I first came to Oakley, although he died in 1971, becomes wiser as I grow older. After a friend of his died following a protracted hospitalization, Jim said to me "It sure isn't as much fun to practice now as it was when my friends were all young and healthy."

I have reached that plateau now. Every thrill, such as delivering a baby for a young woman whom I also delivered, is matched by the grief of seeing a friend inexorably aging and growing weaker, or devastated by cancer, or herself losing a child who lived elsewhere. These are only part of the practice of medicine as I have understood it, an unpleasant part, to be sure, but nevertheless part and parcel of the whole. These I had expected and prepared, as best I could, to face.

I was, and have remained, totally unprepared to confront other unpleasant facets of contemporary medicine; problems that have made me seriously question whether I want to continue my present practice. These are all related and compose the following triad:

- the constraints imposed on my judgment and care by government rules and regulations;
- the specter of a malpractice suit, which always seems to be lurking in the back of my mind; and
- the declining financial rewards of my rural family practice.

Although not necessarily the most important, I will turn to the financial question first. I have never believed that I should get rich practicing medicine, but I did expect to earn a good living while doing what I enjoyed. I did this easily initially, perhaps too easily. My wife and I grew up in post World War II America, with every year bringing more income to our families than the prior year. After we established our practice and home in Oakley we continued to live in that fashion (not wise, but easy to do). We borrowed money to build a large house while our children were still home to enjoy it, and then borrowed more money to travel and help educate those children.

Twin crashes in the farm economy and the oil economy, the two major sources of income in our rural area, forced us to make major adjustments in our lifestyle, tightening our belts. I can't complain about this as everyone else in our community was in the same boat. We decreased our travel and other discretionary spending and paid our debts. Then our financial situation changed dramatically when I was joined by a partner in 1983. I had anticipated that our practice would grow enough to pay his way over a period of a few years. The practice, at least when measured by patients seen, has grown. But net income has been woefully short of keeping pace with that growth. We have not been able to increase our fees as rapidly as our expenses have risen.

Increasing our fees does not bring a corresponding increase in income as about fifty per cent of our patients are Medicare age and we accept assignment, so we end up writing off much of any increase. (Last year about eleven per cent of our total charges were written off for this reason. We wrote off slightly over twenty-five per cent of a Medicare patient's office call fees, for example.) Because we live and practice in an economically depressed rural area many of our other patients find it difficult to pay our fees, especially those for more expensive procedures. We have many patients who do not qualify for Medicaid, but do not have money to spare for medical care. We see very few who actually try to avoid payment. Most will attempt to pay, but pay slowly. This is part of the traditional payment profile of family physicians, and we understand the problems of those attempting to pay us. It is the decreased Medicare payments that are hurting us that we resent, and that may well drive us from Oakley.

The malpractice problem is another major contribution to my present unrest. In spite of the fact that I have developed that ephemeral "rapport" with my patients so talked about in medical school, the fear of a suit, valid or not, is always present, although perhaps not as strong as it might be in other practice circumstances. As the general economic level of the community has fallen I have become a bit more leery. Physicians in surrounding towns have been sued by local residents. Insurance money might look much better to a couple facing bankruptcy than to the same couple if they were well off. A possible reward might push them to actions that would have been unthinkable a few years ago. Try as I will, I cannot always rid my mind of the "What if . . ." as I make my medical decisions.

This, too, is an expected and comparatively minor irritation. The greatest effect malpractice has on my practice is financial. My malpractice premiums have risen by 500% in the past five years. That premium is expected to jump another 50% this year. Obstetrics is responsible for a large part of this increase. Both my partner and I deliver babies, and we believe that is a foundation of family practice. The number of births in our area has declined to only thirty-six in our hospital last year. Yet we must pay the same malpractice premium as a family physician in Wichita or Kansas City, who may deliver a hundred or more babies a year. We continue to deliver babies, but at a financial loss. This seems to be the way our practice is headed; we are doing more, but losing money as we do it. As the old retailer says, "I know I lose money on every sale, but I hope to make it up in volume." I am not sure how much longer I can "make it up in volume".

The remaining factor, and the one that I find most difficult to deal with, is Medicare (and other third party) constraints on the way I practice medicine. It appears to me ridiculous that Medicare will pay referral physicians and hospitals $20-$30,000 for delicate and complicated attacks on the problems my patients develop. They then balk at the $150 a day it would cost to keep that patient in our hospital for a short time to enable her to return to her home. We must see at least one patient a week who has had some brilliant medical or surgical procedure performed elsewhere and been told "Your time is up. You can go home now." Often she (usually) can't go home, because she is not strong enough to care for herself, she is a widow and her children have all moved from the community.

Sometimes, true to tradition, friends and neighbors can care for her and help her regain her strength. Sometimes no one is available to do this, or the care needed is too complicated for untrained and usually elderly friends to provide. This consigns many of my friends to the nursing homes, which are fine as custodial care providers, but not at all good at rehabilitation. It seems to me that this wastes the initial monetary outlay, only prolonging a non-productive life in a custodial institution. I think that either a commitment should be made to provide funds to complete a course of therapy leading to an optimum outcome, or the initial major expense should not be made. (Although I would not like to decide who was to receive what level of care.)

My most difficult decisions regard whom to hospitalize and when to do it, immediately followed by thoughts of "How can I justify this to a Medicare reviewer?" I find myself sorely tempted to fudge and overdiagnose and overtreat when a friend/patient is acutely ill and unable to manage at home, yet perhaps not quite ill enough to justify an admission to those reviewers. What am I to do with that person? I know that it is not safe to leave him at home. My training and experience say that he should be in the hospital, and this is where I would like to place him.

In our community there is no source of intermediate care. On one side lurks a Medicare denial and review of the quality of my care if too many denials are made. On the other skulks the possibility of a malpractice suit if poor old Joe is sent home with a prescription and instructions to return if he worsens, then falls and breaks a hip at home, or does not realize he is worsening until too late, or, even worse, does not call me because he "hates to bother me" again. Many children, often feeling guilty about having moved away and not visiting as much as they think they should, are quick to look for someone to blame if any of these happen. I don't know how to care for my friends when I am placed in this double-bind situation, a situation with which I am sure most of you are familiar.

These are the problems that wear me down; decreasing income with an increasing work load, how to justify actions that a few years ago were considered "good medicine" in that they viewed the patient not only as a sick person, but as an individual in a specific social setting and treated him accordingly, and how best to care for my friends and neighbors without lying or otherwise being dishonest. I do not regret that my children have not chosen medical careers. At this time the rewards of my practice still outweigh the problems. Another doubling of malpractice premiums may make it financially impossible to remain here. More pressure from third-party insurance people may simply make the hassle not worth the reward. Or I may simply age and wear down until I cannot handle the stresses involved. I see my dream of providing a lifetime of care for my friends fading before me. For twenty-six years I have enjoyed living my dream. I guess that I have been lucky, as not many men have been so blessed.

Addendum—Since I completed the above my partner has been lured away to a salaried job with regular hours. This has left me the sole physician in our community of about 3000. I think I am still enjoying my practice, when I have time to think about it. The problems still exist, but do not seem to be as important. Maybe my dream is due to continue for another twenty-six years.

*   *   *

I wrote this in September 1990 and was published in *American Medical News*, March 1991 (Copyright ©1991 American Medical Association. All rights reserved.) as

In Private Practice, Doctor Feels Like a Public Utility

"Oh, Doc, while I've got you would you take a look at this spot on my leg?" And with that the attractive young blond lifted her skirt. Up it went, and up and up. A lacy panty edge appeared. Then I saw white skin, nary a trace of suntan. At last a tiny spot appeared, so small I could barely detect it and looking down through my trifocals was not helping. I was hesitant to kneel on the floor in front of her to better visualize it. I was in a quandary! Why should this be a problem? you ask. It wouldn't in my office, but this encounter was in an aisle of the local supermarket. The number of onlookers was growing in direct proportion to the length of leg showing. Finally I mumbled something about it being harmless and tried to continue my shopping.

I really don't care how much anatomy my patients' display in the supermarket, or anywhere else. This simply illustrates my contention that a doctor has very little privacy, regardless of where he or she is. I have been cornered and questioned at church, at football games, at plays and on the street. My phone rings regardless of the time of day (or night) or my activity. Eating and sleeping have become activities measured by the number of calls. It seems as if the whole community must know when I head for the bathroom. No sooner do I get settled on the throne, journal in hand, than the phone rings. I have conquered that little problem by learning to take a phone with me. My only challenge is what to answer when the caller asks "What are you doing, Doc?"

Some time ago the phone caught me in the midst of some amorous moments with my wife. What was the crisis? One of my patients, evidently forgetting that I had done a vasectomy on her husband, was calling to tell me that the condom her partner (or was it her husband?) was using had broken at a most inopportune time. What could she do? She did not appreciate my suggestion of a cold water douche. But her call had certainly doused my ardor with cold water. All I could do was laugh.

Not that I object too much, this is the way the doctors I knew as a boy lived and somewhat the life I expected in a small town. But my friends in the cities tell similar stories. And we insist on saying that we're in "private" practice.

When I stop to think about it (which I rarely do, as it's too depressing) I believe that most doctors are truly considered and treated as public utilities. We are expected to provide service twenty-four hours a day, seven days a week. No request from the public can safely be ignored. More and more, our fees (read rates) are regulated by the government. There is a growing movement to tell us how to treat each and every disease. What more does one need to define a public utility?

I have friends who say they hate to go to the store, out to eat, to parties, etc. because they are known to be doctors. Questions come from patients and acquaintances alike. Nowhere are we safe. I have not gone to the extreme of becoming a hermit, but a cave, not equipped with a phone, sometimes seems appealing. I have tried a number of dodges to retain some privacy. The old joke about the doctor telling his patient to strip when asked a clinical question at a party used to work. Now I am afraid a nude would confront me if I used that. For years I have told people who called me at home because "I hated to bother you at the office" that I could not answer their questions or prescribe without their charts, which were at the office. Does this discourage them? Not a bit! They simply reply that they will call and remind Theresa in the morning, and she can get me their chart. Nor does playing dumb work. By now everyone knows me too well for that to be successful. As a last resort I have decided that I will just accept my public position and live with it. It takes much less of my time to quickly answer a question or agree to at least look at a chart the next day than it does to hem and haw while searching for a reason to refuse.

What has this attitude brought me? Calls to ask about last years' medicines. Calls to check on the progress of someone in the hospital. Calls to ask about birth control pills. Calls about hemorrhoids, vaginitis, STDs, you name it. It seems like people feel more comfortable calling me at home about truly "personal" problems than about visiting me in the office. Callers ask me to renew prescriptions that I didn't write in the first place, but those are easy to screen and refuse, and then I know who is getting medicines from other doctors. In my absence Carol, my wife, is asked to answer medical questions. Those requiring only a good mother's advice are easy for her to handle; the more complex ones are not. A short while back a patient described in more detail than Carol wanted to hear his troubles with constipation and difficulty moving his bowels. She could not get away from him. Finally, in desperation, she suggested that he actually see the doctor. Apparently this was not the answer he wanted, as he failed to show up.

I do draw the line, however, at having patients drop by my house. I don't believe I have ever seen a patient there and don't intend to. On the very rare occasion when someone has suggested that, I simply say that I have no instruments at home and will meet him at the hospital. This is quite true, although intentionally so.

I have looked at innumerable people at school activities, movies, etc. with no untoward consequences. I am amazed, however, at the intimate details people will reveal to me in a grandstand or a restaurant. Somehow sexual problems, itches, urges and the ilk must be easier to discuss in a non-clinical setting. At least two pregnancies have been announced to the world as the mother-to-be questioned me at a ballgame. One divorce followed a woman's revelations to me at the local restaurant. And many other juicy stories have originated with my public-utility practice.

What have I gained from this? Some satisfaction in helping my patients when they need assistance. I think I have better control of my time. And a rare incident of importance. A young woman who had grown up in Oakley and moved away recently asked me to look at a mole on her shoulder while we both were at her sister's wedding. Her strapless gown uncovered the reddish-black lesion I knew only too well. She followed my recommendation and had it removed, finding it was a malignant melanoma. So far, a year later, she is doing well. Both her mother and I were glad for my public utility practice in that instance.

Addendum—As I review this essay twenty years later, the young woman has had no further problem with her melanoma.

*   *   *

This also was written in September 1990. I don't remember whether I simply had more time or whether I had more urge to write.

Burnout? I Never Had the Time!

I have heard and read a lot about "burnout" in the last few years, but not thought much about it. With a little time on my hands to consider the idea, I feel rather left out. I have practiced medicine in the same repetitious setting for the past 27 years without burning out. I've kept the same wife, raised three kids to more-or-less normal adulthood and not become an alcoholic or developed other addictions. I arise every morning, knowing that I will do about what I do every day. (I don't like non-routine days because they often involve auto accidents, other major trauma, or tasks that involve increased stress for me.) But I continue to enjoy my practice. To what do I owe this amazing good fortune?

I think that most of the thanks must go to my parents and my wife. I was raised in rural Kansas where my parents taught me two important values. One was the work ethic still found widely in the area. The other was that one got out of life about what one put into it. These lessons were quite valuable during my education and have remained helpful throughout my professional life. However, if unbalanced, they might well predispose to early burnout. Carol, my wife, has provided the leavening that my early experience and education needed. Even as a teenager she seemed to have surprising insight into both herself and the world.

Our first major decision came during my senior year in medical school, when I was deciding on a specialty and a career. My two choices were an internal medicine residency and a career in academic medicine or rural family practice. She went to a few meetings held by faculty wives—meetings intended to teach the student-wives how to behave as proper doctors' wives in academic medicine. She then told me that if that were the kind of wife I needed I had better find another woman. As we already had two children and a lot of debt, I didn't think that was such a good idea. So off to rural Kansas we went, and I've not had time to burn out, burn up, or even smolder more than a bit since.

I joined an older man in practice in 1963. After 8 years he died, leaving me the sole physician in our community. I practiced this way for about ten years. Then came a succession of young doctors, including a partner who left a year and a half ago, again leaving me the only physician in our community. During this time I have been fortunate to have stumbled onto many methods of coping with my situation.

Have I ever tired of what I was doing? Certainly! Early in my career a number of problems, concerning both my practice and my family, led me to call the psychiatry department at the medical school from which I had graduated. Did they have an opening in their residency program, perhaps next July 1? A return call assured me that I could start next week. That was too soon and too frightening for me, so I remained where I was. At other times I have considered teaching, locum tenens work, ER work, "Doc in the Box" work, and even quitting medicine to farm. For one reason or another, these have all been discarded. The bottom line is "I like what I am doing too much to leave it."

Family? My family has been supportive, although I have also fought to make time for them. For many years Carol and I argued over her feeling that I put my patients and practice ahead of her. I insisted she came first. I finally had to admit that she was correct. Once I had done this, she found it much easier to live with that situation. Our kids grew up knowing that there were things that came before my activities with them, although I knew that my time with them was important and spent as much time with them as possible. I think they understood and accepted this.

Carol, who has been my source of change, dragged me off to an encounter group, back in the days when those were popular. I found this so stimulating that we returned a couple of years later. These two episodes added a lot to my self-knowledge and willingness to take risks and to change. Carol has also supported me through episodes that might well have driven a less resourceful woman away. Some time after the first encounter session I came home at 2:00 one morning and announced to Carol that I was in love with a younger woman. I had delivered this girl's baby a year before, and then she had been divorced. She had recently seen me because of a depression and we were working on hospitalizing her. After I finished a delivery at our hospital I found a note at the nurse's desk to call her. She wanted to talk to me. The new, risk-taking me said "Sure. Where?"

She said, "Could you come over here? My son is asleep and I don't have any way to leave him."

So off I went, for a four-hour conversation, then home to tell Carol of my new love. Carol's reply was "You're just in lust. Turn over and go to sleep. You have to get up in the morning."

My "love" turned out to be an early morning-fatigue phenomenon, but we did become very close friends. Carol, in her wisdom, also became her close friend, and we all remain friends to this day.

When our kids were young I worked hard to find time to be with them, not just on birthdays and holidays, but every day. This was not out of a sense of duty, but because I liked to play with them, read to them and hear of their activities. But I was not always successful. At first I was angry when the calls of medicine interrupted these activities, but I learned that anger hurt no one but me. I remember one Christmas Eve in particular. My grandmother was visiting and we had just started eating dinner when the phone rang. The bus had dumped a sick young woman and her child off at the bus stop. Someone had taken them to the hospital and I was asked to see her. Fuming at the interruption I drove to the hospital and slammed into the ER, sure that I was being taken advantage of.

What I found was a frightened, sick girl, holding a baby. A few antibiotics for her bronchitis, and my work was done. There remained the question of what to do with her, as the next bus was 12 hours away, and the bus stop was at a now closed gas station. Fortunately the hospital administrator was a friend and he said to let her sleep at the hospital. They also fed her. The police took her to the bus stop in time to continue her trip home the next morning.

Financially I was taken advantage of; the girl had no money. Medically I was not defrauded. She was not seriously ill, but she did need help. I had to eat a cold dinner, not a major loss. Emotionally I profited and grew from experiences such as this. It took several similar episodes before I learned that, as sure as I got angry about being "bothered," I would find a patient that needed my help more than I needed my time off. I then would end up feeling guilty about my anger. So I stopped getting angry. That certainly made me easier to live with and work with. A minister friend who convinced me that people are almost always doing the best they can, and another encounter group session that helped me see some of the reasons for my anger and controlling behavior were also important in this change.

As our kids grew up I tried to attend their school plays, concerts and ball games. The nurses at the hospital learned basic triage and would not call me away from these activities for less than true medical emergencies. I would call them afterwards to see if I was needed for minor problems. Because it was important to me to attend these school activities and since I was in solo practice I could do about what I wanted as far as to when see a patient, etc. Although I initially believed that a good doctor was literally always at the beck and call of his patients I slowly learned that patients could, many times, be asked to wait, or even obtain care elsewhere if it was important enough to me.

However some things, such as deliveries, won't wait. The closest I came to missing one of my boy's varsity basketball games involved an OB. She was in early labor and the game was 50 miles away. I knew that she would deliver before the game was over, so I reluctantly decided that I would miss that game. I sent Carol on to the game then lay down in the room next to the labor room to listen to the girls' game on the radio. Suddenly I heard my patient scream, "Help! It's coming!"

All I had to do was move 30 feet from one room to the other, but the baby was lying in the bed when I arrived. I cut the cord, delivered the placenta, thanked the mother and took off for the ball game, arriving just at tip-off. While that kind of cooperation was unusual, the people of Oakley have always taken care of me.

Whenever I have felt the need for a challenge, I have been able to find an activity outside of medicine to provide it. In my early forties I learned to become a pilot. In my fifties I have had the challenge of computers to master. I have begun to write, which is a great pleasure. Photography has always been a hobby offering distractions and challenges. My rural practice remains a joy and a source of great pleasure.

So I have avoided the specter of burnout. Carol has helped immensely, as have my patients. The fact that I am living where I choose and doing what I like is certainly important. My practice is much as I envisioned it in my early days, but continues to change and grow. I keep developing new interests and new friends. Certainly I get tired. I have never liked the late-night calls. And there are times I wish I were doing something else. But I know of nothing I would rather do. I just haven't had time to burn out.

*   *   *

This was written in May 1991. It was written as a letter to the editor at *Time* magazine but never published.

What a piece of work is man! How noble in reason! How infinite in faculties . . . In action how like an angel! In apprehension, how like a god!

The above lines echo in my mind like some half-forgotten litany, triggered by an amazing confluence of items. Yesterday I watched the news on TV. Our country celebrated our glorious victory over a third rate power in the Persian Gulf with the "largest celebration since World War II." At a cost of $12,000,000, men marched, airplanes flew and 25,000 hotdogs, 40,000 pieces of chicken and 50,000 pieces of candy were consumed. Three tons of trash was left at the end of the day.

Today, I picked up the June 10, 1991 issue of *TIME* magazine. "EVIL—Does it exist—or do bad things just happen?" is the question on the cover. The essay by Lance Morrow is thought provoking as a stand-alone article. But when I read the article *Watching Children Starve to Death*, with the refrain from Ivan Karamazov, "What have children to do with it, tell me, please?" fresh in my mind, I know what one form of evil is. It is the peculiar mind-set that lets our nation celebrate in such an obscene way while we continue to be responsible for the starvation and lack of medical care of children, specifically of the Persian Gulf states, but generically of the world.

No one could be happier than I that only 376 of our troops died in the Gulf, and that injuries were relatively few. Nor do I think that the troops should be made to feel shame for their part in the Persian Gulf fracas. But I do believe that a moral vacuum must exist in our leadership. Is this the "New World Order" of which our president spoke so glowingly? That children starve while we create three tons of trash in an afternoon in Washington? That a can of infant formula costs $60 (if it can be found) in Iraq, while we spend $12,000,000 so that troops can march, airplanes can fly and people can watch fireworks for an afternoon and evening? If that is not evil I contend that evil does not exist.

As I read the articles and pondered my thoughts I drifted, almost unknowingly, to the refrigerator, dished myself some ice cream and ate it. Not just any ice cream, but "frozen dairy dessert," specially formulated with less fat and calories so that my palate and psyche could have the solace of the cold, rich taste without my body having to struggle with even more calories than it already is asked to handle. Infant formula sits in my office, outdated. It was given me by salesmen, for me in turn to give to mothers and infants. On a somewhat smaller scale I, too, am guilty of the evil of self-content, jarred out of my semi-coma only occasionally by something like the juxtaposition of the celebration in Washington and the reality of our world. But, I say, I am not a person of power. What can I do?

I can at least make my position known. I can resolve to be sure that I get all the formula left me to an infant who needs it. Needy children do live in Western Kansas, too. And I can give the money that often goes unnecessarily into my stomach to one of the relief organizations. That seems a bare minimum, but if we all did a bit, perhaps the evil our world inflicts on the weak and helpless would be somewhat mitigated.

I think a quote from Pascal may be more appropriate than the one from Shakespeare with which this essay started.

What a chimera is man! what a confused chaos! what a subject of contradiction! a professed judge of all things, and yet a feeble worm of the earth! the great depository and guardian of truth, and yet a mere huddle of uncertainty! the glory and the scandal of the universe!

*   *   *

I wrote this in August 1991. It had been a tough weekend, so I relaxed by writing it. This also was never published.

We Have a Long Weekend

Would you care to join the new country doc for a weekend? Careful, now, it isn't all fun and games. This is a rural, take all comers, practice, where I'm on call all of the time. A senior from the University of Kansas Medical School accepted my offer, not for just a weekend, but a month as she served her rural precepteeship. This is the story of her first weekend on call with me.

We spent Friday afternoon in my office, a routine afternoon. We did, however, see four kids from the same family for routine physicals. They ranged in age from almost 2 to 6. The family had recently moved to the area and managed one of those cut-rate gas stations that line our interstate highways. The mother seemed fine, although a bit overwhelmed, but who wouldn't be? They had a Title XIX (Medicaid) card to supplement, what I knew from past experience, the meager earnings from the station. I told the student that I thought the family might, with a little luck, be able to survive financially.

Shortly after I arrived home my phone rang. The nurse on duty at the hospital was calling to tell me that the ambulance was heading east to pick up an infant that had been hit by a car. No sooner had I hung up than my daughter called to tell me that it was not my grandson—she had heard the call on their police scanner, and they lived in the area of the accident. I certainly appreciated that call as the evening unfolded. On my arrival at the hospital I was told that it was a code blue, the baby had no heartbeat or respiration at the scene of the accident.

The ambulance soon screamed to a stop at our door. I saw the baby lifted out, noted that she was flaccid but breathing and hurried her to the ER. The monitor revealed a sinus tachycardia; she was breathing in agonal gasps. Her pupils were dilated and fixed, with that glassy look that signifies death. Nevertheless I started to do what I could, only to hear Ann (the student) gasp, "It's the girl from this afternoon!"

Sure enough, it was one of the four kids we had seen for physicals that afternoon. Neither of us could find a peripheral vein. I intubated her then started an IV in her external jugular. The rest of her exam was normal, except for a bruise on her forehead. For a moment I thought she might have only a concussion and be OK, but her breathing became more labored, even with assistance, and she developed a bradycardia. The frustration of not having a neurosurgeon near was never so great. Her heart slowed, then stopped. Rarely have I felt so helpless!

I slowly drove home, to restless sleep. Again the phone rang. One of my OBs had come to the hospital. She was in active labor. Back to the hospital. There the baby came easily. After another hour of sleep it was time for Saturday morning rounds and the office. There were busy, but routine, calls. My student and I planned on going to the movie that night, a comedy, *City Slickers*. We had both seen it before, but thought the laughs might be therapeutic. About mid-afternoon another OB appeared at the hospital. She was in early enough labor that we went to the movie. I had forgotten that the aunt of the father-to-be ran the movie. "What are you doing here?" she demanded. "Where is that baby?"

I assured her that the baby would not come for a while, but she had to know where I was going to sit, and how long it would take me to get to the hospital. No calls came; I almost relaxed and did enjoy the movie. Back to the hospital we went, waited a short while and delivered a charming little girl. While we were in the birthing room, however, an elderly lady came in, complaining of pain in her shoulder, stating it must be dislocated. It did not appear dislocated to me, nor did an X-ray reveal a dislocation, so she went home; as did I. No sooner had I dropped into bed, however, than the phone again rang. My shoulder patient was back. She said that she had "popped" her shoulder trying to get out of the car and it hurt even more than it had. Again it did not appear to me to be dislocated, so I did not call the X-ray tech back for another X-ray. We simply put the woman in bed with an ice pack on her shoulder, as her husband had wanted initially. This time I got to bed, to sleep, and slept the rest of the night.

Sunday morning brought the usual rounds. This morning when I looked at my patient with the injured shoulder she had an obvious anterior dislocation. X-rays confirmed this. After giving her IV Demerol® and Valium® we easily reduced the dislocation and put her arm in a sling. Back to a hospital bed she went. The rest of the day was easy, only a minor laceration and evening rounds.

That afternoon I went to the 75th anniversary reception honoring a couple living in the extended care section of the hospital. Long term patients of mine, he sported black nylon sutures in his scalp, the result of a laceration suffered in a fall a few days before. Everyone enjoyed his insistence that his wife had hit him. A few months before he had been almost incoherent, living in a nursing home, away from his wife. She was adamant that she could cure him, so they both moved into an apartment in the extended care unit which they shared. To my educated surprise, she was correct! He gradually became oriented, began to walk and even joked with us.

That concluded the weekend. I fell wearily into bed, early in the evening. In the morning I would begin a new week.

*   *   *

This was written to present rural practice to medical students who might be enticed into rural medicine. It was published in *KUMCurrents* in September 1992.

An Overview of Rural Medicine By One Who Knows

Rural Medicine. That's what I practice. I don't mean rural as the Congressmen and medical spokesmen use the word when they speak of "rural medicine." No two hundred bed hospitals, no towns of 50,000 or group practices in my life. I practice real rural medicine. I live in a town of 2300, in a county of 3500. I am the only doctor in our community; we have a twenty-two-bed hospital. The next nearest doctor is 25 miles away.

Why do I stay here? Because I love what I do. I don't like being always on call, or having to get up in the middle of the night. But, overall, I love my practice. I take care of my friends, of people I have known for twenty-five or thirty years. I watch the kids I have delivered grow up, go to college and get married. I am delivering the children of children I delivered. That's the kind of doctor I went to as a teenager and the kind of doctor I wanted to be when I went to medical school. If I sometimes work longer than I would choose, or get up when I would prefer to sleep, or miss an activity I'd like to take in, that is the price I pay for seeing one of "my" kids score the winning goal or sing in a concert. The pluses strongly outweigh the minuses in my life.

What does the word "rural" mean to you? "Rural people"—the salt of the earth, or dullards, condemned to a life where nothing ever happens because they do not have the brains or ability to get out of the country? "Rural customs"—are they that different from those of the city? "Rural medicine"—is it a special brand of medicine? I don't think there is much difference between urban and rural. The people are much the same in my experience, some easy to like, some more difficult, but all doing the best they can. Customs are not much different, given the fact that most rural communities are fairly homogeneous and most cities are only clusters of individuals with similar interests. Rural medicine is not much different from that practiced in the city. I use my knowledge and skills as best I can to care for my patients. When I don't know what to do I phone a specialist and ask or refer my patient. The major difference is that my consultants do not just step across the hall; I have to send my patients 90-250 miles to the consultant. That makes the decision a bit tougher, but the basic approach is the same.

Are there challenges unique to the kind of medicine I practice? Of course there are. I am sometimes forced to do procedures I am not entirely comfortable with. I must be alert and skilled enough to recognize and refer many serious and unusual illnesses that I can not treat myself. I have only one brain from which to draw knowledge. I must recognize my own limitations and refer when necessary, before a problem becomes insuperable. (This is probably true of all physicians, not just those of us in the boondocks.) Are there ways to decrease the stress of these challenges? Certainly. The physicians to whom I regularly refer are willing to offer what help they can via telephone if time or weather prohibits an immediate transfer. CME is readily available on audiotape, videotape, printed matter, etc. Patients are usually understanding and will accept an "I don't know, but will find out" as a temporary answer.

Computers and the various forms of electronic communication have done much to make my practice easier. On-line databases provide me with references and abstracts of articles faster than I could find in a library. Drug indications, interactions and new uses are readily available from my desk. Lists of the latest cancer chemotherapy and where the research protocols are used are quickly found. We are close to having interactive TV available, both for CME and for clinical problems. Faxes let me send EKGs for quick over-reads, and we can transmit X-rays from our hospital to the radiologist at Hays, 90 miles away, for immediate consultation. I'm sure that some of these are more quickly available to me than if I were in a large city and asked for a consultation. Patients who do need to be moved can be transported by rapid ground ambulance, or airlifted to Wichita, Kansas City or Denver if needed.

Many of the problems facing physicians in Wichita and Kansas City exist in Western Kansas as well. Government regulations interfere with some of the things I would like to do. Our hospital is financially distressed. The cost of medical care for my patients continues to grow, yet my expenses grow faster. Paperwork requirements continue to increase. I believe many of these are less troublesome to me than to city physicians. You will face even more onerous restrictions and limitations as you enter practice. I'm certain that these caveats will be less problematic for the rural physician. The Federal government presently allows a Medicare bonus for those of us who practice in a Health Personnel Shortage Area. They encourage the establishment of Rural Health Clinics. I think they will find more ways in which to promote rural medicine.

As I mentioned above, I have been in practice in Oakley for thirty years. During that time I have been fortunate to have provided continuing family care to most of the residents of the community. I have delivered babies, seen them grow up and delivered their children, whom I am now enjoying as patients. Unfortunately the practice of medicine is not all roses. The hearty, middle-aged Oakley residents whom I first met have become octogenarians, many of them more in need of my services than either of us would desire. I have cared for some of my friends as they died, never a pleasure, but a task rewarding in its own way. Some of "my" babies have died in accidents, or of other causes, and I have wept with their parents. But these are part of any physician's practice. I think the fact that I am close to all of my patients allows me to be of help to them in ways that a more distant relationship would not provide.

I am practicing the type of medicine that I envisioned as a youth, not a blessing to be taken lightly. There are many rural physicians like me in Kansas and elsewhere. The opportunity exists for you, too, to have such a life. Consider it, visit a rural physician, and see how such a rewarding practice can still be found in the small towns of Kansas.

*   *   *

This was published in *Medical Economics*, Sept 13, 1993 as

Why I Don't Do "Favors" For Patients Anymore

I received a letter from one of my neighbors last week. She couldn't understand why I had refused to order a pro time for her husband at our local hospital. After all, she had asked a favor of me, and she saw no reason, other than sheer stubbornness on my part, why I wouldn't grant it. The fact that I had not seen him in three years and had little idea why she was asking for a pro time did not seem to matter. It was not even as if she were going to the corner market to buy five pounds of sugar. Neither she nor her husband wanted to see me and pay for my services; they just wanted me to call the hospital and order the test that a consultant in Denver (to whom I had not referred the man) wanted done. She was a bit put out that I did not grant her that favor.

Since I live and practice in a rural community with an area population of perhaps 4000, this is a not uncommon occurrence. For several years I was the only provider of medical care in the area and would often accede to these requests if they did not seem dangerous or come too frequently, and if these requests were made by my regular patients. But many came from people whom I had not seen for years. Such calls would include requests for X-rays, antibiotics and pain relievers. Other calls were for insurance papers, etc. Once in a while I would receive requests for narcotics or other scheduled medications "as a favor." Some of these were easy to refuse; others were harder to turn down, and some I would grant.

There are now two nurse practitioners working with me. This gives us more time to see patients with acute problems on the day they call. This relieves much of the pressure to do someone a "favor" by phoning in an antibiotic prescription that might or might not be indicated, or for ordering lab tests or X-rays without seeing the patient.

I still get requests for "favors" however.

"Doc, I just don't have time to come in right now. Can't you just order an X-ray for me and look at it tonight? You can call me about it tomorrow morning."

Then in two weeks the hospital billing clerk gives me insurance papers to complete so that they will be paid for the X-rays. Who pays me for my time? No one.

Or the man whom I saw a few days ago for an on-the-job contusion of his hand calls and says, "I'm OK Doc. Do you really need to see me tomorrow?"

"Not if everything is OK" I reply.

Invariably this request is followed in a month by a request to complete insurance papers certifying that the involved individual was disabled for three weeks. How do I respond to that?

Or Sally calls me at home and says "Doc, I've got my bladder infection back and I'm leaving town early tomorrow morning. The pharmacist said he'd go to the store and get me an antibiotic tonight if you'd call him. Won't you do that for me?"

Two days later Sally calls me from Arizona and says "Doc, I've got a rash from the Bactrim® you prescribed. Does it have sulfa in it? I'm allergic to that, remember? Will you call something to the pharmacy down here to get rid of it?"

Yes, I now remember that she is allergic to sulfa. I'm at my office with her chart in front of me, and it's very plainly marked that way. But it wasn't written on my dinner plate two evenings ago. I know that steroids, combined with the more and different foods and alcohol she is consuming while vacationing, will probably worsen her intermittent acid-peptic disease symptoms. She can get Benadryl® over the counter, but will it help? And the rash she describes doesn't really sound like a sulfa-induced rash, anyway. Again I have dug myself into a hole in an effort to help a friend.

These are all comparatively minor problems. Major problems can arise when the man with rectal bleeding says "Doc, I just don't have time to get that test now. Just give me a prescription for some salve for my hemorrhoids." Or someone else says "My weight loss is on purpose and my ulcer is flaring up again. You just looked at my stomach last year (in reality four years ago). All I need is some of that Zantac® again." This man is bound to show up with a gastric cancer in six months, and the first will have a carcinoma of the rectum. Almost every time I have done a friend such a favor in the past I have come to regret it. These are not minor favors such as calling in a prescription without seeing him, or looking at an X-ray rather than the patient. These favors may involve major problems.

The reasons I have often granted these favors in the past are two. The first is that I hate to think that my friends might have a serious illness. The second has been that I don't like to subject anyone, much less my friends, to the indignities we physicians inflict on others in the name of "healing." In my younger years this led to guessing at what might be going on, treating without diagnosing, etc. I always ended up wishing I had obtained the barium enema or whatever. In my older and wiser years I recommend the tests that I think are needed. When my friends say "Is it really necessary?" I reply "It is if you want me to care for you. I have to know what I'm treating." This seems to do the job.

There is another type of "favor request" to which I often didn't know how to respond. This is the patient who calls, often at night because he "doesn't want to bother me at work," and wants me to refer him to a specialist. He often doesn't know what sort of specialist he wants, much less needs, to see. This leaves me in the no-win position of having to take a history by telephone or guess as to what specialty he needs to be referred. Not surprisingly, my guesses are usually not very accurate. Now I say, "I can't tell exactly what kind of a specialist you need to see without me seeing you first. Call the office and we'll try to work you in tomorrow morning."

I have been known to respond to the "didn't want to bother you at the office" ploy with the response that I expect to be bothered at the office, that's why I go to work, and that's why I keep my records there. But it continued to distress me to divert those "at home" requests. I finally convinced myself that my real friends wouldn't bother me at home except in true emergencies. If my responses to phone requests lead other patients to seek care from physicians in the surrounding communities I really haven't lost much, as I never made a charge for responding to those phone calls anyway.

Rarely will I now do a "favor for a patient/friend, and especially not for a family member. If I am somehow trapped in a situation where this appears inevitable I will usually remind my friend that, as with any commodity, medical care is usually worth what he pays for it. If the requests for "favors" continue I tell the supplicant that if he really desires second-rate care I would much rather that he obtain that care elsewhere.

*   *   *

Members of my family have provided a few ideas for essay. This one was published in *American Medical News,* in 1993 (Copyright ©1993 American Medical Association. All rights reserved.) as

The Patient Was Critical—And a Member Of the Family

Wet and dirty though I was, there was no mistaking the urgency of the call, even received over my low-resolution pager. "Dr. Ohmart. We need you at the hospital. NOW!"

My work on the mower came to an abrupt halt as I ran to my car and raced to the hospital. Entering the ER corridor I saw a couple standing there, holding a child. They did not look too urgent, although they were quite wide-eyed. I opened the closed door to the ER itself. There was my patient! A thin young man, barely breathing, his cardiac monitor skipping and bouncing. Without paying much attention to his face I grabbed the IV someone held out to me and started it in his wrist. Two people were trying to tell me what had happened. Then I glanced at his face.

"My God," I said, "It's Mike!"

Indeed, it was my son-in-law!

I have lived and practiced in a high plains community of 2200 for the thirty years since I completed my internship, much of the time as the only provider of medical care in the area. The community was to hold a recognition ceremony for me in about ten days. Now I was face to face with my worst nightmare.

My wife, Carol, and I raised three children in Oakley without many family accidents. But I was haunted by a recurring dream, especially as they learned to swim, drive etc. Prom and other celebratory nights were especially bad. In my dream I was awakened from a sound sleep to report to the hospital. There I would find one of my children, or occasionally just one of their best friends, seriously injured or dying. In spite of my best attempts my patient would expire. I would awaken in a cold sweat, check to be sure my kids were all safely in bed, and attempt to return to sleep. Fortunately I had nothing worse to repair on my children or their friends than a broken bone or a small laceration; none of them incurred an injury in an auto accident. The closest I came was a call to the ER to "fix a boy's cut head" one evening. On the way to the hospital I drove by the unmistakable purple Barracuda driven by my older son, its front end smashed into the back of another car. But my son was standing by the car. It was his passenger who had sustained the laceration.

This, however, was not a dream, and Mike was critically ill. I knew he was an asthmatic, as well as a hardheaded farmer. He had started out to harvest wheat that morning and continued in spite of increasing difficulties with his asthma. He had exhausted the inhaler he carried with him (and probably overused routinely). But, determined to finish the field before nightfall and the probability of another rain, he had forced himself to go on. Finally he had gone to his parents' house and asked his sister to call me. But I was in the yard, not near a telephone, as I was not on call. He then asked her to drive him the six miles to town. She did that, and later stated that Mike quit breathing about a mile away from the hospital. She could do nothing but drive faster, hoping to get him to the hospital in time.

The nurse on duty quickly grasped the situation, screamed for help, dragged Mike out of his pickup onto the hospital driveway and started CPR. Someone else paged the excellent nurse practitioner working with me who was on call; then managed to get Mike off of the driveway and onto a cart. Then someone paged me.

By the time of my arrival Mike was beginning to breathe for himself, and he had a sinus rhythm with only a few VPCs. I started a second IV; he had already received epinephrine, was breathing oxygen and had an IV carrying a corticosteroid. Slowly he was coming around. An Alupent® aerosol was begun. He was breathing well enough that I did not intubate him. IV aminophylline appeared to give him more relief. He was moved from the ER to the ICU. Thirty minutes later he was asking for water and talking normally. An hour later I telephoned my seven and one-half month pregnant daughter and my wife, who were 900 miles away in Houston, to tell them what had transpired. I still could not talk to my daughter about Mike, but managed to tell Carol what had happened and how lucky we were.

The next morning we were all laughing. Mostly about how the couple with the injured child had reacted on their arrival. They were greeted with the sight of a nurse pulling a 130 pound, 5' 9", unconscious man from his pickup. Then a rather buxom nurse plopped down on her belly on the concrete beside him to provide mouth-to-mouth respiratory support. An LPN was kneeling beside him, providing cardiac resuscitation. What a sight that must have been! But I'm just as glad I arrived a little later. The couple said they had never seen anything like it on TV; my response was that was where those sights should stay. But most of the laughter was still of the tension-relieving variety. Everyone knew what a close call Mike had had, and they were all glad I didn't walk into the ER only to find my son-in-law's body.

He adamantly refuses to quit farming, but has agreed to take more precautions in the future, as well as come to town if he has any sign of asthma. I will provide him with an epinephrine pen to carry with him, and we have had a discussion about how important it is for him to treat his asthma correctly. None of us wish to repeat this experience, although we all learned from it. We might not be so lucky next time!

*   *   *

I wrote this when we attempting to recruit and retain another physician. This expresses some of my frustration in searching for a new physician at that time, but was never published

Musical Docs, A New Game

> Our little town needs a doc.
> The one we have works 'round the clock.
> We just hire one,
> Then he's on the run,
> And our town again needs a doc.

Is that a familiar refrain? If not, you must not be familiar with physician recruiting, either in a large group or a small community. My experience lies in a rural area, (Truly rural, a town of 2200 in a county of 3600, with the next-nearest physician 25 miles away.) so that is what I will comment on, but my city friends tell me the same is true in their groups. It seems that many physicians, both young and old, have discovered a new version of the children's game of musical chairs. It goes this way.

We put out feelers in the way of ads; notices, contacts with recruiters, etc. as do a dozen other towns in our area that are looking for physicians. The prospects come to look us over, some of the more talented and less ethical getting expenses for the same trip from two or three hospitals. We all put on our best faces, shine our shoes and play our most seductive music, hoping the doc will be in our seat when the music stops. Needless to say the "music" involves more dollar signs than musical notes, more vacations than rests and more time off than time signatures in the music.

So the prospect chooses us. Does this end the game? No, it merely raises the ante. Most physicians willing to come to our small rural communities ask for, and get, a one or two year guarantee/salary that is more than I earn after thirty years of practice in the area. It is also much higher than they can realistically hope to make once the guarantee has expired. The guarantee ends and he receives a smaller salary. He then returns to the game, with a new group of communities playing the siren song, while we begin again, playing the same song for a new group of recruits.

We have not really done too badly. There have been four physicians in Oakley in the last ten years, with the shortest stay being about 18 months and the longest six years. Of the four I have been the one constant, staying put on my chair and not playing the game, although I have been tempted. I think I'm too old to learn the rules of the new game. I watch from the sidelines, observing with a mixture of awe and resignation, hoping to see someone land on the Oakley chair when the music stops.

Oakley is a Federal Health Professional Shortage Area, so we have added inducements, like the payback of Public Health Service time, and federal repayment of student loans, but so far we have not managed to recruit a new physician. I think the time will come when he or she will enjoy our rural practice and easy living enough to put down some permanent roots. In the meantime we continue to sing our siren song to older, game-experienced physicians. The only problem is that the inducements have become so high that very few of our truly rural communities can afford them.

Hays, a city of 16,000 with an added college population of 5000, is ninety miles away. For the last twenty years it has been the referral center for Northwest Kansas. In the last five years it has lost all but one of its Family Physicians, two or three internists, an OB/

GYN specialist, two ophthalmologists, etc. Now they are competing for the same physicians as we are. And playing the same game of musical docs. Their entry has merely upped the stakes and made such factors as the university, with all the opportunities it brings, and twenty-four hour emergency room coverage, part of the score. These amenities are lacking in Oakley. We try to overcome these deficiencies with other inducements. The game goes on and the music gets louder and faster. Where will it end?

Some say that it will end with most communities the size of Oakley without physicians, but with mid-level practitioners. The physicians will be concentrated in the larger centers. I am not sure that this is all bad, but it may offer only a short-term solution. Unfortunately the mid-levels are not just learning medicine in school. They, too, are becoming adept at playing medical musical chairs, and for only slightly lower stakes. As they become more in demand these stakes will rise until they, too, demand salaries and perks that price them out of the truly needy small towns' range.

In my worst dreams I think it will end with a national doctor-draft, with all physicians being assigned to the desperately needy areas for a two to five year term when they finish their residencies. I hope this does not occur, as it would be ideal neither for the populace of these areas nor the physicians. But I'm not sure there is a viable alternative. As physicians' practices and incomes become more controlled by the government, the location of one's practice may be assigned.

In the meantime the local docs have developed a new version of musical chairs. A few days ago I received a call from a friend who practices near here. But he wasn't at home; he was spending the weekend working in another town's ER. And his community was paying someone else to staff their ER. A physician from a third town was working in the ER in Town 2. Town 3 hired someone else to take call in their ER. Town 2 talked to me the other day, offering me $3000 for taking weekend call there, a

60-hour shift. For that I would work weekends only, take one weekend off a month and still make more than I am making now. It certainly is tempting.

I am not naive enough to believe that any young physician would choose the life I now lead. I would not intentionally have placed myself in it, either. Varying circumstances and a strong sense of responsibility have twice left me the only physician in Oakley. But two physicians and one or two mid-level practitioners could live quite comfortably in Oakley. They would work hard, but not unbearably so. They would not get rich, but would make a good living, especially if compared to the rest of the inhabitants of the area, rather than our colleagues in Metropolis. I hope to see our litany changed from the jingle that started this article to:

Our town has found a new doc.

It really came as a shock.

We now have two,

And other help, soo

It makes practice here a cakewalk.

*   *   *

This was written in March 1993. It was published in *Cortland Forum* in April 1994.

A Bedtime Story

She moaned, saying "Oh Dick, I hurt so much. Rub my stomach!"

She hurt, that much I was sure of, but what was she doing in bed beside me? Half asleep, I did as she asked. Only later, as I gradually awakened, did I realize how bizarre the entire situation was.

I sleep quite soundly, often not remembering orders I phone to the hospital until I see them on the chart the next morning. Apparently I had done more than phone orders to the hospital during my trance that night. I recalled very little of it. This is the story Carol and Judy told me over coffee, interspersed with riotous laughter. Judy was, and is, a good friend of both my wife and me. This particular night she had come to the door, walked in and told Carol she had this terrible pain in her stomach. Her next question was "Where's Dick?"

Upon hearing that I was in bed asleep she started down the hall towards our bedroom, shedding clothes as she walked. Carol was right behind her, wanting to watch the fun. On her arrival, Judy crawled into bed beside me, asking me to rub her stomach. I think I did, but with a minimum of success.

"Do you think I could have an ulcer?" she asked.

Out of my daze I replied "Judy, there are people who get ulcers and people who give ulcers. You'll never have an ulcer."

She started giggling, soon to be joined by Carol. The giggling turned to guffaws, then howls of laughter. I only wanted peace and quiet so I could return to sleep. Soon Judy exclaimed, "Dick, the pain is gone! You've cured me!"

Nothing would do but that I get up and have a cup of coffee with the two of them. Carol, who has long believed that laughter truly is the best medicine, was ecstatic. Judy and I had proven a point for her. Judy was delighted that she no longer hurt. I was only the grump because I was missing sleep. As soon as possible I returned to bed, warning them that I wanted no further interruptions. I guess they complied, for I promptly relapsed into an uninterrupted sleep.

Two weeks later Judy had an uneventful cholecystectomy. She never returned to my bed.

*   *   *

I wrote this in September 1991 and was published in *Medical Economics* in April 1993.

Richard Ohmart, M. D., F.A.A.F.P.

Why I Never Miss the Good Old Days

I marveled at the report in my hand. Not at what it said, but that it was in my hand. I had seen a young man in the office earlier in the day for diplopia. Wondering what might be happening within his brain, I had requested a CT of his head from our nearest scanner, 90 miles away. He was not back yet, but I held the typed and signed report in my hand assuring me that there was no tumor in his brain. What a change from the scrawled, often misspelled notes on scraps of paper I was used to getting.

You guessed it; we have a new fax machine in our office. Although it was really a few months old at the time this scene occurred, this was the first time it had really come home to me how valuable this technological marvel is. I practice in a rural area and we have long been dependent on telephone consultations, descriptions, etc. The hospital has had a camera that will transmit distinct, clear pictures of our X-rays to the radiologists via phone line for some time, but this is the first time I have had such wonders occur in my office.

Those of you who practice with a friendly cardiologist across the hall, radiologists on the main floor and a lab next door may not appreciate the difference this machine makes. No longer do I have to try to decide what my excellent receptionist (but not a medical librarian) meant with her interpretation of what the radiologist's new typist was trying to say on the phone. Now the radiologist, himself, corrects the dictation, then has it faxed to me. Do I have a difficult-to-read EKG? Fax it to my friendly consultant and get his opinion. Lab results from the hospital? They are now faxed from the lab to my office. I no longer wonder whether that is a GGT or a GOAT on the scrap of paper, or whether the value is 0.26 or 2.6. And I get them at 10:30 in the AM, rather than when I return to the hospital for evening rounds, so there is time to do something if warranted by the report that day.

Am I in love with my FAX? Somewhat. But little more than the rest of the electronic gadgets I use to provide better care for my patients, help my office run more smoothly and make my life easier. I remember the day we stopped typing each statement and began using a peg-board system and a copier to prepare statements for our two-man office. We thought that we were really high-tech. And we were for the times. Our new copier made copying the cards as statements easier and faster than hand-typing each statement. Occasionally, however, a month went by in which our receptionist simply didn't have time to run all those cards through the copier, so no statements were mailed.

Balancing the books at the end of each day was often a problem; the end of the month could be a major disaster. Now each charge is entered into our computer once. At the end of the day the books are automatically balanced. At the end of each month we simply tell the computer to print a monthly summary and the books are miraculously in balance. Tell the computer to print statements and it does so, leaving us only the task of putting them in their envelopes. Want to know how many patients between the ages of 16 and 24 I diagnosed with a URI last month? Just give my trusty computer a bit of time and it will tell me.

The best thing about my computer, however, is that it sends all my Medicare and Blue Shield claims to the Blue Shield office every week. Back come the checks, usually within a week or ten days. The option exists for the money to be deposited electronically in my bank, and credited electronically to my patients' accounts. My office manager simply believes it is easier for her to credit the payments and make the adjustments by hand. No more fighting Medicare HCFA 1500 forms, waiting weeks for my money or getting a claim returned because of a typing error. If the computer accepts it, it is probably correctly typed.

Other insurance forms? We outgrew our first front office computer. It now sits on a desk in a back office. It is slow and clunky, but works. Every night my front office computer talks to the back office computer, telling it what has been entered in the accounts receivables program that day. Most of the insurance companies we deal with will accept the standard HCFA 1500 form in place of their own with no problems. The next day an office assistant puts the HCFA 1500 form in the back printer, tells it what group of patients she would like statements printed at that time, and it spews forth the papers with little supervision from her. It would be possible for a large office to set up a Local Area Network so that more than one person could access the files on the main computer at the same time, but our little jury-rigged outfit works quite well for my office.

Time to pay my bills, or write checks? I have another computer beside my desk that has my bookkeeping system on it, separate from the accounts receivable system. My daughter comes in once a week and enters the week's receipts. When I wish to write the checks I merely put blank checks in the printer, tell it what the amounts of the checks I want to write are, and it merrily clatters away, spending my money while I go see another patient. The only problem with this is that the machine can spend money a lot faster than I can make it. The payroll is handled the same way. Monthly withholding and Social Security deposits are automatically calculated. No more sweating over a pad with a pencil until midnight on the 14th of every month. End of the month and end of the year income/expense statements are ready for my accountant at the push of a button.

Of direct value to patients is a treadmill/Holter monitor unit I have. It is computer-driven and computer-read. I over-read the reports, but they are usually correct. This has saved any number of patients a 180-mile round trip for either a treadmill or a Holter test. At least one cardiologist has commented on the clarity of the printed EKG strips I get. Patient education programs are available on computers, although I have yet to use this service. These can be either computer print outs to be given to the patient or actual programs run by the patient to educate him about his specific problem. On a somewhat lower tech level I do use a VCR and TV set to show patient education tapes in the waiting room, rather than showing the soaps.

Do I have a problem in patient care? Not sure of the diagnosis, what tests should I order or which drug should I prescribe? Why is that gynecologist treating a young woman with interferon? The answer lies in my computer. *Scientific American Medicine Consult*® is only seconds away. This medicine text, updated every three months, lies on a CD-ROM disc. It is an arm's length from my desk chair. I only need to push a few buttons and an answer pops up. Other texts and journals are also available. Can I safely use these two drugs together? Much faster than the *PDR*® is a drug interaction program I have. (The actual *PDR*® is also available on CD-ROM, as well.) My drug interaction program also lets me record the medications and allergies of each of my patients who are on maintenance medications. If I try to record a prescription that she is allergic to, or that doesn't mix with her present medications, it alerts me to the fact that I am about to make a boo-boo. Perhaps I'm at the hospital, seeing a patient at midnight. No more wondering what that patient's meds are. I phone my computer and it tells me what they are.

Until the AMA decided that it would rather build a new building than sponsor its on-line computer network, I had access to a program that helped me construct a differential diagnosis; on several occasions, it also provided me a wealth of other information. Now some of that information is available from *Compuserve*® or other sources available by computer via phone lines. I am also able to query the National Library of Medicine and get abstracts by computer or copies by mail of articles of interest to me. Other programs let me question physicians at the University Of Kansas School Of Medicine about specific problems or treatment regimens. My computer is a source of proscribed CME hours. I am writing this on my computer. In many ways it helps me overcome my geographical isolation.

Another modern marvel is my cellular car phone. Two weeks ago we had our yearly hot-air balloon festival. For the first time I was able to comfortably leave town to follow the balloon I sponsored in my car. Secure in the knowledge that I was available by phone if one of the balloonists, passengers or anyone else needed me. I enjoy photographing the prairie on that I live, but have not been able to spend as much time roaming, as I would have liked. Now with my battery powered phone I can go where I want, in contact with the hospital if need be.

Is everything perfect? No, it's not. In spite of all the talk a few years ago about the "paperless office" my computers grind out reams of papers that have to be stored. Our rural electricity is sometimes undependable, so I have back-up power supplies, but still have to stop work at times. A good lightning storm will see us scurry to disconnect our machines. If the wrong account number or code is typed into the computer it remains there until someone removes it. I have yet to find a computer that will give me more than 24 hours in a day. Both my office staff and I get more done in less time than we would have without computers, however. I believe our work is more accurate, as well.

I have one remaining electronic project. Those of you who use computers may have noted one glaring omission in the above paean. Nowhere do I mention scheduling appointments on a computer. I would like to, but my receptionist of twenty-five years says she won't touch the damned things. I can't get her to change her mind. Although she will use the FAX, she says she can't run a computer. One more advantage to a computer. It does exactly what you tell it to do, with no back talk!

Addendum—As I read this in 2010, adding this to a book I am writing, I realize the marvels I laud above are now prehistoric. Everyone carries a cell phone, or maybe two. All the X-rays taken in our hospital are digital, viewed on a computer screen and transmitted on the internet to a radiologist. They get a digitally signed report. Before I had to retire Hays Medical Center was working on a program where I, in Oakley, could look at my patient's chart if he were in the hospital there and look at his lab results. I was reading of hospitals where the attending physicians carried laptop computers and wrote their orders and progress notes on it. Now in New Frontiers they have similar laptops. I have no idea what the next twenty years will bring.

*   *   *

This was published in *American Medical News* in October 1995 as "As Physicians Grow Older, Their Patient Base Changes" I like my title better. (Copyright ©1995 American Medical Association. All rights reserved.)

Where Have All the Children Gone?

There was a popular song when I was young entitled "Where Have All the Flowers Gone," a ballad about the changes that occur in our lives. As a young man, it appeared to me to be only a song. Now I wonder, in my own practice, where have all the children gone? I have lived and practiced in a small town for thirty-two years. During that time I have practiced in a number of settings; I initially joined an older man in practice; he died and I practiced alone for a few years. I then hired a physician's assistant, then another when the first left. Another physician established a practice in Oakley and my PA left. I then had a partner for a few years and the other physician left. My partner left in 1989 (See "Who Needs Another M.D.? I've Got Partners All Around Me," *Medical Economics*, July 23, 1990.) I was the only medical provider in Oakley from 1989 until September of 1992 at which time we established a community-owned federally approved Rural Health Clinic that employed both an excellent nurse practitioner and me. It was after this that I noticed my practice beginning to change.

I have always delivered babies and have enjoyed those deliveries and taking care of these children as they grew up. I have savored watching them as teenagers in their school sports and music, a part of the small town life I relish. I still enjoy attending the activities. But I rarely see children in the office anymore. Our clinic has grown to employ another physician, a physician assistant and a nurse practitioner. Because I have taken care of many of my older patients for the last thirty years my practice has evolved into a mainly geriatric practice. My patients often schedule their next appointment as they leave from their present visit. Thus I often seem to be booked up in advance. A mother calling about a sick child will usually be seen within two to three hours by one of the other providers, all of whom provide excellent care. If they take care of a child I don't concern myself about them not being compassionate or capable. I just miss seeing the kids. I saw a girl in the ER the other evening after she had broken a finger in a basketball game. I remembered her as a little girl; now she was 14 years old and five feet, six inches tall and playing junior high basketball. When did that happen? I just don't get to see the kids any more. And I miss them.

The young women I knew and enjoyed seeing for yearly physicals because I had delivered them now see one of the women providers for those exams. The women tell me that they feel more comfortable with a woman examining them and that they can get an appointment with one of them much more quickly than they can with me. I know those are the reasons that we wanted to employ at least one woman provider, but it still hurts a bit to sign out on a physical done on one of "my" patients by one of our mid-levels.

I am even losing control, or so it seems, over many of my elderly patients. In my absence (now more frequent) they see another provider and may have their medicines changed. Thus I no longer can trust my memory to tell me what meds they are on. One lady, faced with chronic problems with her arthritis and GI tract, confided to me that her friends told her she should try the new doctor, as he joked with them and made them feel good. Joking has never been my strong suit, and I was certainly glad to have the women wanting to see Dr. Raju, but again, there was pain in being reminded that I could not be all things to everyone. I knew this, and my knowledge tells me that we need a diversity of providers, but my feelings of loss of "my" patients and their care do not always follow my intellect.

I realize that as any family physician ages so does the age of his patients, but that does not make it any easier to accept. I have also been aware for some time that, like most doctors, at least those of my generation, I needed to be in control, not only of my own life but of my patients as well. It has proven harder to share that power than I imagined it would be. Fortunately the other providers employed by the clinic have proven understanding and supportive.

I have the things I wanted when we established the Rural Health Clinic and I became a salaried employee—another physician with whom to share call, more mid-levels, better hours, more time off when I can actually be out of town. But I have had more difficulty giving up the sometimes irritating, usually demanding, but extremely rewarding, role of the community's only medical provider. I think that young physicians, most of whom will never know either these trials or the accompanying rewards, will have an easier life in many respects, but I would not exchange my years with the children of Oakley for less frequent call and shorter office hours.

*   *   *

I wrote this shortly after the New Year, but never published.

A Christmas Miracle

It's Christmas Eve, 1995. As I drive through the small community in which I live and practice I notice clusters of cars at a few homes, usually the homes of my older patients, celebrating with their families. I have beside me a few sheets of paper that I'm taking to a friend. Those pages hold the information I have gleaned from my computer concerning kidney cancer with bony metastases. It is not information I would like to give anyone at any time, much less a friend on this evening, an evening for family and friends and happiness.

I notice other homes where there are cars and lights where I know all is not peaceful. One man, the father of five and grandfather of nine, found out this week that he has cancer of the prostate. Another holds a widow. Three days ago I wished her a Merry Christmas in the office and she burst into tears. Her eldest son, whose birthday it was, had chosen that same day three years ago to tell her that he would have nothing more to do with her. Her Christmases had not been the same since, even though surrounded by her other children. A third home held a woman who had been a long-time patient of mine. Her granddaughter, whom I had delivered, is in Oakley for Christmas. Three months pregnant, she had phoned me a short while ago to tell me she was spotting and asked my advice. There truly are no vacations from the exigencies of everyday life.

Arriving at my friend's home, I am greeted on the walk by a young man who grew up next door to me, his pretty young wife and their little girl. They, too, are home visiting for the holidays and walking to church. He had run on relay teams and played ball with my son. Smiling and awash with the confidence and strength of youth he asks about my son, Dean, and wishes all of us a Merry Christmas.

I knock on Jerry's door, and he admits me. He has his tie in his hand, obviously getting dressed for church.

His youngest son is with him; I do not see his wife. Their house resembles ours in its preparations for children and grandchildren—plates of candy and cookies temporarily protected by Saran Wrap®, a glittering tree, presents lying around the house—preparations for what we know may well be Jerry's last Christmas.

I chat with him for a few minutes about inconsequential matters, then give him the papers I have brought. We discuss them briefly; they don't say much that he was not already aware of. He tells me that he has had a good life and a good family; that everyone's time comes, and that he only asks time to get his business affairs in order for his wife and family. I agree that this is a good idea, even though I have no guess as to the amount of time he has left. As I leave he thanks me, as if I had brought him a long-desired Christmas present, rather than the doleful news of fact.

I go on to the hospital, where my only patient of consequence is Jerry's brother-in-law. He has just completed a course of irradiation for cancer of the lung and was brought in to the hospital after losing consciousness in his bathroom early this morning. Lab work discovered that he was markedly anemic. Because of the day and time we chose to give him two units of blood, and then send him to his oncologist after Christmas. Two or three quick ER visits to sick kids (we're in the middle of a flu epidemic) and I head home to where my blessedly healthy and untroubled family awaits. Memories of Christmas two years ago, celebrated in my home, with my terminally ill father spending his last Christmas with us, stream through my mind.

After dinner, the opening of gifts and some cleanup work done, I am ready to retire. I go to bed, but not readily to sleep. My practice is a joy to me, but with the pleasures come pain. I keep hearing Jerry, with tears in his eyes, wishing me a Merry Christmas as I left his house. I could only reply in irony, my arm around his shoulders and my voice choked, "And a Merry Christmas to you, too."

As an addendum to the above—better news. The lesions thought to be bony metastases on the initial bone scans proved not to be. After a nephrectomy showed a renal cell carcinoma which was confined to the fascial planes surrounding his kidney, my friend appears to be well on his way to a total recovery. Perhaps he did receive a magnificent Christmas gift after all. Who am I to say?

*   *   *

The following article was written in February 1996. It was published in *American Medical News*, May 6, 1996 (Copyright ©1996 American Medical Association. All rights reserved.) as

Loss of Spirit Yields To Renewed Joy In An Ordinary Life

The Rural Health Clinic for which I work provides school health services for the school in Oakley. Last week I had the duty. That means going to the school at 7:30 AM to see sick kids or answer questions as the kids come in. The healthcare office is next to the hall down which the elementary students go to class. I recommend a dose of first and second graders for everyone in February. It's a much better antidepressant than any number of bottles of Prozac®.

Watching the excited, giggling kids come down the hall was a real treat. Laughing and chattering, skipping and dancing, they were on their way to class, excited to greet a new day with its wonders yet to unfold. Two boys dragged their book bags on the floor behind them, bouncing and jostling each other. A girl wheeled another boy in a wheelchair, with his casted leg propped in front of him, down the hall, while a girl on each side of him hopped alongside him using his crutches. I had put that cast on him three or four weeks before, much to his irritation. Now he seemed to be enjoying the attention gained from his accident. A clutch of little girls, already giggly and flirty, teased one of the other boys, who was walking alone. In sum, a sight for my tired eyes!

I played a game I often play with myself as I watch school activities. It's named "How Many Did I Deliver?" Although I could not recognize all of the children, I figured that I had delivered roughly half of them, a somewhat constant percentage, from high school graduation down to preschool Christmas program. In my thirty-three years in Oakley not much has changed.

Or has it? I remember, vaguely, when I was one of those excited elementary students, in Wichita during World War II. I played soldier with the other boys my age, certain that life would soon be better. That is the only time I can remember thinking that killing anything was good. Soon that excitement was replaced by visions of girls, then medical school and marriage. Our children came along and then I was opening new and exciting doors, certain that each new day would bring adventure. I knew that all my preparations, from financial to psychological and technical would grow and improve my family's life. Before long I was whistling as I entered the Oakley hospital, proud to be a "real" doctor, actually stamping out disease and conquering illness.

Now I am mostly tired. Where has that feeling of eagerness to cross the next threshold gone? My practice, while still pleasurable and rewarding, does not give me the high it once did. Perhaps it is because I see mostly the same problems repeatedly. I have learned to handle them easily; much of the challenge seems to be gone. Or else there is too much challenge and I experience moments of terror. There seems to be no in between.

Carol, my wife, and I recently had the pleasure (experience?) of caring for our three and six year old grandsons for ten days. Trying to keep up with two lively boys, practice medicine and cope with the aches, pains and fatigue of my nearly sixty years convinced me that nature was extremely wise in providing young parents for most children. Alternating between rather marked grumpiness and total permissiveness, I must have royally confused the boys. When our children were that age I looked forward to the future as a time to do more and different things with my kids as they grew up. Now I only looked forward to the day I would no longer have to sleep with a wiggly six-year old.

I was certain that, as our children grew up, both they and I would have better lives, richer and more rewarding than prior years. To some extent that has been true; perhaps not as much so as I would have liked, but overall more true than not. Now I am not sure that these little boys will grow up in a world that offers them more than I and their parents have had.

I have an idea that my evolution (regression?) has been typical, not only of my generation, but also of most of the generations before me. I have only one life to live so will not be able to judge first-hand, but much of what I read appears to confirm this. Age seems to bring pessimism and doubt, not wisdom. I hope that the passive exhaustion I see and feel in my generation has not pervaded those younger than we. They need to be the bearers of hopes and dreams that we once were.

Or perhaps I still can be. I still felt the same thrill after delivering a baby yesterday that I did years ago. And the sunset two days ago was as beautiful as ever. I am listening to the music of Handel as I write; it is as grand as ever. My grandson's hug this morning was worth dying for. I am undertaking a new professional challenge that has me excited. Physical fatigue can be conquered; pessimism may not necessarily be the unavoidable accompaniment of age. Perhaps the next ten years will answer my questions.

*   *   *

This was published in *Kansas Medicine* in spring 1996. (Courtesy Kansas Medical Society)

I Practice In A Rural Wilderness

I recently attended an ALSO course in Denver. For those of you not familiar with all of those little devils known as acronyms (all of us?), that stands for Advanced Life Support Obstetrics. It is modeled somewhat after the familiar ACLS and ATLS courses, sponsored by the AAFP, and designed for "rural" physicians. It is the use of the word rural that triggered a series of questions in my mind, questions not new to me and questions many of you have no doubt pondered as well. They begin with "What is rural?"

I believe I practice in a rural area, but I am not certain by whose definition. I have lived and practiced in Oakley since I completed a rotating internship in 1963. The present population of Oakley is about 2200 souls, although there may be those who maintain that the soulless in Oakley lower that count somewhat. Logan County, in its entirety, may have a population of 3000. The surrounding counties and communities are not substantially different. We are predominantly dependent on agriculture for our livelihoods. This certainly would seem to me to be rural, or perhaps remote is a better term.

The nearest community with any supply of specialists is Hays, ninety miles to the east of us, not far by modern reckoning, but more than an evening's stroll. Yet at the Denver course, designed for rural physicians, the instructors were suggesting we ask our OB consultant to step in and review certain problems with us. Somehow I can't visualize one of the already overworked Hays obstetricians spending three hours driving to and from Oakley to offer his opinion, especially if that opinion might be that "All is fine. You just need to continue what you are doing."

Another suggestion was that I alert the local neonatologist if I anticipated problems with a neonate. Our local neonatologist is also in Hays, and I understand she will be leaving soon, leaving the nearest neonatologist in Denver, 250 miles west of me. Alert him/her? Indeed!

These are not complaints, simply facts that are painfully obvious to those of us who have chosen to practice in such a location. I don't believe anyone who has not practiced in a similar setting has much of an idea about what medicine, and life, is in such a more or less isolated community. Certainly few CME courses, articles, etc. appear to me to have much inkling of the way I have spent my life.

Second—why do I stay here, or more correctly, why have I chosen to stay here through thirty odd (in all meanings of the word) years? The obvious reason is that I have always liked what I do, and that enjoyment has grown as the years have progressed. I wouldn't imply that there have not been times when I have considered leaving. In fact, many years ago I went so far as to call the Psychiatry Department at KUMC about the possibility of a residency there. The then head of the department, whose name I have now forgotten, called back the next day, asking how soon I could start. That frightened me away; for better or worse, I will never know. But to go further, why do I like my practice?

I like the people of Oakley, although I assume they are little different from those of any similar community. I have come to know them, their strengths and their weaknesses, and to understand many of the sources of both. I respect their wisdom and opinions, although I sometimes argue long and hard with some who don't care for my suggestions. They are as hardheaded as I am. I have delivered many of them and watched, sometimes wept, as they have grown up. I have seen others go from the strength of their forties to the frailties of their seventies. While not always fun, my practice has always been rewarding, the practice I dreamed of while in medical school.

And there is no reason that it is not the practice of which I dreamed. During my thirty-two years here I have been the only physician practicing in Oakley for ten or so years. That has given me a chance to design both my practice and the patterns at the hospital to conform to my own ideas and desires. The fact that the hospital administrator throughout almost all of my tenure has been the same man has been of utmost importance. He is a good friend. He has been of immeasurable assistance in making many decisions. Now that there are other providers working with me (to be more thoroughly covered in the future) I have more free (even off call) time and can relax in Oakley, knowing that I will only be requested in case of a major emergency. I also get away for more time with Carol, my wife of thirty-eight years.

When I get away from Oakley and listen to, or converse with, others of you in Kansas and elsewhere, I realize other advantages in my situation. To date I have little contact with managed care, although there are hints and heralds of its imminent arrival. My patients see me because they choose me (Carol says it's because I was the only act in town.), not because I am a panel member, or the physician their company chose. When they do call and ask to see me, I am usually accessible, almost always in an emergency. I know that the others with whom I work provide excellent care, and I can relax knowing that I am not essential. My youthful fantasies about being essential have been tamed through maturity and experience. Minor hassles, such as parking near my office, safety in the street outside the office or parking lot, and the intricacies of relationships with nurses and ancillary hospital personnel rarely exist. The people of Oakley respect me and are considerate of me and my time, as they are of the other providers with whom I work. I hope we are as considerate of them.

I do not practice in paradise however. There are the problems common to most medical personnel—of time, increasing paperwork, the specter of malpractice, etc. Many of these appear to me to be less stressful here than they might be in a larger community, but I am no more qualified to comment on an urban practice than those I mentioned above are to understand my situation. The questions asked are all answered with the same basic response—I have spent my life building a practice in Oakley, I like that practice and anticipate that I will continue to enjoy it. And I have discovered another term for the area in which I practice. I understand that the U.S. government considers any area that has a population of less than 6 persons per square mile as a "rural wilderness." Perhaps that describes my locale, but certainly not my life.

*   *   *

This was published in *Jayhawk Family Physician*, Summer 1996 (Courtesy Kansas Academy of Family Physicians) as

You Find Solace Wherever You Can

My wife, Carol, and I kept our grandchildren this past weekend. Sunday morning I heard the two and one-half year-old come screaming down the hall. He streaked (in all meanings of the word) past the shower and into my closet, into the corner under my clothes. Listening to him sob, I was certain that he had broken an arm, at least. As I hurried out of the shower Carol walked in and said that his feelings were the only thing hurt. His older brother had refused to give him the toy he wanted. For solace Rod wanted his "blankie."

Unfortunately that specific item was at his house, not ours. Hence the scream, scamper and seclusion. After allowing him a few moments of sobbing, (And pulling a few clothes on myself, as I am too old to streak.) I went in, sat down on the floor beside him, and asked him what was wrong. I even offered him the use of Grandpa's blanket, a large white one covered with Kansas Jayhawks. No solace there. He did not want any blanket but his own. The rest of the story is of minimal importance to the thoughts to follow; enough to say that no major harm was done to anyone, and the boys were soon playing together in great comradeship.

I have spent a bit of time since thinking about that incident. Carol told me that my closet had become Rod's (the two year old) hiding place when he was upset, a place where he often sought solace. I just had not been here to see him seek it out. We don't know why he chose it, other than that it is dark, quiet and out of the way. I suppose it lets him escape his troubled world when his fears and problems overwhelm him. It provides a physically limited environment, one with little stimulation, where he can regroup and prepare to re-enter our sometimes unpleasant, usually perplexing, world.

How many times have I wished I had such a secret and readily available place to hide while I recovered from some insult or trauma? A hiding place to which I could run, screaming if necessary, and remain until I was ready to face the trials of my world anew. I suspect most of you have had similar longings. We all have our boats, hunting cabins, city spots or whatever, where we can go if we have a couple of days, but often these sites become merely an extension of our homes or offices, another place to work, not to regroup. And even if they are restorative, all too often the hassle of getting there and getting back is more than the value of a day or two away. What I need is a place where I can go if I have only a few minutes, a place I can easily get to, but not accessible by telephone or pager. Not too easy for someone in our profession to find, and impossible to achieve on the on-call days, the days I am most likely to need such a hideaway, even if only for a few minutes.

As a pre-teenager I was taught that big boys didn't run home crying, nor did they scream and hide. Today I wonder how valid that lesson was. I suspect we would all return to our homes in a less stressed mood if we were able to throw a little screaming fit on the bad days. I now enjoy a few moments of solitude, time to regain my composure, then return to my practice renewed, if not refreshed. For some a short prayer, for others a few moments of meditation or contemplation (I doubt that there is much difference.) may do the job. My desktop computer has a CD-ROM that will play audio CDs. I have my shelves well stocked with music that I like, ranging from modern mystical through Wagner. Only a few moments of music accompanying a feet-on-the-desk position will often help me feel better, but there is nothing physical, no screaming, no physical release if that is what I really need. Perhaps I have become too civilized or repressed to admit that I need such an animal abatement.

There may be much to learn from the behavior of our children who have not yet incorporated within themselves the strictures of polite society. If, after a few moments of screaming, then a few more moments of withdrawal, I could be as prepared to return to the activity I had just found so frustrating as Rod did, perhaps I should soundproof and darken a room in my office and let fly.

* * *

This was published in *American Medical News*, September 2, 1996. (Copyright ©1996 American Medical Association. All rights reserved.)

A Family Doctor's Work Sustains More Than the Body

I stood for the prayer, glad for the chance to get out of the pew. I have never understood why church pews have a reverse curve instead of a lumbar support, thus thrusting one's thorax out and providing no support at all for a normal human lumbar spine.

I was attending the funeral of one of my patients, but a man not just a patient. He was a friend of many years' standing. He might have been an in-law, had the cards fallen a bit differently. We had watched our children grow up together, play ball together and leave Oakley for the outside world together.

As I observed the attendees I saw not just individuals who had come to mourn the passing of a man loved by many. I saw four of the starting five on our community's only state championship basketball team, a team that had been sparked by one of Leroy's sons. I saw the boys, now in their thirties, who had run on the track team with my son and another of Leroy's sons. I saw the cheerleaders who laughed when these boys won and wept when they lost. I could not remember all of the activities that my children had enjoyed with that family. I was certain that many of the others mourning our loss saw the same ghosts.

I live in a small community, tightly knit by blood and tradition. These young people had gone to school together at the same time as my children. Most of them were born before I arrived in Oakley, but I had nursed them through their childhood illnesses and injuries. I had supported their parents, Leroy's generation, through disease and despair. Some of these young adults had already lost parents, others will, as the generations continue to unfold.

I have watched them play football and basketball, run in track, sing, act, and, ultimately, graduate from high school and leave Oakley. Many I cared for as my own. They used to hang around our house; we always had a game for them to play or something to eat. I often drove the girls to the boys' games. When they went off to college they returned to our house at vacation time. They were always welcome. My wife and I enjoyed having them in our house and were quite willing to provide food and a place to watch TV or play a game. As they grew up we saw less of them. I delivered babies for the few of those who remained in Oakley. Others would return for someone's marriage and we would have a chance to say "Hi," but often little else. And that was as it should be; their friends warranted more of their time than we did.

Then came a span of years when I saw little of them. They might return to Oakley for Christmas or another holiday, but their families filled that time. Sometimes they would bring their own children in to see me, either because the child was sick, or just as proud parents, wanting me to meet their child. I was always glad to see these little ones, sick or well, just as I had seen their parents.

Now they return for funerals. The kids whom I cared for as infants and elementary students have matured. As they have aged so have their parents. The doctor who could heal a broken bone or cure pneumonia cannot defeat aging and death. They look at me with tears in their eyes, not accusingly, but perhaps disappointed that I have let this thing happen. Although we all know that death is inevitable, none of us is ready to see a loved and loving parent die. I can hold a hand, or offer a comforting hug, but little else. Perhaps the presence of a man they have known for years makes the farewell to a loved one easier for those remaining. That, too, is my job, a task that always reminds me of my own mortality. It is a task that is made easier by the little ones whom my one-time kids bring with them. Life continues, and none of us can, or probably would want to, avoid the end as we know it.

Medicine is certainly not as much fun as it was when my friends and I were young and healthy and tomorrow would always be better. But, as a physician, my duties involve accompanying and easing my friends and patients through the sad times, as well as the glad times. There are always the laughing faces of the young to remind me that the cycle began before I was here, and will continue after I am gone. I am fortunate, and honored, to have been allowed into so many of their lives.

*   *   *

This was published in *Kansas Medicine*, Fall 1996. (Courtesy Kansas Medical Society.)

Kansas Is Like Its Wheat, Tough and Firmly Rooted

It's the first weekend in March and I'm driving across Kansas, actually zigzagging across Kansas. As a native Kansan, reared and educated in the state, it's nothing I haven't done a multitude of times. Yet there are certain scenes and sounds, both familiar and unfamiliar, which thrust themselves at me on each trip. I am alone today, so perhaps am more sensitive to some of these stimuli.

My trip started with a call on the Farm Services office in Scott City, then east on Highway 4 and a stop or two at wheat fields. After wandering out into the fields I stooped to pull some of the sparse, foreshortened plants. Dry they may be, but firmly anchored in the soil, with a good taproot. In spite of all the dire predictions, moisture at the right time might yet bring a tolerable crop to fruition. Of course, wind with no moisture will prove disastrous.

Following Highway 4 through the small towns that dot its eastern path demonstrated again an apparently dying town, composed primarily of uninhabited, tumbling-down buildings, curiously juxtaposed with an occasional new home or business. The Ransom hospital, of course, has become well known for its healthcare EACH/PRCH arrangement with Hays Medical Center.

To my right I see a remarkably green and vigorous field of wheat; it stands out like a flag in the tan and gray landscape. As I pass it I see the pipes and ditches that tell me it is an irrigated field. No wonder! I stop to take some pictures of a decrepit house, and the lone tree next to it, wondering what joy and sadness once reverberated through that home. On my walk back to my car I startle a pheasant, and once again am struck by that bird's impressive color scheme.

At WaKeeney I join Interstate 70, both for ease of driving and to speed my journey. But my reveries about Kansas are not over. I usually drive a "safe" five miles above the speed limit of 65 and pass three cars for every one that passes me. Today, at the same speed, I am passed by ten cars for every one I pass. The ratio increases as I near Topeka and Lawrence, in spite of a roiling wind that moves me across the two lanes of traffic as it desires. Evidently our drivers, true to their tradition, are not waiting for March 22, the day our new, improved and more dangerous speed limits take effect.

It is state basketball tournament weekend. I meet the buses from the small schools headed west for Hays and Manhattan, each painted with signs indicating that it, and only it, contains the best basketball team in the state. Each is followed by its own convoy of painted cars, vans etc. I pass bus convoys from the larger schools headed for Salina and Topeka where the large school tournaments are held. One McPherson bus appears to have a trailer in tow, perhaps carrying band instruments. I dimly remember my high school days and similar trips. Much brighter are the memories of my children's high school days, and the excitement felt by the entire community when our high school team actually won the state basketball tournament.

I stop at a Stuckey's for gas and a brief rest. Inside I notice a tee shirt stating:

I Love
To See
Kansas
In My Rearview Mirror

Clever, perhaps, but I don't agree with it. There is also the usual assortment of OZ shirts, jokes, etc. For good or bad we are inextricably entwined with Baum's book.

Back on the road I do a little bird watching. Red-tailed and red-shouldered hawks as the most numerous large birds I see have replaced the harriers of Western Kansas. A red-tail, hovering over the highway in the wind, veers slightly, revealing the magnificent tail coloration that gave him his name. Perhaps the earth and plants are not yet showing their spring colors, but the birds certainly are.

Driving past a winery, Fields of Fair, brings a smile. I am just back from a four-day CME in the Napa Valley. But our Kansas wine has its own bouquet. This also kindles memories of my wife singing a folk song about dry Kansans, voting liquor out while "drinkin' all they kin." (*Oh, They Say To Drink's a Sin In Kansas*) She especially enjoyed singing that ditty for the Rev. Dick Taylor, then head of the Kansas United Dry Forces. Dick, a man with a sense of humor, always seemed to enjoy her gentle ribbing.

Dotted across the state I noted the ubiquitous "ABORTION STOPS A BEATING HEART" signs. The KU and K-State logos were displayed in various fashions; one farmstead apparently has ties to both. I noted a barn with "No God, No Peace; Know God, Know Peace" painted on the side. At the end of the barn was a large round hay bale with a sheet with a KU Jayhawk painted on it. I enjoyed the juxtaposition. As I neared Topeka I was struck by several signs I had not seen before. One large billboard advertised "Vasectomy Reversal, Money-Back Guarantee," and listed a Houston phone number. I wondered how many of the men zipping past me, no doubt in a hurry to get home to their wives, would be interested in such a procedure.

Another billboard, featuring a scantily clad (or perhaps unclad, her hair was strategically arranged) blond urged me to stop at "The Best Gentlemen's Club in the Midwest." I wondered whether this was a high-class strip joint, a house of prostitution or merely another "Hooters," but I wasn't curious enough to follow the posted directions to the club itself. I also wondered whether they cared there whether one's vasectomy had been reversed or not. "Potawatomie Bingo! Big Bucks!" read another. I wondered whether the play on words was intentional or accidental.

The radio provided equally diverse entertainment. Music ranged from "Rockin' Jesus" through the travails of a man "Old Enough to Know Better But Too Young To Care" to Debussy's *Le Mer*. The unctuous tone of the National Public Radio announcers analyzing Bob Dole's chances in the New York primary the next day was counterbalanced by the hoarse exhortations to be found on the Christian stations.

The only non-changing factors across the state were the wind, the need for rain and the colors of the earth and plants, various shades of tan and brown. All told, a fascinating journey through the microcosm that is Kansas.

Reflecting the climate and geography of their state, the people of Kansas, with whom I have lived my entire life, are a hardheaded, similar, but yet diverse, group of individuals. It is little wonder that they have a strength and endurance that sustains them through hardship and suffering, an exuberance that, in good times, bursts out in excess. There is an optimism that spring is just around the corner, and the wheat will survive. They are as tough as that hard winter wheat, which struggles across the state this year. These characteristics are nowhere better demonstrated than in rural Western Kansas. Practicing medicine here is frustrating, rewarding, all consuming, and fun. It is never boring.

*   *   *

Not everything I have written had a tinge of sadness in them. I usually wrote when I was emotionally involved. Often sadness was my dominant theme. This was not a time of sadness; it was about my sixtieth birthday, a

Disneyland For a Sixty-Year Old.

I turned sixty on May 29. Carol had promised me a birthday vacation that I would enjoy and remember, and I had visions of late mornings in bed, time to read and a generally relaxing time. Instead I found myself in Disneyland with our four grandchildren! Fortunately three of their four parents made the trip as well. In spite of this I did things that I had never done before. I think my good sense deserted me as I left my fifties.

For a start my first ride was on one of those rocket-shaped things that go around in a circle, with one of the riders able to control the height of the orbit, swooping it up and down. Not only was this a ride that my good judgment, even as a teenager, had kept me off of, but I had ridden an elevator some fifty feet into the air to the boarding platform. Charlie, age 5, said "Let's go, Grandpa," and I found myself in one of those contraptions with him in the pilot's seat, taking me up and down at a fearful rate. Noting the fact that I had turned green and stopped talking to him, he did cease swooping. I staggered out and down the elevator, vowing that that was my last such ride of the trip. Henceforth I would ride with the three-year olds.

The next day, however, Nicki, age nine, needed someone to ride Space Mountain with him, and I was the only one available. With much more hesitation than prior to the rocket ride, I went off with him. I should have learned the first time! I have known since I was a child at the state fair, that roller-coaster rides are not for me. I refuse to ride such things, at least if I know in advance and/or can see what is coming. As the line we were in entered the building, I should have had an inkling of what awaited us. Nicki, who had been there before, was giggling. The pictures were NASA pictures of their rocket excursions. And the theme music was a very much-jazzed up rendition of "Ghost Riders In the Sky." You're right. It was a roller coaster! But not just any roller coaster. This went through a darkened mock-up of the sky—planets, stars and all; at least as best I can remember it. I don't think I breathed during the ride. As we walked out Nicki looked at me innocently and asked, "Did you like that, Grandpa?"

I mumbled my response, something about ripping his head off if he seduced me into another such ride. Back to the three-year olds!

Even the little kids posed problems for me though. Roderick decided that he had a broken leg and couldn't walk. Dale carried him. When this ceased to work he developed two broken legs. Fortunately Kira wouldn't let me carry her. Even renting strollers didn't solve all the problems of carrying tired children. One of the primary reasons for going this year is that this is the last year they will present the light parade. That meant we had to see it every night we were there. In order to let the little kids see we had to hoist them to our shoulders. I did that when I was much younger with my children; it's much more of a task now. But no less enjoyable.

Nicki did talk me into one more ride with him, a ride for which the other kids were too small. The Indiana Jones Adventure is well worth it. The ride is a trip in a fake Land Rover, through an amazing display of what can be done with computers and animation. While bumpy and jerky, the ride is not too much bouncier than a fast trip through one of our pastures in a pickup. But the special effects are breathtaking! It is technological toy making at its best.

As grumpy as I try to sound, Carol was correct. It was a vacation I will always remember. My feet and legs have never ached so fiercely. It took me longer to recover than anything I have ever done in the past. But the feel of a little hand in mine, or a sleeping child on my shoulder, are with me yet, and the aches have disappeared. It was worth every bit of effort I expended, and can never be repeated.

*   *   *

Back to sadness. This was written following my Dad's only sibling, Bernadine Ohmart's death in November 1996.

The weather has been beautiful this weekend, as only a fall weekend in Kansas can be. I told my brother yesterday, "It's a beautiful day for a funeral." We were in McPherson for the memorial services for our aunt, our Dad's only sibling. At age 81, she had lived a long and, I hope, peaceful life. I had not been exceptionally close to her at any time, and she had been a nursing home resident in McPherson for some time, so I had even less association with her than in the past. Nevertheless her passing was a milestone in my life. She was the last of my parents' generation to die. I am now the oldest living member of my immediate family, a position I am not especially happy to accept, but one that, I suppose, was inevitable.

There was no funeral, there was to be only a simple graveside memorial service, a service which turned out to be more than I had anticipated. Our family, as many Kansas families, has found itself spread across the country, so I expected few attendees, probably my brother, his wife and their son, and myself and my son, whom I was to pick up on the way. A cousin, on the other side of my family, had offered to fix lunch for us at her home in McPherson. She and her husband also attended the services.

However, true to tradition, a number of others showed up as well. Bernadine, my aunt, had been raised in McPherson and nearby communities. Two friends from her childhood appeared, both bringing their husbands. Two other men, friends of hers, my father's and their parents, also were in attendance. I remembered their names, as I did the names of another couple, long-time residents of McPherson, as ghosts from the past. Bernadine had been in the WAVEs in World War Two, so, something I had never expected, she was buried with military honors, complete with a color guard, a rifle salute, and the saddest of all melodies, *Taps*. I did not cry until the lonely notes wafted across the beautifully maintained cemetery. Then I wept, perhaps as much for the generation to which she belonged, as for Bernadine.

Only one or two of the men in uniform had known Bernadine. A sense of duty and comradeship for someone who had shared an experience with them brought them all to the cemetery, veterans of much more than

WW II, to "honor a fallen comrade." Who will play taps and fire the rifles for these men? They were all well into their seventies and eighties, but they turned out to perform, one more time, the duty that must always remind them of their own advancing years and mortality. I can only marvel at their strength and sense of propriety, of the necessity of doing what must be done. I thank them all, although they are, and probably will remain, unknown to me. I do not know in what marble the strengths of that generation must be rooted, perhaps their churches, perhaps their families or perhaps just a simple sense of what is right and proper, but I fear those strengths may disappear as that generation does.

After the ceremony I spoke to one of the men, whom I vaguely remembered from my own childhood. I had been born in McPherson, but had lived there only until we moved to Wichita at the start of WW II. Nevertheless, with grandparents on both sides of the family and the few uncles and aunts I could claim all living in the area, we returned frequently. I looked at the elm trees in the cemetery, the milo field beside it ready to harvest, and the beautiful flowers adorning most of the gravesites, and told him that McPherson still, after 50 years, felt more like home to me than any other place. He told me that there must be others like me, as many people were returning to Mac to retire.

That sense of place and family still exists, at least to some extent, in those of my age. Two months ago we had a reunion attended by all seven (admittedly not a great number) of the cousins of my generation. This was on the farmstead I had visited as a boy, now the residence of a cousin. While the buildings were different, the atmosphere was not. Ready acceptance, good food, reminiscences; all the pleasures associated with a reunion of friends were there. Yet I, at least, enjoyed it with a tinge of sadness, regret that I could not live my entire life in that atmosphere.

The knowledge that I had to return to my world and my work, although of my choosing, colored my enjoyment of the comradeship of the moment. Perhaps by returning to Kansas communities such as McPherson, the communities where our family, social and church roots lie deep, we can, in our later years, recapture some of that sense of friendship and acceptance so important to us in our youth. Perhaps, as the oldest surviving family member, I feel more need for that comradeship now than in the past. It is amazing how, as I get older, I understand better the feelings and actions of my parents.

*   *   *

There are two essays I wrote before my fall and stroke in January 2001. One of these was written in Oakland, California. I was visiting Carol's remaining aunt, who was dying of a malignancy, in her home. Hospice was assisting her. I knew I would not see her again. This was included in my first book, *An Amazing Adventure*. I was going through some old papers yesterday (October 6, 2010) and found a copy of the *Kansas Family Physician*, Spring 2002. In that issue I found this essay entitled "The Struggle of Life." I don't know whether I submitted it prior to my fall/ stroke in January 2001 or submitted it in 2002, at a time when I had few of my wits about me.

Dying In Oakland California

I sit here writing in a room designed and built specifically for me to write in. Sadly, the woman who owns the home is dying as I write. I am merely temporarily occupying the room as I await her death. She is my wife, Carol's, aunt; ninety-four years old, with terminal cancer, but too tough to let go. Someone needs to tell her that it is now all right to die. There is no need for her to suffer further. I think it is a task that is mine.

It is Friday, the fifteenth of December, in Oakland, California. The sky is bright blue. The sun is shining. The schoolchildren are playing. And Eddie is dying. We were called from our hotel early this morning with the words that she could not last much longer, which I am certain is true. But she hangs on. Yesterday afternoon my daughter and I arrived from Kansas, bringing with us Edna's three great grandnephews, including the two-month old that she had never seen. She had enough strength to hug and kiss the ten and seven-year olds, a procedure which they handled like the gems they are. Then their mother, Susan, put the baby on Edna's bed, in her arms. Edna held his hands, played with his fingers and cooed to him, as if he were the baby she had never borne. Then we left her to rest. Throughout the night I would awaken, wondering at the fact that we had received no call from her attendant.

This morning the call came, but death has yet to come. She is obviously weaker and hanging on through sheer determination, in spite of discomfort and extreme difficulty breathing. She will appear to doze, but awakens with any stimulation. How long can a heart beat, or lungs expand?

Afternoon comes, and Edna appears much stronger. Carol tells me this has been the pattern; weak in the morning, stronger and receiving guests in the afternoons. I leave her bedside to walk in her back yard. The sun is still shining, the sky a beautiful blue. The oranges and lemons are bright on the trees, and a few roses still are in bloom. My mind drifts back to the first time I saw this house and met the women who called it home. The forsythia bush in which I watched the hummingbirds and the very steps upon which I sat are gone, but my memories are not. These women, Carol's three aunts and her grandmother, welcomed me into their family, appearing to ignore the fact that I was taking their cherished granddaughter/niece from them. Never once have I felt I was an intruder. Now Edna thanks me for all that I have done for them and Carol.

Evening has come. Twice I have thought Edna would die. She had been waiting on two things. One was to see an end to the messy presidential election. A good Kansas Republican transported to Democratic California; she had been delighted by the announcement that Governor Bush had won. She had seen and held the children so dear to her. It was time to give up the fight. The hospice nurse arrived. She is as good as Carol had described her. After speaking with Edna and listening to her heart, she recited the 23rd Psalm and Lord's Prayer with her, and then came to us. Telling us that Edna was ready to die, but concerned that Eddie could not keep her mind quiet, she instructed us on how to grind her lorazepam tablets and dissolve them, telling us to give it every four hours. She showed us how to draw her morphine into a syringe, telling us to give her that along with the lorazepam. If she needed it more frequently, we were to give it as she needed.

Edna is at peace; her breathing almost still, her body growing cool. She could take her last breath at any moment. I have told her, my voice choking, that Carol, Barb and I would be all right, that she could stop fighting and go to her Lord. But still she resists. A friend calls to ask if she can come to sing a special song for Edna. I say OK, but privately doubt that Edna will last until her arrival. She does, and, amazingly, rouses and claps time and mouths the words. Her friend calls her daughter and the two of them sing Christmas carols to Eddie, which she obviously enjoys. After her friends leave, Edna again goes to sleep, her breathing slow and shallow. She does occasionally moan, as if in pain or having a bad dream.

Now it is the middle of the night. Carol, exhausted after a month of this, is asleep in the "writing room" and the attendant drowses in the living room. I sit in Eddie's bedroom, holding her hand and thinking. I have always believed that "physician assisted suicide" was beyond the pale, forbidden by both the oath I swore and the church in which I grew up, something I would never consider. But if ever there was a terminal patient, Edna was it. She was not in severe pain most of the time, but, perhaps even worse to the woman I had known and loved, she was totally dependent on others for even her simplest needs. She was diapered, as she could no longer be helped to the commode. She had to be handed a glass of water, so she could suck a little moisture through a straw. She clutched a moistened swab, with which she occasionally rubbed her lips, as one last defiant thing she could do for herself. Never would she have desired to live like this.

The morphine was there. The hospice nurse had told me to use it "as needed." Had the accompanying glance meant "Doctor, you know the effects of this medicine. Your aunt is ready to die. Use it to speed the process if you desire."?

How easy it would be. Take the syringe, fill it, and drip it into Eddie's parched mouth. Do it again, and again, until she finally finds the release she seeks, the peace that her beliefs promised her. Why should she have to continue to endure the indignities of life, the struggle to breathe? The transition would be so easy. Just a little action on my part. I remembered one of the singers saying she had heard so much about me—that Edna had described me as "a wonderful doctor, but a better person." How would either respond to this situation? My anguished decision was that I could do nothing but hold her hand. She moaned and gently squeezed my hand with her cold, withered one.

Saturday came, and Susan and the boys and I came to say goodbye, as we had to return to Kansas early Sunday. Again surprising me, Edna knew all of us, and said "Goodbye" to each. We flew out of Oakland Sunday morning then started the four-hour drive to Oakley from Denver. Edna died shortly after we arrived at our homes.

* * *

I must have written this in January 2001 shortly before my fall and stroke, late January of that year. I don't remember writing it. *The Cortland Forum*, published it in January 2002, more than a year after I wrote it. Either John Bosserman, or Troy, their son, brought a copy of it to me after my return to Oakley. I cannot find it on my computer but have copied it from the journal.

When a Best Friend Dies

I have practiced in Oakley, Kansas, a community of 2500 citizens for 36 years. I first met Carol when I was a medical student doing my rural precepteeship there. After

I returned to Oakley to practice, Carol and her husband, John, became two of my first patients and close friends. Our children were about the same ages. We went through Cub Scouts, Little League and a multitude of school experiences together. Later, I diagnosed her husband's bladder cancer, from which he recovered, and I delivered some of their grandchildren

About two and a half years ago, Carol developed abdominal pain. Our scans revealed an intra-abdominal mass. Surgery proved it to be ovarian cancer, which had seeded her peritoneum. She proved amazingly strong throughout an illness I cannot describe. A trip to Houston led to chemotherapy and care by gynecologists in Wichita.

Chemotherapy stole her hair soon after Elizabeth Taylor had experienced the same side effect. We joked about her looking like Liz. A year ago Carol wished me a "Happy New Years" as we danced. I was afraid to wish her the same.

The year was a wonderful year for me. I received an award as Rural Practitioner of the Year and two other awards from the University of Kansas, my medical school. My family was in good health. But Carol's health was slowly deteriorating.

Just before Christmas Carol was hospitalized with an obstructed bowel and ascites. With the help of her family, the public health department and friends, she spent two or three days in her home, including Christmas Day. That evening she returned to the hospital.

I knew it was for the last time. I would have traded my awards for a healthy Carol, not a choice I could make. As I have grown older I have realized the truth of a statement made many years ago by my partner, "Medicine was a lot more fun when all my friends were young and healthy."

I had never cared for a patient/friend die that had been as close to me as Carol. I know that pain and death go with the life I have chosen. But it still hurts and I don't like it.

For years I had kissed Carol at midnight and wished her a Happy New Year. This year, on New Year's Day, she asked if there was nothing more I could do for her. When I told her we were out of options, she said "I guess I'm in God's hands then, Dick. I love you." I could only kiss her good-bye.

Chapter 11

Partners In Health

After Dr. Adams left Oakley Carol and I tried different approaches to our practice. We realized that I didn't have enough time to care for the sick and injured, time to answer questions about medical problems and have any time for Carol and my children. We hit upon answers—Partners In Health and *Dialogue With Your Doctor*. We would ask our patients to become our partners in caring for themselves. Carol and the office staff would also be involved in our office as partners. We would write and print a bi-monthly newsletter. I had written articles for various publications and enjoyed writing. Carol also had some writing experience. We could say what we thought important and disseminate the information widely without spending an inordinate amount of our time. Later, as Tracy and Ramona joined the practice, they wrote a few articles. No one had the nerve to tell me he didn't care for either the idea or the newsletter but we received a number of compliments on our newsletter. A few of my favorite issues follow.

This was our first newsletter, July 1989

"Partners In Health"
"Huh? I meant to dial Dr. Ohmart's office?"
What is all that about? We have been asked that several times since Dr. Adams left. No, unfortunately it doesn't mean that we have a new doctor in sight, or even in mind. What it is meant to imply is a shift in the way we approach healthcare and help you solve your problems. Acute, well-defined illnesses will be handled much as they have been in the past.

But of more importance is that we would like to work with you to help you maintain your health and avoid the illnesses that put you in my office or the hospital and cost you time and money.

Thus, the title is meant to imply that you and I are partners in maintaining your health. The third partner is Carol, my wife. She has spent a lot of time and effort learning about many of the approaches and techniques we will be using. These number, among others, humor, relaxation and nutrition. The fourth partner(s), perhaps the most important, are the women who work in this office. As well as making the office as warm and welcoming as a doctor's office can be, they all have technical tasks to perform that are extremely important in achieving our goals. I believe that we must all be equally involved in sharing responsibility for the outcome of our endeavors.

It is no longer to be Dr. Ohmart's office. It will be the office of "Partners In Health." Of prime importance is the fact that partners must communicate with each other. That is why we have named this newsletter *Dialogue With Your Doctor.* Too many doctors (certainly including me at times) are too hard to approach, tending to brush off other's ideas and opinions with a doctor-knows-best attitude. I will try not to do this. That's my side of our initial bargain. Yours is that you will attempt to tell me what is bothering you. Not just what your symptoms are, but what you think they may mean. What it means to you to have to undergo some of the unpleasant procedures doctors do to people. What your hesitations and fears are. Only then can we truly begin to be partners, and only then can you get my best advice.

We will print a newsletter on a monthly (more-or-less) basis. All of us would appreciate any comments or ideas you may have. If you know of someone not on our mailing list that would like to receive it, please let us know.

HELP US HELP YOU!!

Ask a question or suggest a topic to discuss in a future newsletter. Just write it down and bring it to someone in our office.

OPEN HOUSE Thursday afternoon, July 27

PARTNERS IN HEALTH & the Oh/MART will host an open house at 123 Center from 2-5 p.m. Hear the music, see the books and tapes that we think are helpful. Snacks will be from the recipes featured in *The Slim Chef* by Arlyn Hackett. Enter your name and win a free copy of *The Slim Chef*. Come join our partnership and visit our new approach as you have fun at the Logan County Fair.

*   *   *

In 1992 Rod and I founded New Frontiers Health Services. Tracey and I worked in the 123 Center building where I had practiced for fourteen years. Dr. Raju and Ramona staffed the clinic at the northwest corner of the hospital building. I continued to write having a bit more time.

June 1996

Diet? No . . . It's a Four Letter Word

I read, at least most of the time, several medical newsletters meant for people who have not been blessed with the letters "MD" behind their names. Surprisingly (or maybe not so) I gain a lot of knowledge from them, and much of what I learn finds its way into this newsletter. (And you all thought every idea in here was the result of my own research, didn't you?) Two of them which I find to be of value and to provide balance are the *University of California, Berkeley, Wellness Letter*, and *Dr. Andrew Weil's Self Healing*. For the month of April both featured articles on weight loss and both agreed in much of what they said. This occurs quite often, somewhat surprisingly, as the UC letter is a fairly traditional publication and Dr. Weil is probably the country's best-known advocate of non-traditional therapies.

At any rate, since they shared the same opinion of many of the "new" diets, I thought I might spend a bit of time on those. This thought was enhanced by the fact that I also share these ideas, and I always like to see that the experts agree with me. They were specifically talking about *Dr. Atkins' New Diet Revolution*, which is little different from the diet he promulgated 30 years ago. It is based on his idea that we should eat a high fat, high protein diet, avoiding carbohydrates. There are now several other diet doctors (Eades, Sears and Heller) with similar programs. Even

Suzanne Sommers has her own low-carb diet plan for sale. These diets have been around for most of the twentieth century, and appear set to boom in the early twenty-first as well. Why?

For starters, Americans are bigger than ever before. Movie seats and stadium seats are being made bigger. Airplane seats haven't changed, but they seem to me to be smaller than they used to be. It couldn't be that I am bigger, I'm sure. We are less active than a generation or two ago. I feel deprived if I have to get up to change the TV channel; where did the grandkids hide the remote? We eat more, meals have larger portions and we eat more snack food, usually high calorie, low quality eats. I wonder how many of us eat a whole bag of chips during Oprah, or a box of crackers during a tight ball game? As I watched KU basketball games this winter I found myself roaming the kitchen in the close or losing games, looking for something, anything, I could eat. Often I didn't even realize what I was doing. And I knew the calories I consumed weren't going to put the ball in the basket.

For whatever reason, we're bigger—and all looking for an easy way to get smaller. Hence there is a large and growing market for magic bullets. Unfortunately, none of them work for the long term. The Atkins diet mentioned above is typical. During the first two weeks you can eat as much protein and fat as you desire, but no more than twenty grams of carbohydrates a day. That is the amount of carbohydrate in one small apple! You can not eat any bread, fruit, starchy vegetables, milk, rice or other grain products. That little squib of carbohydrate can come only from vegetables such as asparagus, broccoli and cabbage, foods loved by all of us! During these two weeks weight loss may be precipitous—much of it is water. And your body will burn its own fat, but carbohydrates are necessary for the body to burn that fat completely. Without the carbohydrates, we produce ketones (acetone, which we used to use in model building, is one) accumulate in our blood. These ketones cause ketosis, which decreases our appetite and may actually cause nausea, thus making dieting easier. If you remain on the diet longer than two weeks any continued weight loss is probably due to decreased caloric intake, simply because you are too sick to eat. Long-term, this diet may damage the liver and kidneys, as well as leading to calcium loss and osteoporosis. Supplements are advised, but don't provide the fiber, phytochemicals and other natural nutrients found in fruits and grains.

O.K. So how do I lose weight over the long run? You already know. It's very simple. You eat fewer calories and burn more calories. How's that? If only it were that easy! Be nice to yourself; lose weight because you want to, not because I tell you to lose, or your spouse nags at you, or your boyfriend pinches you and remarks on the soft stuff there. Congratulate yourself for each walk you take, each time you eat a fruit rather than a chocolate or each time you manage your "emotional" hunger with something other than a dozen chips. Set a reasonable goal, 10-20% of your body weight. Be happy with a 1-2 pound per week weight loss. Celebrate that loss with a glass of sparkling water rather than a milkshake. Decrease the size of the portions you eat (or serve your spouse). Eat plenty of fruits, vegetables, whole grains and beans. They are all filling and high in fiber, as well as good sources of complex carbohydrates. Eat fewer foods made with sugar and white flour; these refined carbohydrates carry few nutrients for their caloric value. Drink lots of water. Get regular exercise. It doesn't have to be strenuous, but consistent. Weight training is good, not to get "ripped" but because muscle burns more calories, even at rest, than does fat.

Most important of all, diet truly is a four-letter word. I should not diet. I should learn better eating habits for the rest of my life, if not to prolong it (perhaps) at least so that I can enjoy it more.

* * *

September 1996

The Good, The Bad, and The Ugly

First the good. Dr. Raju took and passed his American Board of Family Practice certification exam in August. He is now Board Certified. While this means little to his practice in Oakley, it does testify to his knowledge and skill. Not that we needed any further proof that he is a fine physician; we have known that for a long time. But it is nice to have proof that he compares well with the other physicians in this country.

The bad? Dr. Raju suffered a mild heart attack in mid-September. He is doing well, recuperating at home with his wife and children. He will resume his practice in Oakley October 28th.

The ugly? That is a description of my life at present. I had not realized how much it helped to have another physician around. Not just to provide me with coverage so I could have some free time and another job which I have come to enjoy, but for the knowledge that he could provide. No matter how you look at it, two heads are better than one. Or, in our case, since we have Ramona and Tracey, four heads are better than three. The more information we have to consider the better care we can provide. We will be glad to see four weeks pass and Dr. Raju return.

*   *   *

January 1997

Rip-Off?

A year or so ago Carol came home with a couple of carbon monoxide detectors. After my usual derisive remarks about being ripped off and who needed those things in this day and age, I hung them in the basement and promptly forgot about them. This summer we replaced our twenty-five year old furnaces with new, closed combustion, burners.

One cold Saturday early in January we got up and went to Carol's office in the morning. When we came home at noon we were met by a piercing screech, truly enough to wake the dead. Both basement alarms were howling! After shutting them down we opened the doors, almost freezing us in the process, but airing the house out. We called Walter Hughes, who had installed the furnaces. By the time he got here the answer was obvious. Because Carol hadn't wanted long vent pipes running up the sides of the house he had left only about an eight-inch vent pipe. We could see the condensation from those vents, and presumably the carbon monoxide, being blown right back down into the air intakes left from our old system and into our basement.

We were to keep our three and six year old grandsons that night. Who knows what might have happened had we not had the alarms? The little boys might well have gone to sleep in our carbon monoxide laden air, only to become statistics. With enough time, Carol and I might have joined them. Modern equipment or not, perhaps we weren't ripped off.

*   *   *

February 1997

Cigars, Women and Glamour (Or Is It Cancer?)

I guess the idea that smoking a cigar is glamorous has been building for some time, but it is only in the last few weeks that I have become aware of the campaign. Shows where I keep my head, doesn't it? Virginia Slims® has for some time used the slogan "It's a woman's thing," but now cigars, too, are being pushed as a woman's thing. It doesn't seem enough that cigarettes have made lung cancer, which was a man's disease when I was in medical school, an equal opportunity cancer. Now cigars, and the "glamorous" women shown smoking them, are trying to give women that same opportunity to develop cancers of the lips and mouth. Hurry out and get yours!

While advocates argue that it is safer to smoke cigars than cigarettes because such smokers usually don't inhale, most cigarette smokers who switch to cigars *do* inhale. Holding the smoke in your mouth before blowing it out is probably the reason for the increased incidence of oral cancers. Cigars are also much more polluting than are cigarettes. One cigar produces more carbon monoxide than three cigarettes, worse both for the smoker and others in the room.

This is an opportunity women should pass up. Oral cancers occur most frequently in men over forty, about twice as many in men as in women. Now, those of you seeking gender equality have a chance to catch up with men in that race, too.

*   *   *

February 1997

Ten Red Flags of Junk Science

Confused about a new health or nutrition claim? Check out these warning signs, all of which cast doubt on the validity of the claims you are evaluating.

- Recommendations that promise a quick fix.
- Dire warnings of danger from a single product or regimen.
- Claims that sound too good to be true.
- Simplistic conclusions drawn from a complex study.
- Recommendations based on a single study.
- Dramatic statements that are refuted by reputable scientific organizations.
- Lists of "good" or "bad" foods.
- Recommendations made to help sell a product.
- Recommendations based on studies published without peer review.
- Recommendations from studies that ignore differences between individuals or groups.

These come from *The American Dietetic Association Complete Food and Nutrition Guide*. While none of them alone means that the claims are not valid, if a number of them are applicable you might be a bit suspicious.

*　　*　　*

March 1997

I Hurt! What Shall I do?

This is probably one of the most commonly asked questions in medicine. First, and most important, is to ascertain why you hurt. Pain is a warning symptom. It means something is wrong. Where you hurt is also important, both in determining why and what to do about it. I would like to consider only musculo-skeletal pain in this article. These aches in the muscles and joints usually follow fairly minor trauma or overuse. Apply cold to the area immediately after the injury; follow it with heat in 24-36 hours.

If medication is needed, I'm old enough to think that old-fashioned aspirin is hard to beat for this kind of discomfort. It's cheap, effective and safe. It is in the same classification of medications as are ibuprofen, Aleve®, etc. These are all known as non-steroidal (non-cortisone) anti-inflammatory medications. Those, other than aspirin, are as effective, probably as safe, but usually quite a bit more expensive. The major problem with aspirin, if taken for the relief of chronic pain, is that it upsets many people's stomachs, causing nausea, heartburn and, rarely, bleeding from the stomach. All of the other non-steroidals may do the same; they may simply do it less frequently, or not at all in someone who is sensitive to aspirin. Acetaminophen (Tylenol® and others) is a fairly competent reliever of pain, but has no anti-inflammatory effect. Choosing an analgesic is just a trial and error process. If the over-the-counter medications do not do an effective job of relieving your pain it may be worthwhile checking with your healthcare provider to be certain that you don't have a more serious injury than a minor sprain or bruise.

If, as many of us over-the-hill guys are, you are already taking an aspirin a day in hopes of keeping the bogeyman of a heart attack at bay (Isn't it amazing how myths, or facts, change? I grew up with the catch-phrase "An apple a day keeps the doctor away." Now it's an aspirin.) You probably should not take any of the other non-steroidals along with aspirin. More aspirin or acetaminophen is the best approach. Better is prevention. Warm up, stretch, and use care when doing anything that is unusual activity or might be injurious. And beware of the weekend athlete syndrome!

*   *   *

The exam room can sometime be a humorous place. After asking her to take her clothes off, I glanced at her and her tight fitting clothes. "You'll have to diet," I said

Her response, as quick as a wink, was "What color?"

Another way to look at our health . . .

A patient the other day told me "I'm sick from top to bottom. My head pounds, my eyes flicker, my heart jumps, my stomach gurgles, my knees crack, my ankles swell, my feet burn and I, myself, don't feel so good."

"That's quite a list," I replied.

"I know," he said. "If I weren't so healthy I couldn't stand the pain."

The following poem is by Shel Silverstein, an artist and writer frequently featured in the *Playboy* of my younger days. I don't even know if *Playboy* is still published, but I do know that Shel Silverstein still writes and draws. The poem is from the Northwest Kansas Area Agency on Aging *NEWS* and I thank them for its use.

Life Enrichment through Reminiscence

Said the little boy,
"Sometimes I drop my spoon."
Said the little old man, "I do that, too."

The little boy whispered
"I wet my pants."
"I do that, too," laughed the little old man.

Said the little boy, "I often cry."
The old man nodded, "So do I."

"But worst of all," said the boy, "it seems grown ups don't
pay attention to me."
And he felt the warmth of a wrinkled old hand.
"I know what you mean," said the little old man.

*   *   *

March 1997

Retirement? Not For Me!

I don't know why, but it seems that rumors fly of my imminent retirement as soon as spring arrives. Juday says she is getting at least one question daily, and a few brave souls have even asked me if that is my plan. Definitely not! I enjoy my practice more than ever, and my part-time job with the University of Kansas Medical Center, while it does take me away from Oakley more than I might like, adds to the pleasure in my practice when I am in town. Perhaps I have grown grumpy along with aging and you are thinking I should retire because of that, but there will have to be a concerted effort to move me out before I quit on that basis. I figure that, at age 60, I'm good for another five years, at least, and probably longer. My Dad was managing a fairly active insurance agency at age 80; I may just emulate him. At any rate, don't mark me out yet.

Addendum—As I compile the articles I wrote into a book I realize I almost made it to 65. I had a stroke in January of my sixty-fifth year, never again practicing medicine.

*   *   *

For those who believe that the miracles of modern medicine are only for humans, this was brought in by a friend.

The old couple watched as Rover ran out into the street and was run over. The old man picked up his limp body and placed him in the pickup and rushed Rover to the veterinarian. The vet took a look at Rover and said "I'm sorry, sir, there's nothing I can do."

"Are you sure?" the old man pleaded. "Rover's been a long time companion and I just can't stand to lose him."

"Well," the vet replied, "I do know that some dogs who hate cats have been revived by placing a cat near them. I have a cat in the kennel out back. Let's see what we can do."

The vet placed the cat near the dog and allowed the cat to walk completely around Rover. Next he rubbed the cat on Rover's nose with no response. "I'm sorry," he said. "There just isn't anything more to do."

"Okay," the old man said. "I'll take him back out to the pickup. Figure my bill."

The man returned, took his bill from the vet and exclaimed "$300.00! What in the world is this for?"

"Well," the vet replied. "$10.00 is for the office call and $290.00 is for the CAT scan."

*   *   *

June 1997

Time, Where Does It Go?

Do you ever wonder where time goes? I don't mean as in "How did I get so old so fast?" although I wonder that, also. I mean, "Why don't I have more time to relax and enjoy life?" I have all the latest time saving devices—computers, a car phone, etc. Yet it seems as if I have less free time (whatever that is) than I did twenty years ago. I'm writing this newsletter late, because I didn't have enough time in May. I'm usually just one step ahead of my deadlines, and I don't like it.

When our kids were in school we went to high school and junior high events, often three or four in the same week. We also went to other local events more frequently than we do now. I was the only physician in town at that time, and at least my memory tells me that I worked longer hours than I do now. I think I should have more time now, not less. But that does not seem to be the case.

For years, in the wisdom of youth, I told many of you that you couldn't expect to do as much, or as quickly, as you did twenty years ago. Could it be that I have now reached that stage? Or does that stage really exist? Perhaps we just slowly add more to what we want to do, not realizing that every task requires more of our available time, until we reach the point where, apparently without warning, we have undertaken more than it is possible to do in the time allotted. I know I am slowing down, but I refuse to admit that I can now do less than I used to do.

Paperwork appears to be a major troublemaker, both at the office and at home. In spite of computers, copiers, and the fact that I dictate my office and hospital notes, I spend more time on paperwork than ever before, more time than I do in actual patient contact. That is not why I entered medicine! At home it seems like putting my financial records into my computer and handling other papers takes all of my spare time. Used to be I tossed all of my checks, bills, etc. in a basket and dug through them at the end of the tax year. Now I have all the information neatly arranged on my computer. I can certainly find it more easily than in the past. One would think that preparing my tax return would take less time than it used to, but I think it takes more total time than ever.

What have my new toys gained for me? I do generate more paper and records than a few years ago. I can now find a specific item much more easily than I could. And the whole shooting match is a lot more fun than it was. But time? It has always been hard to find, and it's a lot harder now. How about you?

*   *   *

August 1997

Vacation? Yes. Rest? No.

Carol and I spent the last week in June vacationing. Somewhere cool and restful? No. I did something I had sworn I would never do again. I returned to Houston in the summer. Not only did Carol and I go to Houston; we drove, and took our grandchildren with us. Charlie (age 6) and Roderick (3) appeared to enjoy the trip down, probably more than I did. Then, to add fuel to the flames, more or less, we brought Nicki, our 10-year-old grandson, back up with us. Kira, our three-year old granddaughter, did not join our trek to Kansas. Carol had wanted to drive her old Dodge van, which she has turned into a kids' travel wagon. Since it has over 170,000 miles on the odometer, I did not trust it. I placed my foot down and said that we were not going that far from home in a rolling wreck, kept running only by the magic performed in Oakley Motors' back room. Little did I know, but that was to be the only discussion I won on the entire trip.

After renting a suitable van, taking the middle seat out, and strapping in Carol's VCR/TV, we loaded the boys and set out. This was to be an animal trip, so we stopped at the zoo in Wichita. Of course it rained on us, but what's a little water? We ran through the deluge to the herpetarium, and admired turtles, lizards and snakes through most of the rain. The rain forest was our next stop. As Carol had been particularly interested in bats, we searched carefully for the fruit bats in the Rain Forest display. Finally we found them, clinging upside down (as expected) to the topmost branches of the trees. Closing time finally drove us from the zoo to the nearest McDonald's (the first of many) for dinner (what flattery!). Once spied the boys were determined to play in the McDonald's playground. The boys rarely ate the food but certainly enjoyed the play. After the boys played and Carol and I ate a bit we hit the road. We stopped in north Texas for the night and arrived at Dale and Minette's the next afternoon. Carol played videotapes about bats most of the way south. Dinner was at a pizza place.

The next day Carol went to do a little shopping, leaving me alone with all four kids. That was no problem. What came next was! I thought it took her a bit longer than she had expected, but that is not unusual. But trust Carol to do the unusual. I next heard her calling for the kids to come outside, so I went too. There, surrounded by four dancing, screaming kids, was a chunk of mossy mud or rock. Then it stuck its head out and moved! She had found a turtle, later to be identified as a Red-Eared Slider, on Dale's front walk. And not just any turtle. This old mossback's (I now know where they get the name.) shell was 10 1/2 inches (measured) in length. She is strong, fast and very quick to use her mouth and jaws. A real find! And nothing would do but that we bring her home with us. So Oakley has a new resident.

The following day brought a different kind of excitement. While getting ready to go miniature golfing, and in a bit of a hurry, I slammed two of Carol's fingers in the car door. She yanked them out, clasped them to her chest and started whimpering. I, being a well-trained physician, thought her chest was the cause of her obviously severe pain. I was ready to send Nicki to call 911 while I administered CPR, and was a bit let down to find that nothing so dramatic was needed. The damage was done. There was little anyone could do. Carol has a nasty looking finger as a souvenir. I hope her memory of how she came by it fades as the swelling and color subside.

Miniature golf was a washout, literally. It rained and blew. After another dinner, hamburgers, if I remember, I tried to repair a lazy Susan for Minette. After my ministrations the metal base still did not slide, but my thumb did. Fortunately I was working in the garage so didn't get blood in Minette's house, but it did bleed a bit. After reassuring myself that I had not cut the side entirely off my thumb I convinced Carol to use her one good hand to wrap a Band-Aid tightly around it. This held the flap in place and almost stopped the bleeding. It is now healing, but it is a race to see whether Carol or I have full use of our right hand first.

The next day we left for Oakley. Carol had found the location of Bat Conservation International (BCI) in Austin, not too far out of our way. So we headed west, bound for the bats. The BCI was an office, not too interesting for the kids, but they did have a couple of bats there in cages, so they weren't entirely disappointed. They each paid to adopt a bat. After convincing Roderick, with some difficulty, that he couldn't take his adopted bat home with him, we left for our bit of culture, the state capital. As boys are, they were more interested in the pigeons and squirrels on the lawn than the stories of Davy Crocket and Sam Houston inside the building. Once inside, the candy at the shop took precedence.

Then we were ready to head out on our great adventure. Carol had found a site where bats would stream from the cave at dusk and we could watch this phenomenon, if only we could find the place in the hill country of Texas. Carol had called and carefully written down directions. The one that stated that we had to follow a dirt road didn't bother me too much. After all, I'm from Western Kansas and have driven dirt roads for decades. The direction that we "ford a river, go slowly, the bottom is solid rock" was a bit more disconcerting. But the directions said that a car could successfully do this, and we were in a 4-wheel drive van, so surely we could cross it. What the directions didn't say was what to do if it had rained 11 inches the week before, as it had.

As expected, our excellent highway became a graveled road, then little more than a path.

No problems to this point; it was not muddy. Then we crossed a trickle of water that ran across the road. Even I knew this was not a river. Next came a gully with water running in it, with a "detour" beside it. Down the bank, across a few feet of shallow water and up the other bank we went. Still no river. At last a river came into view. About 20 feet wide, flowing fairly rapidly and with a rock bottom, it had to be the stream we had been awaiting. I could see the road climb out of it on the other side. The only problem was that the streambed had a two-foot drop running across it just downstream from the road. But, remembering the words that it would be OK if we were careful and went slowly, I plunged in. No problems. We climbed out the other side and searched for the sign and parking lot that was to be found half a mile further on. No sign of either. We continued, and came to a river that was a real river. At least fifty yards wide, and flowing fairly rapidly, it did not look like anything this guy from Western Kansas was about to ford in anything less than a ferryboat. And there was nothing that looked like that around.

We retraced our steps, looking for anything that we might possibly have bypassed that resembled, even remotely, a parking lot or entry to a cave. It was growing darker, and we knew that the bats would soon be leaving their cave. We must have seen forty or fifty deer, many fawns, and two sets of twins. There were a lot of jackrabbits. But no bats. We found another car of people that also was looking for the bats. They had no better luck than we had. Finally Carol insisted that we return to that major waterway, certain that it had to be the river mentioned in the directions. To me a "river" is any water that flows at least part of the year. I thought this river looked to me as the Red Sea must have looked to the Israelites, and I did not expect these waters to be parted for our passage.

I stopped on our side of the torrent. In the distance, on the other bank I could see what appeared to be a set of tire ruts climbing out of the water. That was a little reassuring. As it darkened we realized that it was now or never. Carol offered to walk ahead of the van, saying that if she disappeared we would know it was not safe to drive. So into the water she waded, with me following closely behind in the van. I could see the bottom, and it was rock. The water appeared to be only a foot or so deep. I waved Carol back into the van and we slowly crossed, none the worse for the water. The other car remained on the bank behind us. Pulling out on the far bank we could see the "Bat Cave" sign.

As we pulled into the parking lot I looked up. There, in the northern sky, was an unbroken procession of bats, rising to the east on their nightly hunt. We could hear the beat of their wings and little squeaks as they flew. We rushed the boys down the path to the cave and there they were! Never before had I seen such a sight! A literally never-ending stream of Mexican Freetailed bats was rising from their cave, making one circle and heading into the sky. It was well worth the trouble of getting there. The man who ran the exhibit was glad to see us, as we were the only ones brave (or foolish) enough to come through the river, which he did say was considerably higher than usual. He caught a bat for the boys to touch, talked to them about their habits and told them about the snakes, raccoons and owls that came to catch and eat the bats. Everyone was happy but me. I was thinking of driving back across the river in the dark.

That proved to be no problem. Nor was the rest of the trip home, other than the expected problems of traveling with three tired, wiggly boys. We stopped in Fort Worth for a visit to the zoo there, stopped again at the Wichita zoo, and arrived home safely, if not quite soundly. All told, it was not a bad trip. The bat cave was worth the effort, and Carol and I have shared another adventure. But next vacation I get to rest!

* * *

Probably 1998

Dr. Raju

During my term in Oakley I have had the pleasure of practicing with three fine physicians, and the pain of seeing all three depart. While nothing will match the shock and distress of Dr. Marchbanks' sudden death, the departure, first of Dr. Adams, and now Dr. Raju come close. I have come to treasure my association with Dr. Raju in the three years he has been here. He is not only a fine physician, but a good man and a friend I will miss. New Frontiers and Oakley have indeed been fortunate to have him here as long as we have.

I have known all during his tenure that he has been a lonely man. It has been clear that he has missed his family. He has found the professional opportunities here that he desired. All he needed to make his life in Oakley perfect was the presence of his family. More than once he has told me that he could not be happier in his practice, but that he remained alone, a status he did not want. He tolerated the separation from his family better and longer than I could have withstood such a situation.

Yet I can not blame his daughter for wanting to remain in Saskatoon. A very bright, beautiful girl, she had her high school career laid out before her when he decided to come to Oakley. Who would want to move and start over? She has visited, but never become convinced that Oakley could offer what she wanted. I think perhaps we could have, but we will never know.

Our initial plans are that I will continue my part-time job with the University Of Kansas School Of Medicine, a job that I enjoy very much and find rewarding and relaxing. I am playing a part in building something unique in Kansas, a medical school without walls, one that truly will involve all areas of the state in the education of our young physicians. I will be scheduled to be in the office three days out of the week. Part of the time I am not in the office I will be working locally doing paperwork in Oakley, and able to provide backup for Tracey and Ramona. When I am away from the area another physician will provide backup services for them. We hope to have temporary physicians in Oakley much of this time.

We have what we believe is a firm commitment from Celeste (Bussen) Rains, D.O. to come to Oakley to practice in July of 1999. While that looks like a long time on paper, it is not really so long. She is a local girl, married to a local man, so I think we stand a good chance of her staying here for a long time. I hope you will assist us as we provide you with service in the interim.

*   *   *

December 1998

Outracing Middle Age Spread. Can You Do It?

I know I can't!

Is it possible to run enough pounds off to avoid the inevitable weight gain of the 40's and 50's? Probably not, at least for most of us, because of the sheer amount of jogging necessary. Just imagine, if you can without laughing too hard, that I am a 45 year old man who runs four times a week, for three miles at a stretch, and eats healthily. Further sustain your disbelief, and imagine that I have been following this regimen faithfully since I was 18. I am not eating any more than I was at that age. But I have still gained weight. Why?

It is because my body's metabolism slows as I grow older, to the tune of needing 100 fewer calories a day with each passing decade. How can I counteract this insidious attempt by my body to subvert my weight-gain prevention program? There are two ways that come quickly to mind, neither easy. The first is to increase my exercise. This sounds simple, but not so easy. I would have to increase my weekly running distance by 1.4 miles with each passing year. This figures out to about 54 miles a week, based on 12 miles a week at age 18. That would wear out a lot of shoes, not to mention knees and hips in a 48 year old man. (I knew there was a good reason I quit running when I graduated from high school.)

The other way is to eat less. This also sounds simple, but again it is not easy.

*   *   *

February 1999

Love or Depression?

It's February, the month for lovers. But I sit here writing this, and I'm depressed. I also have the aches, fever and chills that warn me I'm coming down with that viral illness mentioned elsewhere (the flu). I'm certainly not badly depressed, but it seems that February always brings a feeling of the blues, in spite of the red fete of St. Valentine's Day. So I'm going to put an extra helping of humor in this issue of the newsletter. Most of it has come to me over the Internet, as did the "Taller Buildings" essay. I hope you enjoy them, laugh at them, and perhaps get a boost in mood.

We have taller buildings, but shorter tempers; wider freeways, but narrower viewpoints; we spend more, but have less; we buy more, but enjoy it less.

We have bigger houses and smaller families; more conveniences, but less time; we have more degrees, but less common sense; more knowledge, but less judgment; more experts, but more problems; more medicine, but less wellness.

We spend too recklessly, laugh too little, drive too fast, get too angry too quickly, stay up too late, get up too tired, read too seldom, watch TV too much, and pray too seldom.

We have multiplied our possessions, but reduced our values.

We talk too much, love too seldom and lie too often.

We've learned how to make a living, but not a life; we've added years to life, not life to years.

We build more computers to hold more information, to produce more copies than ever, but have less communication; we've become long on quantity, but short on quality.

We've been all the way to the moon and back, but have trouble crossing the street to meet the new neighbor.

We've conquered outer space, but not inner space; we've done larger things, but not better things; we've cleaned up the air, but polluted the soul; we've split the atom, but not our prejudice; we write more, but learn less; plan more, but accomplish less.

We've learned to rush, but not to wait; we have higher incomes; but lower morals; more food but less appeasement; more acquaintances, but fewer friends; more effort but less success.

These are the time of fast foods and slow digestion; tall men and short character; steep profits, and shallow relationships.

These are the times of world peace, but domestic warfare; more leisure and less fun; more kinds of food, but less nutrition.

These are days of two incomes, but more divorce; of fancier houses, but broken homes.

These are days of quick trips, disposable diapers, throwaway morality, one-night stands, overweight bodies, and pills that do everything from cheer, to quiet, to kill.

It is a time when there is much in the show window, and nothing in the stockroom.

Indeed it's all true. Think about it . . . . read it again.

$$* \qquad * \qquad *$$

February 1999

To Antibiot Or Not, That Is the Question

In this era of wonderful antibiotics it would seem that a pill, or at most a shot should easily cure all infectious diseases. Unfortunately, such is not the case. We are presently (Feb 10) in the midst of an epidemic of a viral respiratory illness. Amazing as they are, antibiotics, or at least the routine ones, will do nothing to help these infections. Those illnesses are characterized by up to a week of high (102 degrees) temperature, cough, runny nose and general aches and pains. This episode is probably influenza, we do not yet know for certain. We try not to treat these symptoms with antibiotics for three reasons:

- They are not effective;
- They may cause side effects, some serious; and
- Unnecessary use can lead to the creation of bacteria resistant to their effect.

This does not mean that all fevers and sore throats should be neglected. We are also seeing some strep throats, proven by a rapid strep test. These do need an antibiotic, usually a form of penicillin, as treatment and rheumatic fever prevention. If the above symptoms hang on for a week or longer, if your child complains of an earache, or develops a worsening cough or purulent drainage from his/her nose, it may be time for an antibiotic. Then it's time to let one of the New Frontiers providers see her,

* * *

March 1999

Summer Is Coming

Summer is on its way, and with it comes old sol, for the good or bad. I spent an afternoon working on a yard project a couple weeks ago and got my first sunburn of the spring—and it was still winter! While we all need a little sun to provide us with Vitamin D, too much sun is not only damaging to the skin, it leads to keratoses, basal cell cancers, squamous cell cancers and, most dangerous of all, malignant melanomas. These last cancers were so rare that I was told in medical school that I would probably never see one. Now I discover at least one new one a year. Several have been in young women, usually blondes who have spent time and money acquiring a "beautiful tan." While lovely to look at, such skin is not medically advised. So, as the Australian campaign says: **Slip** on a shirt, **Slap** on a hat and **Slop** on the sunscreen.

* * *

March 1999

To Pop or Not To Pop, Your Choice

When I was in medical school, and for many years thereafter, I was taught that America had the most vitamin-rich sewers in the world; that Americans popped a lot of vitamin pills and promptly excreted them in their urine. We also wasted a fantastic amount of money enriching the flushings. While we may still have the most vitamin-rich urine in the world, some of the vitamins we pop in pill form may be essential to our health. I don't recommend spending all of our time taking vitamins in one form or another, but there are some that we probably don't get enough of in even a good diet, and those we might supplement. Some of what follows is fairly well proven, some is a bit tenuous as yet. But as noted above, the information presented to me as gospel a few years ago has undergone vast changes, so what if this isn't yet carved in stone?

Even those of you who eat lots of fruits and vegetables probably have trouble getting enough B vitamins. Folic acid, especially, is in the news. Adequate levels of folate decrease the level of a chemical in the blood (homocysteine). High levels of homocysteine have been connected with an increased risk of coronary disease and Alzheimer's dementia, as well as a known connection with certain birth defects. Supplements providing all of the Bs, but especially B_6, B_{12} and folic acid are probably important.

Vitamin D (seems to keep popping up, doesn't it?) is another vitamin which may need supplementation. It is calcium's silent partner in building strong bones. Adequate levels are necessary in staving off osteoporosis and for everyday well being. Some experts say that up to 40 % of all Americans over the age of 50 do not get their recommended doses. With the emphasis on avoiding sun (expressed elsewhere in this newsletter) this figure may increase.

Vitamin E, which I was taught had little, if any, use, is another big gun in our contemporary arsenal. It is an antioxidant that probably protects against heart disease, and may also deter Alzheimer's, Parkinson's and other diseases that we usually associate with aging. But these benefits accrue only if Vitamin E is consistently ingested in amounts well above those provided by a sensible diet. Supplements again appear to be the answer.

But there are problems, also. Vitamin C is another antioxidant, reputed to head off coronary artery disease and is certainly necessary for many processes in the body. But a recent study, although somewhat questionable, indicated that a daily dose of 500 milligrams, less than many of us take, may cause the kind of genetic damage that can lead to cancer. Too much D can cause headaches and fatigue. And we know that too much Vitamin A can cause liver damage. So what does one do?

A one-a-day multivitamin usually provides 400 mcgm of folic acid, 2 mg of B_6 and 6 mcgm of B_{12}. Along with a good diet that should provide adequate intake of those vitamins, along with the rest of the B group. That same pill will usually provide 400 mg of Vitamin D, enough for young people. Those of us over 50, however, who probably do not get a lot of sun, might add a calcium-Vitamin D supplement, to total 600-800 mg daily. Do not take two multivitamins to achieve this level, however. That might lead to too much Vitamin A. Most multivitamins contain only about 30 International Units vitamin E of the 400 recommended by most experts. So a 400 IU supplement is definitely suggested here.

So it looks like "To Pop" is the correct thing to do. Slip me a handful of pills as you go by, will you?

*   *   *

May-June 2000

The letter below is from Tracey. I am as sorry as any of you to see her leave, but a reduction in providers is a necessity for New Frontiers. From our standpoint, the staff we had is the right mix and number. Two Nurse Practitioners, one full-time physician and two half-time physicians can provide 24 hour, 7 day coverage for the Oakley area without much strain on any of us. Unfortunately, our patient load has not grown as rapidly as we had hoped and planned. We do not see enough patients to be able to afford all the providers we have had for the past year. Tracey has an opportunity to teach close to home, where she could also work for New Frontiers on a part-time basis. We are all sorry to see her leave, and wish her the best in her new position. We will be delighted to have her in the office on the occasional basis she has planned.

Dear Valued Client,

"If I only had a crystal ball." This idea has consumed my thoughts over the past few months. The administration of New Frontiers has been very candid about their uncertain financial situation and the clinic's inability to continue employment of all providers. "If I only had a crystal ball."

With this uncertainty in mind, I allowed myself to envision a future separate from New Frontiers. Fortunately, a position at Colby Community College opened and I was offered the Director of Nursing position. As much as it grieves me to leave direct patient care, I look forward to my other love-teaching. In addition, I will be instrumental in the transformation process of "civilian" people into nurses. What could be better?

My full time status will change to a casual position on May 30th. I will continue to work 1-2 days per week for the summer and take occasional call. By fall, vacations will be over and I will be well into my new position. I hope to occasionally "fill in" as needed and work one afternoon per week.

Thank you will never express how grateful I am to those of you who allowed me to be a part of your lives. It has truly been a blessing that will be with me always.

Tracey A. Stark, ARNP
Family Nurse Practitioner

*   *   *

Problems Faced by the World

Always remember, you are unique, just like everyone else.
The hardness of the butter is proportional to the softness of the bread.
Why do bills travel through the mail at twice the speed of checks?
The problem with the gene pool is that there is no lifeguard.
What happens if you get scared half to death twice?

*   *   *

Beautiful Land of Kansas

This was brought in to me by one of you. Since it matches my prejudices exactly, I am happy to print it.

Once upon a time in the Kingdom of Heaven, God was missing for six days.

Eventually, Michael the Archangel found him, resting on the seventh day. He inquired of God, "Where have you been?"

God sighed a deep sigh of satisfaction and proudly pointed downwards through the clouds, "Look Michael, look what I've made. It's a planet, and I've put LIFE on it. I'm going to call it Earth and it's going to be a place of great balance."

"Balance?" inquired Michael, still confused.

God explained, pointing to different parts of Earth, "For example, Northern Europe will be a place of great opportunity and wealth while Southern Europe is going to be poor; The Middle East over there will be a hot spot. Over there I've placed a continent of white people and over there is a continent of black people." God continued, pointing to different countries. "This one will be extremely hot, while this one will be very cold and covered in ice."

The Archangel, impressed by God's work, then pointed to a beautiful land in the center of a large mass. "What's that one?"

"Ah," said God. "That's Kansas, the most glorious place on Earth. There are beautiful lakes, rivers, streams, and prairies. The people from Kansas are going to be modest, intelligent and humorous, and extremely sociable, hard-working and high achieving. They will be known throughout the world as diplomats and carriers of peace. I'm also going to give them a super-human, undefeatable basketball team which will be admired and feared by all who come across them."

Michael gasped in wonder and admiration but then proclaimed. "What about balance, God? You said there will be BALANCE !"

God replied, wisely, "Wait until you see the loud-mouth people I'm putting next to them in Missouri."

*   *   *

Watch for the Big Move!

Be prepared. Your next appointment may be at our new office. Our tentative moving dates are June 8th and 9th. Most of the new equipment is in and getting set up. No guarantees, but keep this in mind. More to follow next edition.

We moved. All of us now had offices and practices in the New Frontiers clinic adjacent to the Logan County Hospital. I no longer had to hurry from my 123 Center office to the hospital for a delivery or a heart attack. I could walk to the lab or X-ray department to see the results of the tests I requested. If you had an injured ankle and wandered into my office I could put you in a wheelchair and have you wheeled to the hospital for an X-ray. The best part of the move was that, for the first time in my life, I had a window in my office! That lasted six months. I slipped on the ice, sustained a head injury and was flown to Denver for the care of a neurosurgeon. There I had a stroke.

Chapter 12

My Post-Stroke Life

My stroke early in 2001 left me unable to walk, talk or speak. After a month in an ICU and almost six months in Mediplex, a rehabilitation hospital, Carol took me home to an apartment we had maintained in Denver. During the three months of outpatient therapy I remember most vividly the morning of September 11, 2001.

There I slowly improved. I could again walk. With hesitation I could speak. Physical therapy, occupational therapy, speech therapy, music therapy and an acupuncturist all played important parts of my recovery. My neurologist told me to continue writing. This was written in May 2003, about the same time my first book was published. This has not been edited for this book; the mistakes I made then are still present.

Return To Mediplex

Carol and I drove back to Denver to attend and more or less lead the Brain Injury Support Group. I had a bit of a talk prepared and thought we could use some of the music therapist's equipment. We thought this might be somewhat new as all of the patients have been through physical and occupational therapy rehab. Karen DeBrine [speech therapist who cared for me while I was in the rehab hospital] was to be the facilitator. She was a bit late. While I wondered whether to start or wait for Karen one of the members was all set to start. Tami had a brain injury in an auto accident. She was in a wheelchair and had difficulty speaking. She jumped right in, however, and started asking the members' names and what their problem was or had been. Many of the members had been there before; Andy had a bicycle accident, Jesse had a motorcycle accident and one of the stroke patients had been in the SRS group with me. When she asked me what had happened to me I said I was to have been the leader. She was not fazed. She just said "Good. Get going."

That was a good way to get started, as I had been a bit nervous. Karen entered and she just let us go on. With Carol and Karen (and Tami) helping me the evening was a success. One of the members asked Carol how she had coped during the time I was in the hospital. Carol said it was not too tough. Our children visited when they could. She had friends who spent time with her. And shopping in the thrift shops was always a boost. I still wear many of the T-shirts she found while I was still in the hospital. Someone asked if I became angry while I was in the hospital. I said "No," meaning that I didn't get romping-stomping mad. Karen said that I did sometimes get "frustrated" with Karen when she couldn't understand what I had said. She also said that I became frustrated with myself when I wasn't able to say exactly what I wanted to say. Karen says I had trouble looking for words. I might use a medical term, perhaps "appendicitis", when I meant to say "car." We all got a laugh out of that, but many of us had been in that situation.

I always get a big boost from talking about the amazing recovery I have made, and individuals who are still on their road to recovery also appear to get a boost. As always, I learned something about my own stroke and my recovery. One and a half years after my dismissal from the hospital I still feel as if Karen is my teacher as well as my friend. Karen named several of the members and said that she is always glad to see any of us return because that is the only way any of the therapists get to find out how we are doing. All in all it was a good evening.

Carol and I had hoped to see Dr. Ravi [the neurologist who cared for me] that evening, but he could not come. He had told us that he would be on my old ward, 100, Thursday morning, so we managed to get there. Many of the staff was still there, as was Dr. Ravi, so we had a reunion. I could not remember some of the staff members at all; others I could vaguely remember and a few I remembered very well. I think those I could remember the best were people I had talked to while I was returning to Mediplex as an outpatient, or later when I met some of the staff members when I was visiting the hospital. They all seemed glad to see me and thought I was in much better shape than I had been when I had been a patient.

I was almost in tears. I had been helpless when I first arrived, and little better when I had been discharged to Carol's apartment. They fed me, bathed me and dressed me. One memory I do have is of being in the ward and eating breakfast. I vomited and someone had to clean me up and again dress me. My feelings toward these folks are much as if I care for parents or larger siblings, taking care of me and protecting me. I would like to have the opportunity to sit down with each of them and hear of their tears and laughter as I struggled to recover. Carol says that Dr. Ravi provided an immense amount of support for her during the months that Carol visited me. When Carol says that Dr. Ravi said he was "optimistic" without the qualifier "cautiously"; she wanted to throw her arms around him and kiss him. Maybe she did, I don't know. After I met him, probably during my SRS stay, and later at his office, I found him to be a physician whom I wish I had known while I had practiced. Kind, gentle and intelligent physicians were always hard to find.

Our grandson Rod, now nine years old, but only seven when I fell, went to Mediplex with Carol and me to go to one of the Brain Injury Support Group meetings, probably in March. He was willing to let me go, but he didn't want to go into the hospital. Then he said he would go to the meeting, but he wouldn't go to the ward. We didn't push him. The next morning I wanted to see who was working that morning and he agreed to go to the ward, but he wouldn't go to my old room. Later I asked him what he thought about all of that. He just wouldn't say much. A classmate told him at school that I had died, I'm sure not to be vindictive, just mistaken. Fortunately Rod did ask Susan about that and she handled it well. He will still just come up and give me a hug for no reason at all. I hope our children carried two lessons from this episode. First, never give up. Second, kindness and gentleness should always be valued.

Charlie, now twelve years old, had to write an essay as an assignment in the fifth grade. He again had to write a report in the sixth grade and used grandpa's stay in the hospital as his subject for both. He did an excellent job. I was talking with him about his papers and his thoughts, but he didn't say much. When I asked him about his fears when I was in St. Anthony's he said only that it was scary. Susan had brought both of the boys to see me at St. Anthony and Mediplex but they appear to have survived their visits to Grandpa.

How my Grandpa is doing after his accident

By: Charles Marl Bloom, Jr.

Like most of us know my grandpa was in the hospital, in Denver, for a long time. Still a few don't know how it all started. One night in January, 2001, he went outside to get in the Ram Charger and slipped on the ice. A few days later he was driven to Colby in an ambulance to get a CAT scan. A CAT scan shows tissue, not just bone. The CAT scan showed that he had a Subdural Hematoma, blood clot between the skull and bone. So he was brought back to Oakley and loaded in an Eagle Med airplane and flown *Flight For Life* to Denver to St. Anthony Hospital to have surgery to get the blood clot out. To do this, they had to make him sleep, then drill holes in his head to let the blood drain. After that, he was placed in I.C.U. (Intensive Care Unit.) While he was there, he had a stroke and went into a coma. A stroke is a blood clot in the brain. A coma is an unconscious state.

A few days later, he caught pneumonia and was placed in the S.I.C.U. (Surgical Intensive Cars Unit).While he was there we were allowed to visit him. While visiting we had to wear gowns and gloves to prevent the spread of germs. While in the hospital he had to be fed gross green stuff through his stomach. While in the hospital he had a trache (tracheotomy) tube to let air pass to his trachea so he could breath but he can't talk. On the wall were many signs and pictures of my cousins, brothers and me. One of the signs said things you could do to make him feel better. Things such as: you could sit in his room; you could sneak him a pizza; you could plan a hospital breakout; you take off or put on his glasses; you could give him aback rub; you could give him a water swab for a dry mouth; you could work his joints for him; you could read to him; you could turn on the TV or music; you could call a nurse for him or you could read his writing if you wanted to.

After four weeks at St. Anthony's hospital, he had improved enough to be moved too Mediplex rehab (rehabilitation) hospital. When he first got to Mediplex he was very sleepy but still they started working with him right away. Also when he got there the Mediplex nurses gave him a shower so he wouldn't smell bad. After they did that they started with three kinds of therapy: speech, occupational and physical. In speech therapists tried to teach him to talk. Since he couldn't put sentences together he babbled mindlessly. The first things he did in this therapy were like being in preschool. In O.T. (Occupational Therapy) he learned to get dressed, comb his hair, brush his teeth, tie his shoes and eat again. In physical therapy at the beginning all they could do was stretch his arms and legs out in bed. (This is because of muscle atrophy; when someone doesn't use their muscles for a period of seventy-two (72) hours (three days) or more they begin to rot and start to turn soft.) When they were able to get him in the wheelchair they would put him in it and take him to the P.T. (Physical Therapy) room and lay him on a mat and help him sit up. When he was still at Mediplex he still had the tube to eat from. Then he started to eat chopped up normal foods. Then to drink any clear liquids the rehab center had to put some stuff in it so it was like syrup but it made it taste really bad. He could not drink clear liquids because they are the hardest to swallow, because if they go down the wrong pipe they are hard to either get out or in because you cough and cough and cough. Then he got really thirsty so they gave him plain water through the stomach tube every day. Then they decided to do a swallow test. A swallow test is where they take an x-ray of him swallowing. Swallowing is a very complicated process. It requires the shutting of one valve (the epiglottis) and the opening of another. The epiglottis lies between the larynx and the esophagus so that when you swallow it blocks the food from going into the larynx.

Later in Mediplex he got to do Music Therapy. In Music Therapy the therapist would sing and he would finish the last word(s). Then she would play percussion instruments and he would repeat the beat. Also they used music to get his walking even and smooth.

In April he stopped making progress in his therapy. At this point he still didn't realize that he was in the hospital even though he was doing at least three hours of therapy a day. On April 12th they went back to St. Anthony's in the ambulance to get another CAT scan. The CAT scan showed that he had hydrocephalus (water on the brain). To relieve the pressure that it was causing they put in a permanent shunt to drain it. This shunt as a plastic tube in his head put in from inside the skull down to the peritoneal cavity (the place where the intestines and stomach) to drain the water. This time if we wanted to go in and visit him we had to wear masks, gowns and gloves. He was only supposed to stay there for two days, but he had a bad comeback from surgery and had to stay a week instead.

After a week, on the 19th of April, (their 43rd wedding anniversary) they went back to Mediplex rehab center. When they got back to Mediplex they started all the therapies over again. On May 15th he became medically stable so they upgraded goals. The speech therapist said that he got body parts right 40% of the time.

On May 16th he had his first visit with the acupuncture doctor Dr. LiXin Zhang (le-shin zong)). The acupuncture doctor said that he thought that he would have a good recovery in eight or nine months. So they decided that he would see the acupuncture doctor twice a week (Tuesdays and Thursdays (with a few exceptions)). Each time the acupuncture doctor used twelve needles.

On May 29th he had a birthday party celebrating his 65th birthday. When he came to the party he walked, with a little help, straight and upright. That night he had a lot of food because he had just gotten the stomach tube out. He seemed to have a good time then, but has no memory now of anything before sometime in June. At this point in Speech Therapy he was just learning to speak whole sentences (fish-fishing-let's go fishing). At this point in Physical Therapy they were trying to teach him to go up and down stairs, and trying to increase his walking speed from 58 steps per minute. At this point in Occupational Therapy they were working on getting rid of his double vision, so they referred him to an eye doctor who said to do Vision Therapy. At this point in Music Therapy they were working on balance so they made him reach to play the drums.

On the 13th of July they let him go with my grandma to their apartment in Denver, though he still continues his therapy. After ten months of doing therapy and working very hard, he is now doing very well. He can do most of the things he used to be able to do, though he has a little trouble talking.

About Doctor Richard Verle Ohmart

His wife for 44 years is Carol Ann Ohmart.

He has three children—Dale, Dean and Susan.

He has five grandchildren—Nicki, Charlie, Rod, Kira and John.

He is a Family Practice Doctor in Oakley, KS and has been for 39 years.

He is a published author of articles about his practice.

He is a licensed pilot.

He is a graduate of K.U. (Kansas University)

He is an avid Jayhawk fan.

He played tuba in the K.U. pep and marching bands when Wilt Chamberlain played for K.U.

He was the National Rural Physician of 1999 and the Family Practice Physician of 2000.

He is a whiz on a computers (though he can't type).

He is an accomplished photographer.

He is a mentor and teacher to students and interns.

He loves jazz and classical music.

He also loves theater—season tickets to Denver Garner Productions.

He teaches K.U. Medical Students and Wichita State
Medical School Students.

I think Charlie did a pretty good job. And he has made good use of
a class assignment. I sometimes wish I could use something that is useful
when I am trying to write. I don't think either of my two grandsons in
Oakley has been particularly damaged by my accident. And many kids
have grandparents, parents or other relatives who have been killed or
injured. I'm sure that any child who has such an episode remembers it,
just as any other memory in his childhood.

*   *   *

June 19, 2003

Charlie has had to do some math assignments this summer that he
didn't complete when school ended. Mostly I think he just didn't work
at it. One of the teachers told Carol that he was too sociable to really get
into school. And he wasn't doing much better this summer. Carol said
she was not very good at math but I had been a whiz. (Maybe not a whiz,
but good.) When I told Charlie I would try to help but I wasn't sure that
I was able, he offered to teach me. So we sat down to do his assignments.
Some of it I should have been able to do, but I made errors in addition,
subtraction, etc. Some of the problems I just couldn't remember—what
the volume of a sphere would contain. And some of them were quite easy.
But Charlie did a great job of teaching me. He's good at telling me what I
should do and how to solve the problems.

*   *   *

In August 2005 I was asked to speak at a Relay For Life to support cancer.
Again I have not edited this for the present book.

Relay For Life

When the committee planning the Relay For Life in Oakley initially
asked for a donation I thought we would contribute a bit of money and

that would be done with it. It has always been easier to donate money than time and energy. Carol's sister has participated in the Scott City Relay for several years, but I knew little about it.

Then one of the organizers asked me if I would speak a few words at the Relay. I have never liked to speak to a group of people but had learned not to fear the podium as I once did. I hadn't spoken to a group since my stroke and wasn't certain that I could, particularly about my own prostate cancer. But it was a long time until I actually had to face the audience so I said, "Yes."

As the evening drew near I became more anxious. Eventually the evening arrived. The Relay was to be held at the high school football field. It drizzled intermittently throughout the day. "Maybe it would be rained out. But they would probably postpone it. I would still have to speak. Might as well get it over with."

The evening was overcast and it continued to drizzle a bit. But the affair was to continue. The infield was dotted with tents. Team members were clad in varied-colored tee shirts. I was given a purple survivor's shirt to wear. As I slipped my green shirt off, replacing it with a purple T, a friend said men could change shirts in public but women couldn't. I told her to go ahead and change hers, I didn't mind. She didn't take me up on the dare. We all might have done this thirty years ago but now we're too sedate.

Another survivor, Eleanor Meitl, said she thought she was the longest survivor there. I remembered when I first met her. I was a medical student and was a preceptee in Oakley. Jim Marchbanks, the only doctor in Oakley, had found cervical cancer on her prenatal Pap smear. He had sent her to KU for a C-section/hysterectomy. I met her during a well baby checkup on her son. That baby grew up to run on the high school track team with our son. When Jim died I inherited her care. She was proud to be here.

The Girl Scouts, wearing pink tee shirts, carried a flag around the track, fastened it to the flagpole, and raised it. The flag was flying. A high school girl sang the "Star Spangled Banner." The Methodist pastor prayed for strength and guidance in hopes that cancer could be defeated. Lue Ellegood read a prayer she had written for those who have had cancer. After a few introductions, I was on.

As I began my voice quavered and I thought I might break into tears. However my voice strengthened and the microphone carried my words to the crowd. This is my speech.

When the printed program said I was to be an inspirational speaker I thought they had made a mistake. I have been called many things but never an inspirational speaker. I would hardly call myself a speaker at all. But I will tell a story. It is our story, Carol's, as well as mine. Although she, of course, didn't have prostate cancer.

I have a bad family history for cancer. My father was diagnosed as having prostate cancer in his early sixties. In his eighties he died from lung cancer. My mother had breast cancer. My paternal grandfather died of stomach cancer. I have two younger brothers, three years and nine years younger than I, both of whom have had prostate cancer and prostatectomies in the early 1990's.

In 1996 I had a PSA of 3.3. In 1997 I had a PSA of 3.8. In 1998 I started peeing small orange stones. I didn't like that so Ramona sent me to a urologist, Kevin McDonald, in Hays for a cystoscopy. I was expecting a cystoscopy, a procedure I was sure I wouldn't enjoy. But the nurse told me to take my pants and shorts off, lie down and I would be ready for a prostate sonogram and biopsy. I told the nurse what I was supposed to have. She checked the schedule and she insisted she was correct.

I still objected. I was not used to arguing with a young woman while I was the one lying naked on the table, but she agreed that she would ask Kevin. She returned, wearing an evil smile, and said I should have kept my mouth shut. I would get both! When Kevin entered he said he would sleep better if I had the prostate exam. He didn't worry whether I would sleep better or not. He found no cancer, including biopsies.

I had no further problems. I ignored me rising PSA level. In January 2001 I slipped on the ice and struck my head. After three days of stumbling around someone at the hospital sent me to Colby for a CT scan. I had a subdural hematoma, a clot inside the skull but outside the brain. Carol and I were airlifted to Denver in a blizzard where a neurosurgeon removed the clot. He told Carol I would probably be home and working in a week or so.

The next morning I had a stroke. Carol and I spent over a year in Denver before we returned to Oakley. Again Ramona checked my PSA. It was 8.3. We went to see the urologist in Denver who had taken care of me when I was in the hospital. I had worn a catheter for about six months and he thought I simply had prostatitis. He placed me on an antibiotic for a month and rechecked my PSA. It was 6 or so and he was satisfied with that, but said my prostate was somewhat large.

Ramona kept watching my PSA level. By the spring of 2004 Ramona couldn't tolerate my constantly increasing PSA. At 6.8 she again sent me to Dr. McDonald in Hays. He did a cystoscopy, sonogram and biopsies. He told me I had a huge prostate but he found no evidence of cancer. Carol and I had planned to go to Denver with our son-in-law and grandson, moving our furniture out of our Denver apartment and moving it to a house we had built close to Dale in Fulshear, Texas.

On our return from Denver I expected to hear Kevin's nurse on our answer phone telling me the biopsies were clear. Instead I heard Kevin saying I needed to talk to him. I knew what that meant. Carol and I hauled our van full of furnishings to Hays and talked to Kevin. Yes, I had prostate cancer but there was no great hurry about treating it. So Mike, our son-in-law, followed us, taking John, our four-year old grandson, along to Fulshear. We unloaded, they left, and we got things somewhat organized. Carol and I tried to decide what to do.

Carol did not want me to have another general anesthetic. In Denver they weren't certain whether the anesthetic had been connected with my original stroke or if a second anesthetic had worsened my condition rather than improved it. We talked to Dr. Ravi, the neurologist who cared for me in Denver. He said he didn't think an anesthetic was advisable if anything else could be done. I was, and am, a coward so I didn't really want surgery. With all of us telling Kevin that we didn't want an anesthetic, Kevin agreed.

Dr. Prasad, the Hays radiation therapist, was encouraging. So we began the procedure. I again had to be catheterized but at least the catheter was not to be left in. I was to have 45 treatments. Carol and I wanted to be in Oakley with our grandchildren as much as possible so I daily drove from Oakley to Hays and back for the treatments. I drove 90 miles, walked into the hospital and dropped my drawers. A young woman treated me for five minutes. Then I dressed and drove 90 miles home.

We spent most of the summer of 2004 in that manner. I had no problems with the radiation so we were able to take the kids to Hays to the Sternberg Museum, the water-park and other things in Hays. Carol took the three boys to Texas and brought Kira, our granddaughter back to Oakley for the fair. I stayed in Hays while Carol was gone. I also had about six weeks of physical and occupational therapy in the Hays Rehabilitation Center since I was going to Hays daily anyway. That rehabilitation effort certainly helped my balance. At the end of treatment my PSA was 3.2. In June this year it is 0.6.

I have a few thoughts about this episode. Things have changed immensely since I was in medical school or my early years in Oakley. We then simply ignored prostate cancer; or if something had to be done we used estrogen. That same estrogen was used for women's hot flashes, breast cancer and for birth control pills. Breast cancer, colon cancer, lung cancer—all had dismal prognoses. Great changes have come about. Much more can be done, surgically, with radiation or chemotherapy. Prevention and early detection are extremely important. I'm not a particularly good example; I'm just lucky. If you are told you have cancer you shouldn't, as an ostrich, put your head in the sand. You should be proactive, learn about your disease and its treatments. Then plot a path. Fear is of no help. Concern is warranted. We all live with concerns of all sorts. But we need to continue our lives.

After my talk, the survivors gathered on the track to walk a lap. I recognized many of my friends whom I had cared for. Many others were cancer survivors who had been diagnosed and treated after my stroke. A young woman wearing the purple shirt of a survivor carried an infant. As the survivors walked, the sun burst out, spraying us with its rays. Even nature was saying to us that we could survive.

As I left a fifteen year old girl whom I had taken care of as a child walked up to me and said she had enjoyed my talk. She said her mother, her grandfather and her grandmother had all died of cancer. I hadn't cried for myself but I had tears in my eyes as she walked away.

*   *   *

This was published in *Kansas Family Physician*; Fall 2005. (Courtesy Kansas Academy of Family Practice.) I wrote this essay four years after my stroke. Again I have not edited this essay.

Awakening

I awakened, slowly, remembering bits and pieces of a dream, much as if I were reconstructing my life. Indeed, that is what I was doing. My life was quite different from what it had been. For thirty-eight years I had been a rural physician. I had planned to spend another five years in my practice. Then I would be seventy years old, time enough to retire.

I suffered a subdural hematoma in January 2001. Nothing dramatic. I didn't get thrown from a horse. I didn't fall on the slopes of Aspen. Nor in any of the exciting, contemporary manners in which one's head might be injured. I slipped on the ice in my driveway, hitting my head on the concrete. I discovered that the concrete was less yielding than my head. After two days I was willing to consult a physician other than myself. A CT scan revealed a subdural and I was flown to Denver in a blizzard. There the hematoma was evacuated. The neurosurgeon told Carol, my wife, that after two or three days in the hospital she could take me home and I could return to work in a week or two.

Plans often go awry. My plans for practice and retirement and the surgeon's plans for my recovery all were blown away in the wind. I had a hemorrhage (actually three) in my brain, a brain of which I had been inordinately proud. I spent a month in an ICU, the next six months in a rehabilitation hospital. There is where I was reawakening, finding how extraordinarily my life had been changed.

I remember nothing of the first few months of my new life, much as an infant remembers little. Carol tells me I had an endotracheal tube and was on a respirator. I was fed through a gastrostomy tube. I had a catheter. Someone bathed me and, when I could swallow, fed me. They dressed me. Not as an adult but with a diaper, a tee shirt and socks. I couldn't walk. I couldn't talk. And, if I could think, I have no recollection of those thoughts. Probably that is just as well.

Susan, my daughter, had delivered an infant son three months before my accident. I'm sure Susan and Carol thought they might well have two infants on their hands; but at least they could look forward to Susan's infant maturing. I might be in a perpetual infantile state.

Imperceptibly I improved. Carol was thrilled when I wiggled a toe. Then I smiled. Soon I could use a word or two, although it was months before I could speak. The physical therapists managed to sit me up in a chair, then onto my feet. The speech therapists taught a child's words to me—comb, pen, stethoscope. Strangely, I could learn familiar medical words more readily than I could learn to use a child's articles. The occupational therapists taught me to dress myself, brush my teeth, and tie my shoes. Little of this do I remember.

I remember sitting in a wheelchair and fiddling with anything within reach, much as a one-year old. Much as I watched Alzheimer's patients fiddle in their rooms when I was a physician. I remember trying to walk in the gym between parallel bars, up and down a four-step stair, and walk slalom style between small pylons. I was shown individual words, then was to arrange them into a sentence. I was asked to match two objects, two colors or two shapes. Sometimes I did. Sometimes I didn't. Usually I improved. Occasionally I slipped back a bit. But I slowly was recovering. Then I lost a lot of ground. The neurologist thought I had developed hydrocephalus. The surgeon placed a shunt in me to drain spinal fluid from my brain to my peritoneum. Unexpectedly I got much worse; then I again improved.

Six months after my accident the speech therapist helped me learn the names of my grandchildren. They were to be here for Fathers' Day and we were going out for dinner. I hazily remember a storm when they moved all of us into the hall, away from windows. Carol, an entertainer, sang to us, trying to calm some of the patients. Carol and I were on a ship in a storm, Carol singing to calm the passengers, much as on the Titanic. On July 4th, always one of my favorite holidays, I watched some fireworks then wanted to go to bed. Just as my young grandchildren when they were tired.

Carol took me home to an apartment in Denver, still in a wheelchair, minimally verbal and virtually an invalid. She drove me to the rehab hospital as an outpatient three days a week. Monday, as we were preparing to leave for the hospital, the radio announced that an airplane had crashed into the World Trade Center. It was September 11. Still attempting to orient my new life, I had to face another, larger reality. A world that had changed immensely while I was absent. My memories of that tragedy are my first vivid memories.

I was promoted to the Social Reintegration Services in October. This was a four-week course helping me fit back into the real world. I think I remember most of this. Much as an infant, but much more rapidly, I grew up. There were six to eight of us in the course, all brain injured. We were taught to read, and then discuss the articles in the newspaper. We were taught to use a map. We had to design a schedule, when and where to go and how to fit in time to move from one to the next. We had to learn to add and subtract, then how to balance a checkbook. As an outing we were taken to a large store where we were to find a few objects and list their costs. Then we were taken to another store and to compare the costs. Wednesday we planned a lunch menu, Thursday we purchased the items needed and Friday we prepared lunch. And learned to clean up.

After four weeks I graduated. I didn't want to leave the therapists. They were my parents. But as any parent, they knew I had to move on; I had to learn to care for myself. With Carol's love, pushing, pulling and sometimes whipping me to continue my improvement, I have persisted in my recovery. But my life is not the same. I have not been able to resume my practice. Carol and I spend half of the year in Houston where our son's family lives, the other half in Northwest Kansas. We avoid ice and snow if possible.

Carol and I were both undergraduate students when wed, soon to become parents. Medical school was a full time job. Then I was in practice. Since my accident I have had time to spend alone with Carol, a time for the two of us to talk, watch a movie or work on a project. We rarely had that opportunity.

I have much more time to spend with our grandchildren. John, my grandson now four, is learning to write his name, how to manipulate numerals and how to solve jigsaw puzzles. As I watch him I recall many of the steps I have retraced in the past four years. I am fortunate to have had a second chance, a life quite different but very pleasant.

Postscript

I practiced in Oakley for 37 years. As a young physician, I was told by the older physicians that I had missed the golden years of medicine. Insurance companies, Medicare, too much paperwork and too many people attempting to supervise your care, all combined to ruin the practice of medicine. I didn't believe that then, nor do I believe medicine is now ruined. I believe that I practiced in the golden age of medicine, just as most physicians now practice in a golden age. Nevertheless, the golden age has evolved. Science has overtaken art as a part of medicine. However, as the old men complained to me during my youth, I now believe that insurance companies, too much paperwork and too much oversight have driven much of the pleasure of caring for friends from the profession I loved.

I entered medical school as a boy, although already married. I graduated as a man, father of two boys. School was enjoyable, although hard work. Before me lay a year of internship, then a family practice in northwest Kansas. I was anxious to get started, ready to care for people. For most of my career I have loved that practice. The last few years of my practice weren't as much fun as the earlier years, but I still enjoyed caring for my friends.

In medical school I had learned all of the latest diseases, medicines and techniques, the science of medicine. Penicillin and streptomycin were the only antibiotics. The tetracyclines were just being used. The up-to-date doctors were switching from digitalis to digitoxin, then to digoxin. Oral diuretics were just over the horizon. In Kansas City a cardiologist was electronically monitoring men who had a coronary, occasionally resuscitating a patient. We used glass syringes and steel needles to draw blood or give injections. Those syringes and needles were then washed, sterilized in an autoclave in our office and used again and again. Bone scans, CTs and MRIs were far in the future. I gave the diptheria-pertussis-tetanus shots to my boys and knew of tetanus shots for adults. Carol and I took our boys to get polio shots while I was interning.

As well as teaching science, my instructors taught me to talk with, not to, my patients. This was the art of medicine. Doctor Delp, the grand old lion of the medicine department, told me that if I listened attentively, a patient would tell me what was wrong with him, giving me the diagnosis I needed. A little blood or an X-ray would confirm the diagnosis. Medical treatment was limited; if a surgical problem was found a surgeon removed it. But listening to a patient was the foundation of medical care.

I continued to learn throughout my practice. I grew in both the art and science of medicine. New medicines were discovered and used. The few cubic centimeters of blood I was told to draw at KUMC increased until several tubes of blood were required for the myriad tests available. Then a small amount of blood was needed to perform a multitude of tests in a machine. A rare confirming X-ray became a host of X-rays and scans. In the last few years of my practice the time allotted for a patient visit was ten or fifteen minutes. In that time I was to listen to my patient's problem, diagnose, prescribe and write down (or dictate) what had transpired during that span. Since I had now known many of my patients for years I could often complete that in that span.

My original blueprint for my life was to practice in Oakley until I was seventy years old. Forty-three years in practice, age seventy; that seemed an appropriate stopping point. But my life was changed by a fall on the ice, followed by a cerebral hemorrhage. At age sixty-five I spent most of a year in a hospital. The therapists encouraging, often cajoling, sometimes scolding, taught me to again walk, read and speak. They were, and are, my heroes. I am still recuperating from that.

From the sidelines I see medicine failing. It appears to me that the time constraints now forced on a doctor-patient visit must rush a physician through that visit, allowing no time for a detailed history, much less idle conversation. The enjoyment in caring for a friend is decreased by the myriad other things a physician is now required to do. As a student at KUMC I saw the nurses training there, trained to manage papers as an administrator. In my internship at Wesley Medical Center in Wichita, I saw the nursing students taught there to take care of people. I fear too many physicians are now being trained as administrators while the physician assistants and nurse practitioners care for people. That may now be necessary. But I was not trained to be a paper shuffler. I was taught to listen to people, to touch living, breathing, and, yes, dying people.

About the Author

The author was born in McPherson, Kansas, May 29, 1936. His brother, Bob, was born in McPherson two years later. At the start of WW II his family moved to Wichita, Kansas, where Verle, his father, was a supervisor at Boeing. When the war ended the family moved to Buhler, Kansas, where Verle coached and taught. Shortly after moving to Buhler his youngest brother, Harold, was born. After three years there they moved to Scott City, Kansas, where Verle coached for three years, then became an insurance agent. Fern, his mother, began teaching in a one-room schoolhouse a short distance from Scott City. She then taught chemistry and physics at Shallow Water High School. Verle and Fern remained in Scott City until their deaths.

After completing high school in Scott City Dick enrolled in the University of Kansas and received a bachelor's degree in 1958, with majors in English and chemistry. He played in the KU band for three years. While there he was elected to Phi Beta Kappa, chosen a member of Phi Lambda Upsilon, the chemistry honor society and received Honors in English. During his senior year at KU he also married his high school sweetheart, Carol Socolofsky.

In the fall of 1958 Dick entered medical school, also at the University of Kansas, graduating in June 1962. Dick and Carol, along with their two boys, Dale and Dean, moved to Wichita where Dr. Ohmart interned at Wesley Medical Center. In June 1963 the family moved to Oakley, Kansas, and joined practice with James Marchbanks. M.D. Susan, their third child, was born shortly after they arrived in Oakley. Dr. Ohmart practiced in Oakley until his retirement in 2001.

He is a member of the Kansas Medical Society, the Kansas Academy of Family Practice and a Fellow of the American Academy of Family

Practice. He has been president of the Northwest Kansas Medical Society. He was a preceptor and Clinical Assistant Professor of Family Practice at the University Of Kansas Medical School until his retirement. He was a Clinical Preceptor for The Wichita State University Physician Assistant program until his retirement.

In Oakley Dr. Ohmart has been scoutmaster, a member of the school board, Medical Director of the Logan County EMS service and District Coroner. He has been a board member of the Kansas Blue Cross/Blue Shield insurance company and a board member of the High Plains Mental Health Center. In 1992 the hospital administrator and Dr. Ohmart founded the New Frontiers Health Services and was medical director until his retirement. From 1996 until his retirement Dr. Ohmart was Director of Medical Education, Northwest Region, University of Kansas Medical School.

Dr. Ohmart was elected to Alpha Omega Alpha, the medical honorary society. He was chosen Rural Practitioner of the Year in 1999 by the National Rural Health Association. In 2000 the Kansas Academy of Family Practice selected Dr. Ohmart as Family Physician of the year.

An ice storm was brewing. Dr. Ohmart fell on the ice in January 2001, sustaining a subdural hematoma. Following a flight to Denver, surgery to remove the hematoma was successful. The next morning Dr. Ohmart suffered a stroke. After spending six months in a hospital, Carol took him home to an apartment in Denver for rehabilitation. Two years after his stroke Dr. Ohmart and Carol published a book about their experiences as *When I Died, An Amazing Adventure*. Along with Carol, he continues his recovery spending the warmer months in Oakley and the winter months in Texas.